# CDISC Implementation

## Lessons Learned from
## Real World Examples

## Sy Truong

Fremont, California, USA

ISBN 978-0-557-71148-2


Printed in the United States of America.

# Contents

introduction

## Data Standards Beginnings

Prior to using CDISC, my first experience with data standards was working on a project which transformed hundreds of legacy clinical trial studies into one uniformed safety database referred to as the Unified Corporate Safety Database or UCSD. I had recently graduated from UCSB and initially thought this was referring to a university but soon learned that it was an initiative that was transformative for many years to come. We had used SAS version 6.12 on VMS at that time so there was no XML or fancy GUI (Graphical User Interfaces). The computing environment was dramatically different then, but the core fundamental tasks we had to perform of organizing the clinical trials metadata, transforming it into a standard structure and then documenting the final results are the same challenges we are faced today with implementing CDISC data standards.

The large Pharmaceutical company I had worked with wanted to gain the ability to run standard safety reports such as adverse event summary by severity or relationship to drug. Before the existence of the UCSD standards, we had to develop custom analysis programs for each study. The need for standards became apparent when we needed to perform an ISS, which are integrated safety summary reports combining multiple studies. For that project, we had to develop huge complex algorithms to transform multiple data sources from each individual studies into one standard structure in order to perform the analysis required. Management soon recognized that this was resource intensive and wasteful. We pondered if the data from the various studies were standardized, we no longer needed to re-invent the process and analysis programs for each study.

The value of having the ability to perform analysis across multiple studies using standard data structures compared to having to perform custom analysis for each study was recognized even as far back as 1990 when I worked on UCSD. What I did not know at the time was that the FDA was soon to experience similar challenges and what I was working on was a microcosm of something larger that was going to span across the entire industry.

The challenge that we were faced with in our internal data standards when trying to perform safety analysis across studies was analogous to the same efforts from the FDA. For years, the FDA needed to be able to do a safety review and analysis of data when there are safety concerns. This proved to be pivotal when the FDA was trying to evaluate if heart attacks were being caused by a popular pain killer drug. After many cases of cardio vascular complications, the FDA needed the ability to analyze a class of drug comparing the popular pain killer and compare it across others in the same class. They needed to determine if this drug was truly the cause of the cardiovascular problems or was it some external causes before recalling the drug. Without any data standards, they had to do what we did prior to having internal data standards; that was to spend tremendous efforts transforming each individual study data from each separate company that was submitted to the FDA. This prove to be nearly impossible since the FDA was not the owner of the original source data and their domain of expertise was in the statistical review of a clinical study and they did not have the resources in performing many data transformations into a uniform standard. What evolved in the ensuing years was the development of CDISC as a new data standard that the FDA could use to perform these types of analysis and draw conclusions by looking at a standard data warehouse named Janus. The UCSD database I was working did not have the same scope but it had a similar purpose as the one the FDA was working on.

## Metadata Essentials

As I continued to work on projects which automated the performance of analysis and reporting of clinical data through the 90s, Microsoft Windows and then the Internet revolutionized how we worked. Instead of writing cryptic code to perform these tasks, user friendly interfaces enhance the efficiencies. Although the way users access the data changed, the underlying data warehouse remain the same. The semantic level of how we access and use clinical data was updated but its core essence of the clinical data analysis remains the same. An early example of this was when I was assigned to a project to prepare data to be transferred to a collaborating partnering Pharmaceutical company. We performed PROC CONTENTS and used a binary comparison report using a checksum to ensure the data transfer retain its integrity. Most of the effort was documenting things like the number of records in the dataset and what variables it had and its attributes. There was no such DEFINE.XML at the time but what we were preparing as documentation before we sent the clinical data to the collaborating partner was in essence the same things needed today when we submit data to the FDA. The goal remains the same and that is to document the data with all of its metadata in a way that the recipient can easily understand what is included. This help to understand what has been transferred and verified that the transfer did not alter the data in anyway. The efforts that I had spent for years preparing data to be transferred to other companies using different computing operating systems are analogous to the standards which CDISC had organized in its SDTM model along with the DEFINE.XML to document the metadata during transfer. I now appreciate the elegance of the platform independence and organized schema files within DEFINE.XML and how it is used document metadata and controlled terminology. This is very different from the early PROC CONTENTS in SAS 6.12 and data being transferred on tape backup but the essence of the capturing and documentation of metadata is the same.

The efforts I had worked on for years before paralleled the same goals that CDISC is trying to accomplish. This is one of those rare instances where an initiative such as CDISC is supported and promoted by the FDA since they can benefit from having the ability to perform safety analysis; while also well accepted by the industry. Once the recommendations from CDISC move from a set of recommended guidelines and become a regulation, all companies will adhere to using the standard data models for their submissions. Progressive organizations can see beyond the regulatory requirements and are adopting the standards since they can see benefits internal to their organizations. Some of the internal benefits which I have noticed for years included things such as performing integrated summary analysis, using the same software on multiple studies or effectively communicating data transfers. There are numerous other benefits that in the final analysis, can contribute to a significant savings for the pharmaceutical companies implementing CDISC standards. This is a case of a win win since all parties involve can gain for using this standard.

If this was such a win for all companies and the FDA, why is there still a challenge in implementation of CDISC? If managers view this only in the short term, they see many changes in their work flow involving investment in training and transition from what they have done in the past. This can be overwhelming and by reviewing hundreds of pages from the CDISC guidelines, they become discouraged. What you have to keep in mind is what the FDA and many organizations recognized. That is, the investment placed into the implementation of CDISC standards will have significant returns for each and every study implemented in this format moving forward. It is only when you can gain this longer term view and see the total return from all the future studies that you can see the total return on investment for CDISC implementation.

Since CIDSC standards can affect many departments involving a multi-disciplinary approach, it is not just a technical challenge but also one that involves many people and processes. Each organization has their own legacy standards and their own SOP (standard operating procedures). The adoption and implementation of one standard data structure such as CDISC requires working through many technological and procedural details. When I first started with initial implementation from the early releases of CDISC guidelines, I had to leverage on experiences on implementing previous data standards. I find that the lessons learned from other real world implementation were a tremendous help in avoiding pitfalls and easing the learning curve. The purpose of this book is to present to you many such examples so you can learn from paths that have been previously paved. It is a collection of papers that I have written and other colleagues have developed to share their experiences and the issues they run into. Since every company and its employees are unique, there will not be one "user manual" that you can follow by the letter. Instead, this book is intended to share with you different approaches that you can learn from. It is as if you can gain tens of years of experiences through lessons learned from other approaches so it will make your implementation much more effective.

## Changing the World with CDISC

On a lighter note, I was captivated by the first Matrix science fiction movie with the protagonist named Neo who had to battle enemies in a virtual reality world of the Matrix. The really fun trick that Neo was able to do with the help of his friend Morpheus was to gain years of martial arts training by simply downloading the knowledge directly into this brain. With a few minutes of fluttering eye lids, he can battle the enemy with the skill of a master martial artist. I then pondered would not it be nice to be able to do this for any challenge that I run into in real life. Perhaps implementing CDISC data standards is not as exciting and glamorous as saving the world compared to Hollywood's portrayal of Neo. However, if you can "download" the information gathered in this book and learn from it, I hope you can implement your data standards like a master and change the world.

# one

# CDISC Implementation by Examples

## CDISC and Data Standards

Data standards have existed long before CDISC was ever established. The goal of data standards is to enable different users to have the ability to access and work with the data without having to re-inventing the wheel. This reduces the amount of time spent in software development and training required since all users would only need to be trained on the same set of data standards and its related metadata. Prior to CDISC, there was a plethora of data standards throughout the industry. Each company had their own set of standards and even each department within an organization had their own variation of data standards. At that time, it appeared that there was no compelling business need or driving force to motivate the need to establish a global standard since clinical data represented the intellectual asset of each organization; and this was hidden and guarded as a competitive advantage between companies. Some intercompany standards existed in instances when two organizations used the same CRO to perform the same task and the CRO recommended the same set of standards for ease of interoperability. However, in many instances, standards were modified to fit each company's needs so the end result was a mixture of different standards. The approach of having multiple standards within each organization ultimately defeats the purpose and goes against the benefits of having a uniform standard.

One of the motivations behind CDISC is to provide the FDA a more efficient way to review data across sponsors. This came to light when safety issues arise from drugs that are already in the market yet there were many deaths due to safety issues. Since the data submitted to the FDA were not in a standard structure, there was no way for the FDA to easily perform analysis spanning across sponsors. At moments where thousands of patients are at risk of heart attack due to a drug that the FDA has already approved, it became essential that a timely analysis be performed across large sets of data in order to decide if a recall of the drug was necessary. Without data standards, it was difficult to analyze data from different studies coming from the same sponsor company, let alone comparing drug across different sponsors. This can only be successfully done if the data from various sponsors are stored in a uniform standard data such as the one established by CDISC in the format of the Janis data warehouse. This will allow the FDA to make a ruling in the event that a safety issue arises for a particular drug. This will allow for a timely analysis to be performed across different drugs that may span different companies without having to do extensive data transformations that would be resource prohibitive. This motivates many companies across the industry to adhere to one set of standards.

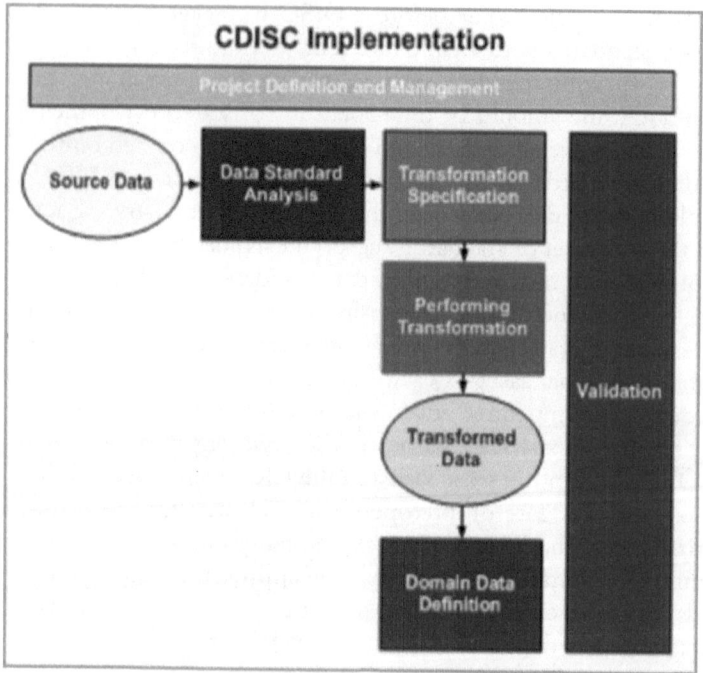

Within the set of standards, there are many CDISC models including examples such as: ODM, LAB, SDTM and ADaM. Each model is intended to be used for different purposes within phases of a clinical trial. This chapter will focus on the implementation of SDTM since it is the format in which the FDA will require companies to submit their data in this format. The guidelines are made available for download at the CDISC.ORG website. Rather than reviewing the guidelines section by section, this chapter will use it as guidance in an implementation. The implementations will use examples to demonstrate the challenges and rewards that are gained from using the standards.

## Why Implement CDISC?

Implementation of the CDISC data models is no longer a theoretical academic exercise but is now entering the real world. This chapter will walk you through the steps and share lessons learned from implementations of CDISC SDTM version 3.1.2. It will cover both technical challenges along with methodologies and processes. Some of the topics covered include:

1. Project Definition, Plan and Management
2. Data Standard Analysis and Review
3. Data Transformation Specification and Definition
4. Performing Data Transformation to Standards
5. Review and Validation of Transformations and Standards
6. Domain Documentation for DEFINE.XML

Regulatory requirements are going to include CDISC in the near future. It will therefore be mandated that the submissions be stored in this format. It is wise and prudent to establish procedures on how you would apply CDISC data standard techniques and processes. This would prepare your organization so when the regulations take effect; you are not starting from scratch and thus delay your electronic submission and ultimately the scheduled drug approval.

CDISC standards have been in development for many years. There have been structural changes to the recommended standards going forward from version 2 to 3. It is an evolving process but is beginning to be more stable and has reached a point of critical mass that organizations are recognizing the benefits of taking the proposed standard data model out of the theoretical and putting it into real life applications. The complexity of clinical data coupled with technologies involved can make implementation of a new standard challenging. This chapter will explore the pitfalls and present methodologies and technologies that would make the transformation of nonstandard data into CDISC efficient and accurate.

It is important to have a clear vision of the processes for the project before you start. This provides the ability to resource and plan for all the processes. This is an important step since the projects can push deadlines and break budgets due to the resource intensive nature of this effort. The organization and planning for this undertaking can become an essential first step towards an effective implementation.

## CDISC Project Management

Before any data is transformed or any programs are developed, a project manager needs to clearly define the project for CDISC implementation. This is an essential step which will clarify the vision for the entire team and will galvanize the organization into committing to this endeavor. The project definition and established plan works on multiple levels from providing a practical understanding of the steps required to also creating a consensus among the team members to function together. This can avoid the potential political battles which sometimes do arise among distinct departments within an organization. The following steps will walk you through the project planning stage.

### STEP 1: Define Scope

The project scope should be clearly stated in a document. This does not have to be long and can be as short as one paragraph. The purpose of this is to clearly define the boundaries of the project since without a clear definition; the project has tendencies towards scope creep. It can therefore potentially eat up your entire resource budget. Some of the parameters to be considered for the scope of the project include:

1. **Pilot** – For an initial project, it is a good idea to pilot this on one or two studies before implementing this broadly. The specific study should be selected based on the number of datasets and number of rows of each data.

2. **Roll Out** – This could be scoped as a limited roll out of a new standard or a global implementation for the entire organization. This also requires quantifying details such as how many studies are involved and which group will be affected. Not only does this identify resources in the areas of programming and validation, but it also determines the training required.

3. **Standard Audience** – The scope should clearly identify the user groups who will be affected by this standard. It can be limited to the SAS programming and Biostatics group, or it can have implications for data managers, publishing, regulatory, and electronic submission groups.

4. **Validation** – The formality of the validation is dictated by the risk analysis which needs to be clearly defined separately. The scope of the project would then determine and define the proper level of validation.

5. **Documentation** – The data definition documentation (DEFINE.XML) is commonly generated as part of an electronic submission. It is a task that is implemented with a CDISC implementation. The scope would identify if the data definition is part of the project or considered another project all together.

6. **Establishing Standards** – The project may be used to establish a future set of standards that will be implemented with this new standard. The scope should identify if it is within the scope to establish global standards or just meant as a project specific implementation.

The scope document is analogous to a requirement document which will help you identify the goals for this project. It can also be used as a communication tool and sent to other managers and team members to set the appropriate level of expectations.

## STEP 2: Identify Tasks

Capture all the tasks that are required in implementing and transforming your data to CDISC. This may vary depending on the scope and goals of this project. If the project is a pilot, for example, the task would be limited as compared to a global implementation. The following is an example list of a subset of tasks along with the associated estimated time to performing the task.

### Data Transformation to CDISC

| Project Tasks | Estimated Work Units |
|---|---|
| Initial data standards review including checking all data attributes for consistency. Generate necessary reports for documentation and communication. | 17 |
| Reconciling internal data standards deviations with my organization's managers. | 18 |
| Data Integrity review including invalid dates, format codes and other potential data errors. Generate reports documenting any potential data discrepancies. | 16 |
| Initial data review against a prescribed set of | 15 |

| Project Tasks | Estimated Work Units |
|---|---|
| CDISC SDTM requirements and guidelines. Generate a report with recommendations on the initial set of CDISC SDTM standards. | |
| Reconcile decisions on implementing initial CDISC SDTM data review to identify tasks to be implemented. | 17 |
| Perform a thorough review of all data and associated attributes. Identify all recommended transformation requirements. This is documented in a transformation requirement specification. | 42 |
| Create transformation models based on the transformation specifications for each data set. | 25 |
| Generate the code to perform transformation for each transformation model. | 50 |
| Generate test verification scripts to verify and document each transformation program against the transformation requirement specification. | 42 |
| Perform testing and validation of all transformations for data integrity. Reconcile and resolve associated deviations. | 42 |
| Execute the transformation programs to generate the new transformed data into CDISC SDTM format. | 25 |
| Perform data standard review and data integrity review of newly created transposed data into CDISC SDTM format. | 17 |
| Document summary reports of all transformations. This also includes a summary of all test cases explaining any deviation and how it was resolved. | 17 |
| Project management activities including coordinating meetings and summarizing status updates for more effective client communication pertaining to CDISC SDTM data. | 25 |
| Total Estimates | 370 |

This initial step is only meant as an estimate and will require periodic updates as the project progresses. It should be detailed enough so that team members who are involved with the project would have a clear picture and appreciation for the project. The experience of the project manager will determine the accuracy of the tasks and associated time estimates. In this example, it has not been specified how many person hours this will be but in the real world, this will more closely reflect your team's efforts in estimated hours.

This document is used to communicate with all team members who are going to potentially work on the project. Feedback is then incorporated to make the identified tasks and the estimates accurate and reflective of the available resources.

## STEP 3: Project Plan

Once the tasks have been clearly documented, the list of tasks will be expanded into a project plan. The project plan is an extension of the task list including more of the following types of information:

1.  **Project Tasks** – Tasks are grouped by function. This is usually determined by the skills required to perform the task. This can correlate to individuals involved or whole departments. Groups of tasks can also be determined by the chronological order in which they are to be performed. If a series of steps require that they be done one after another, they should be grouped.

2.  **Tasks Assignments** – Once the tasks have been grouped by function, they are assigned to a department, manager or an individual. The logistics of this depends on the SOPs or work practices of your organization. This however needs to be clearly defined for planning and budgeting purposes.

3.  **Schedules of Tasks** – A time line is drafted noting at a high level when important deliverables or milestones are met. The titles of the tasks are the same as the title for the group of tasks. This will allow users to link back to the list of tasks to understand the details from the calendar. The schedule is also shown in calendar format for ease of planning.

A subset and sample of the project plan is shown here:

Study ABC1234 CDISC Transformation Project Plan

## Overview

This project plan will detail some of the tasks involved in transforming the source data of study ABC1234 into CDISC SDTM in preparation for electronic submission. The proposed time lines are intended as goals which can be adjusted to reflect project priorities.

## Project Tasks

The following tasks are organized into groups of tasks which have some dependency. They are therefore organized in chronological order.

Data Review
Evaluate variable attributes differences within internal data of ABC1234
Evaluate variable attributes between ABC1234 as compared to ACME Standards
Evaluate ABC1234 differences and similarities with CDISC SDTM v3.1
Evaluate potential matches of ABC1234 variable names and labels against CDISC SDTM v3.1
Initial evaluation of ABC1234 against CDISC evaluation
Generate metadata documentation of the original source data from ABC1234
Data Transformation Specifications
Perform a thorough review of all data and associated attributes against CDISC SDTM v3.1. Identify all recommended transformation requirements. This is documented in a transformation requirement specification.
Create transformation models based on the transformation specifications for each data domain.
Have transformation reviewed for feedback.
Update the specification to reflect feedback from review.

Task Assignments

| Project Tasks | Project Manager | Team Managers |
|---|---|---|
| Data Review | James Brown, Director of Data Management | James Brown Billy Joel Joe Jackson |
| Data Transformation Specification | Janet Jackson, Manager of Biometry | Elton John Mariah Carey Eric Clapton |

Schedule of Tasks

| August | | | | | | |
|--------|-----|-----|-----|-----|-----|-----|
| Sun | Mon | Tue | Wed | Thu | Fri | Sat |
| | | 12<br>Data Review | 3 | 4 | 5 | 6 |
| 7 | 8 | 9 | 10 | 11 | 12 | 13 |
| 14 | 15 | 16 | 17 | 18 | 19 | 20 |
| 21 | 22<br>Data Transformation Specifications | 23 | 24 | 25 | 26<br>Final review of Data Transformation | 27 |
| 28 | 29 | 30 | 31 | - | - | - |

## STEP 4: Validation

Validation is an essential step towards maintaining accuracy and integrity throughout the process. Depending on the scope of the project, it can be determined to be outside the scope of some projects since it is resource intensive. The following lists some of the tasks that are performed as it pertains to validation.

1. **Risk Assessment** – An evaluation of each task or groups of tasks is performed in a risk assessment. This will evaluate and determine the level of validation effort to be performed.

2. **Test Plan** – This will document the testing approach and methodologies used during the validation testing. It describes how the testing will be performed and how deviations are collected and resolved. It will also include test scripts used during testing.

3. **Summary Results** – This will document all the findings as a result from the testing. It quantifies the number of deviations and documents how they are to be fixed.

The following example shows a form that is used to collect the tasks and associated risks.

| Risk Assessment Title | | Risk Assessment of analysis files for sample study. | |
|---|---|---|---|
| I identify the task where the programs reside which contributes to the risk. | ⇨ | **Task Name and Location** | *Interim Analysis on my server* |
| I identify the groups of programs to see which categories they appear in. | ⇨ | ☒ **Analysis Files (20)**<br>☐ **Listings (5)**<br>☐ **Summary Tables (10)**<br>☐ **Graphs (10)**<br>☐ **Edit Checks (5)**<br>☐ **Other:** | *This is a subset of the analysis files Just as an example.* |
| | Score: | 20 | |
| From the group of studies identified, classify the types of programs. | ⇨ | ☒ **Single Use Program in One Study (5)**<br>☐ **Single Use Program (10)**<br>☐ **Multi Use Program in One Study' (20)**<br>☐ **Multi Use Utility or Macro in Multiple Studies' (30)**<br>☐ **Multi Use Utility or Macro in All Studies ' (40)**<br>☐ **Other** | *This is a single use program and it is going to be used in this study only.* |
| | Score: | 5 | |
| What is the likelihood that the program would produce errors or incorrect results?<br>• Are the specifications not clearly defined?<br>• Does the program use custom logic versus SAS PROCs or standard macros? | ⇨ | ☐ **Error Likelihood Detection (0-20)** | *Since there are some derivations and hard coded values in this code, I will give it some degree of likelihood.* |
| | Score: | 10 | |

The test plan can vary depending on the amount of details and level of formality as determined by the risk assessment. The following example shows you a subset of a more formal test plan. This can be abbreviated to handle transformation tasks that are deemed to be of lower risk.

An example of the table of contents for the test plan is shown here:

Table of Contents

This document is used to both instruct team members on how to perform the testing and also used to define how things are to be validated. The following is an example of the validation testing approach and execution procedures.

## 4.  VALIDATION TESTING APPROACH

Operational Qualification (OQ)

OQ will provide assurance that the system meets minimum requirements, required program files are executed and the resulting reports and data produced are operational according to the requirements.
Testers will follow the instructions provided in the Test Scripts to perform the tests as documented in Appendix 1.
All supporting documentation (printouts, attachments, etc.) must be saved and included.

Summary Report

After all the tests scripts for this validation plan are executed and all deviations have been resolved, a summary report of the test results will be prepared. This summary report will include a discussion of the observed deviations and their resolutions, and the storage location of any data not included within the summary report.

## 5.  GENERAL EXECUTION PROCEDURES
Prerequisites for testing are described in "Test Scripts Setup" in Appendix 1. Once these steps have been completed, the programs for the Test Scripts can be run.
The testing will be executed either with a batch program or through an interactive visual inspection of reports. For each test, the results will be compared, manually or with the aid of comparison tools, to the expected results, and the results of such comparisons will be recorded by the tester on the Test Scripts.

> Deviations that occur during testing will be recorded in the Deviation Report, a template for which is included in Appendix 2.

## Test Scripts

The format of the test scripts can also vary depending on the formality of your testing. It is important to have each test case contain a unique identifier such as a test case number. This is what a tester and reviewer use to perform the test and its associated deviations.

| System Name and Version: | Wonder Drug ABC1234 CDISC | Functional Area/Module: | Standardize E123 Data |
|---|---|---|---|
| Test Script Number: | 1 (Requirement 4.1) | | |
| Overall Test Objective: | Verify the variable attributes of the existing source data of Wonder Drug ABC1234 | | |
| Specific Test Condition: | Tester has read access to input data. | | |
| Test Program Run Location: | Test Area | | |
| Test Program Name(s): | difftest_avf.sas | | |
| Test Script Prerequisites: | None | | |

| Step | Instruction | Expected Result | Actual Result | Initials/Date |
|---|---|---|---|---|
| 1 | Right mouse click on test script program and select batch submit. | Script file is executed. | | |
| 2 | Evaluate log file for errors. | No errors are found. | | |
| 3 | Evaluate output files to verify that the attributes results match with the report that is performed using %difftest as part the summary report. | Output is verified against output. | | |
| Recovery: | Resubmit the program. | Signature/Date | | |
| Final Expected Result: | Verify the variable attributes of the existing source data of Wonder Drug ABC1234. | Actual Result: ☐ Pass ☐ Fail | | |
| Comments: | | Reviewed By: | | |

The format presented in the test plan such as the summary report can follow the same format. The examples of this chapter show only a subset of the entire test plan and are intended to give you a conceptual understanding so that you can apply the same concepts to all the other parts of the documentation.

## STEP 5: Transformation Specification

The specification of the transformation towards CDISC standards is a detailed road map that will be referenced and used by all team members during the transformation implementation. There can be different technologies used to perform this task. The following example utilizes tools including MS Excel and Transdata™. Dataset transformation is a process in which a set of source datasets and its variables are changed to meet new standard requirements. The following list describes some of the attributes and types of changes that are specified during transformation:

1. **Dataset Name** - SAS dataset names must be updated to match STDM standards, which require them to be no more than 8 characters in length.

2. **Dataset Label** - The descriptive labels of SAS datasets must be modified to conform to SDTM standards.

3. **Variable Name** - Each variable within a SAS dataset has a unique name. Variable names can be the same across different datasets, but if they share the same name, they are generally expected to possess the same attributes. Variable names are no more than 8 characters in length.

4. **Variable Label** - Each variable has an associated label that describes the variable in more detail. Labels are no more than 40 characters in length.

5. **Variable Type** - A variable's type can be either character or numeric.

6. **Variable Length** - A character variable can vary in length. The guidelines do not explicitly require a length but in general, it is from 1 to 200 characters.

7. **Format** - Variable format will be updated.

8. **Yesno** - If the value of the variable is "yes", it will produce a new

row with the newly assigned value of the label.

9. **Vertical** - Multiple variables can be assigned to one variable that will produce a row if it has a value.

10. **Combine** - Combine values of multiple source variables into one destination variable.

11. **Drop** - The variable from the source dataset will be dropped when creating the destination data.

12. **Same** - The same variable with all of the same attributes will be kept in the destination data.

13. **Value Change** - This can have either a re-coding of values or a formula change. This will change the actual values of the variable.

There may be other types of transformations, but these are the common transformation types that are usually documented in the specification. The transformation specification can be stored in an Excel spreadsheet and is organized by tabs. The first tab named "Tables" contains a list of all the source tables. The subsequent tabs contain the transformation specifications for each dataset as specified in the initial tables tab.

## Tables Tab

The Tables tab contains the list of source datasets along with descriptions of how each one transforms into the standard data model. It also records the associated data structures such as Relational Records and Supplemental Qualifiers.

ABC1234 Data Transformation

| Source Data | CDISC Data Name | SDTM 3.1 Label | Related Records | Supplemental Qualifiers |
|---|---|---|---|---|
| Ae | AE | Adverse Events | AE | AE, CM, EX, DS |
| Ccancer | DC | Disease Characteristics | | DC |
| Conduct | DV | Protocol Deviations | | DV |
| Death | DS | Disposition | DS | DS |
| Demog | DM | Demographics Domain Model | | DM, EX, DC |
| Discon | DS | Disposition | | DS |
| Elig | IE | Inclusion/Exclusion Exceptions | | MH |
| Lcea | LB | Laboratory Test Results | | LB |

The example spreadsheet lists all the source datasets from the original study. It is not always the case where you would find a one to one transformation. That is, there may be instances where many source datasets are used to create one transformed CDISC data. In that case, it is referred to as a many to one relationship. The first page in this specification will act as an index of all the data and how they relate to each other. The relationship is not limited to relationship between source and destination data, but also how it relates to CDISC domains such as in the case of "Relational Records" and "Supplemental Qualifiers". These related data structures are used within SDTM to include data that contains values which do not fit perfectly into existing domains.

## Transformation Model Tab

Each source dataset will have a separate corresponding worksheet tab detailing the transformation. The following is an example of an adverse event transformation model tab.

| Adverse Event Data Transformation from Study ABC1243 to CDISC SDTM 3.1 | | | | |
|---|---|---|---|---|
| Variable | Label | Transformation Type | Update To | Domain |
| PATNUM | Subject ID (Num) | name label length | usubjid label="Unique Subject Identifier" length=$15 | |
| STUDY | Clinical Study | name label length | studyid label="Study Identifier" length=$15 | |
| ADCONATT | Con Med Attribution and Name | name label length combine | aerelnst label="Relationship to Non-Study Treatment" length=$140 | CM |
| ADCTC | Adverse Event CTC | name label length | aeterm label="Reported Term for the Adverse Event" length=$150 | AE |
| ADCTCCAT | Organ System CTC | name label length | aebodsys label="Body System or Organ Class" length=$30 | AE |
| ADCTCOS | Other Specify CTC | Drop | | AE |
| ADDES1 | AE Description 1 | name label length combine | aeout label="Outcome of Adverse Event" length=$1000 | AE |
| ADDES2 | AE Description 2 | name label length combine | aeout label="Outcome of Adverse Event" length=$1000 | AE |
| ADDES3 | AE Description 3 | name label length combine | aeout label="Outcome of Adverse Event" length=$1000 | AE |
| ADDES4 | AE Description 4 | name label length combine | aeout label="Outcome of Adverse Event" length=$1000 | AE |
| | | | | |
| Key | | | | |
| Relational Records | | | | |
| Supplemental Qualifiers | | | | |
| Comments | | | | |

In this example, the source variable ADCTCOS is moved to the supplemental qualifiers structure. Most of the transformations are pretty straightforward attribute changes. However, the transformation of type "combine" will concatenate multiple source variables into one target variable. Most of these are going towards the AE domain except for the variable ADCONATT which is being transformed into the CM domain. This example illustrates how various details of data transformations can be expressed concisely with great detail in the form of a transformation specification.

## STEP 6: Applying Transformation

In an ideal world, the specification is completed one time and then you would apply the transformation according to the specification. In the real world however, the specification goes through changes throughout the duration of the project. You would therefore need to make an executive decision at specified times to apply the transformation even when things are still changing. Because of the dynamic nature of the data, a tool such as Transdata™ can be very useful since the transformation specification needs to also be dynamic to keep up with the changing data. Changes to the transformation would also have implications for re-programming the transformation logic. This is where manually programming transformation can lead to constant updates and become a very resource intensive task. To automate this process, the same transformation specification that was previously defined in an Excel spreadsheet is captured in a SAS dataset within Transdata and managed with the following screen.

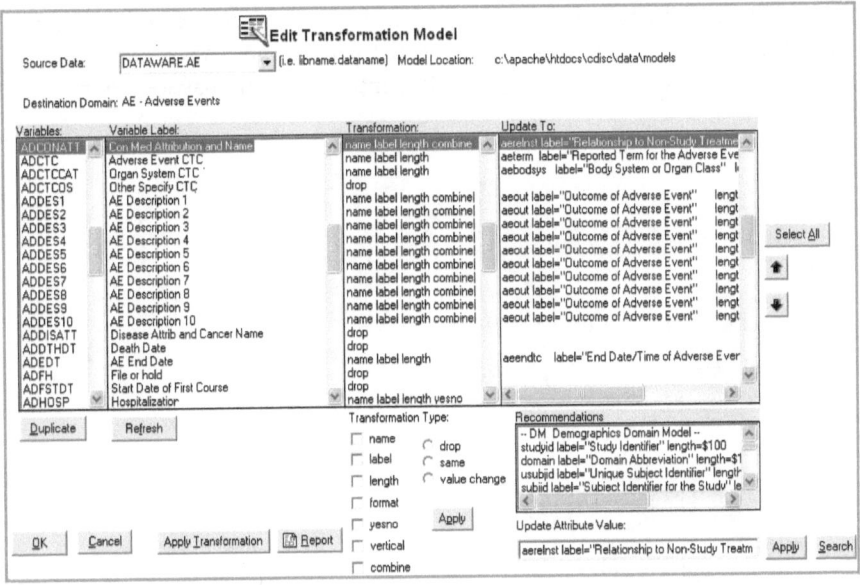

All the source variables and associated labels can be managed and displayed on the left two columns. The type of transformations including the most commonly used ones are listed with check boxes and radio buttons for ease of selection. The new attributes of the target variables which were seen from the specification spreadsheet can also be captured here. Besides being able to edit these attributes, standard attributes from CDISC are listed as suggested recommendations. The advantages to managing the specifications in this manner as compared to storing it in a spreadsheet include:

- **Audit Trail** - An audit trail is kept of all changes.

- **Selection Choices** - The selection choices of transformation type and target attributes make it easier to generate standardized transformation.

- **Code Generation** - Transformation logic coding and algorithms can be generated directly from these definitions.

- **Data Refresh** - A refresh of the source variables can be applied against physical datasets to keep up with changing data.

## Program Transformation

Once the transformation specification has been clearly defined and updated against the data, you would need to write the SAS program that would perform this transformation. A sample program may look like:

```
*************************************************;
* Program: trans_ae.sas
* Path: c:\temp\
* Description: Transform Adverse Events data
*              from DATAWARE.AE to STDMLIB.AE
* By: Sy Truong, 01/21/2006,  3:49:13 pm
*************************************************;
libname DATAWARE "C:\temp\DATA";
libname STDMLIB "C:\temp\DATA\SDTM";
data STDMLIB.AE (label="Adverse Events");
   set DATAWARE.AE;
   retain obs 1;
   *** Define new variable: aerelnst that combined by old
   variables:   adconatt adoagatt;
   attrib aerelnst label="Relationship to Non-Study
   Treatment" length=$140;
   aerelnst = trim(trim(adconatt) || ' ' || adoagatt);
   drop  adconatt adoagatt;
   *** Define new variable: aeout that combined by old
   variables:   addes1 addes2 addes3 addes4 addes5 addes6
   addes7 addes8 addes9 addes10;
   attrib aeout label="Outcome of Adverse Event"
   length=$1000;
   aeout = trim(trim(trim(trim(
   trim(trim(trim(trim(trim(
   trim(addes1) || delimit_aeout0 ||
   addes2) || delimit_aeout1 || addes3) ||
   delimit_aeout2 || addes4) || delimit_aeout3
   || addes5) || delimit_aeout4 || addes6) ||
   delimit_aeout5 || addes7) || delimit_aeout6 ||
   addes8) || delimit_aeout7 || addes9) ||
```

```
delimit_aeout8 || addes10);
drop  delimit_aeout0 delimit_aeout1 delimit_aeout2

delimit_aeout3 delimit_aeout4 delimit_aeout5
delimit_aeout6 delimit_aeout7 delimit_aeout8
delimit_aeout9  addes1 addes2 addes3 addes4 addes5
addes6 addes7 addes8 addes9 addes10 ;
run;
```

This is only an example subset since normal transformation programs can be more complex and longer. Some programs involve multiple transformations applied to separate target datasets which are then later merged into a single final target dataset. Transdata acts as a code generator so all of the code shown above is automatically generated. In the event that the transformation requires multiple datasets to be merged, you can develop code manually by performing PROC SORT and MERGE, or you can use the following interface in Transdata.

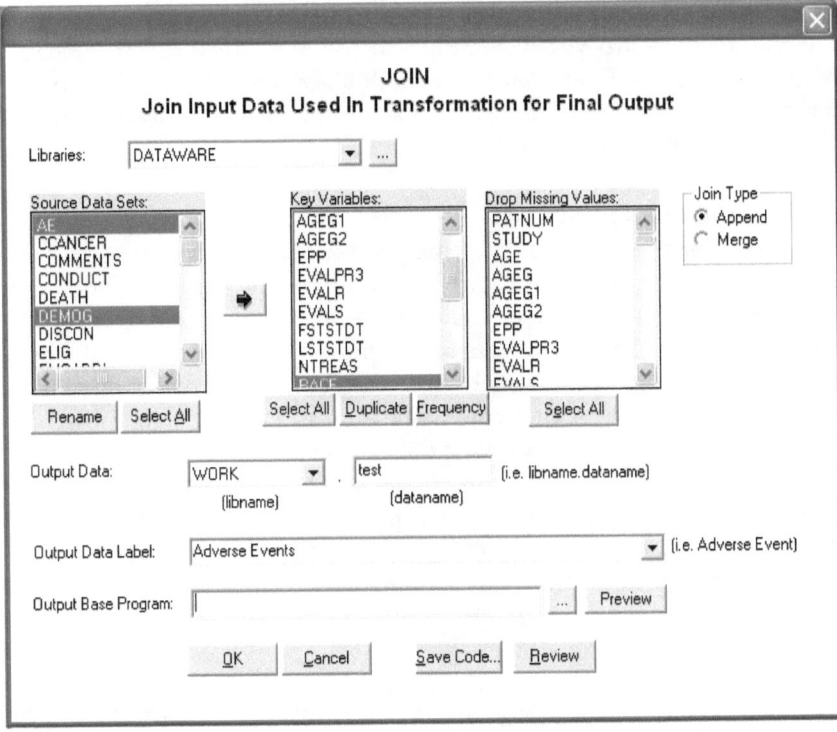

The two most common types of joins are classified as "append" or "merge". The append stacks the data on top of each other with the SAS code being something like:

```
data WORK.test (label = 'Adverse Events');
    set
        input1(in=input1)
        input2(in=input2)
    ;
    by RACE;
run;
```

The other type of merge is when the two data are actually "merged" by a particular key. The code for this is more like:

```
data WORK.test (label = 'Adverse Events');
    merge
        input1(in=input1)
        input2(in=input2)
    ;
    by RACE;
run;
```

The difference is that you would need to use the "MERGE" statement rather than the "SET" statement. In both cases, Transdata will generate this code for you so that you do not have to perform the PROC SORT and merging data step manually.

## STEP 7: Verification Reports

The validation test plan will detail the specific test cases that need to be implemented to ensure data integrity and quality of the transformation. A common report that can be generated to verify the transformation is referred to as the "Duplicate Variable" report. This report lists all the transformations that contain more than one source variable which is being transformed towards the same destination variable. The purpose of this report is to catch the following potential deviations.

The target variable attributes between the data sources are different and therefore not standard. You can therefore identify transformations that are unintentional since they may be duplicates. An example output of such a report is:

| | | Duplicate Variable Report for Transformation Variable: aereinst | | | |
|---|---|---|---|---|---|
| Obs | Source Dataset Name | Variable | Update To | Transformed Variable | Destination Table Name |
| 1 | AE | ADCONATT | aereinst label="Relationship to Non-Study Treat- | Aereinst | STDMLIB.AE |

| | | | | | |
|---|---|---|---|---|---|
| | | | ment" length=$140 | | |
| 2 | AE | ADOAGATT | aerelnst la-bel="Relationship to Non-Study Treat-ment" length=$140 | Aerelnst | STDMLIB.AE |

*Generated on: 01/21/2009, 4:27:24 pm, Sy Truong*
*Model located at: C: \CDISC\DATA\MODELS*
*Report located at: C:\cdisc\*

Part of a review process for any transformation involves doing spot checking. This is accomplished by reviewing the data before it was transformed as compared to the corresponding target transformed data. This will catch value changes that may have been incorrectly transformed due to values that are cropped or formatted incorrectly. This review is referred to as a "Sample Print" report where a PROC PRINT is produced with a subset of subjects. The user can then scroll and review, catching potential deviations. A sample output would look like:

In addition to the sample print report, another common report for verifi-

--- Source Data: DATAWARE.AE ---
Subset by subjects: 32001 32002 32003

| Obs | PATNUM | STUDY | ADCONATT | ADCTC | ADCTCCAT | ADDES1 | ADDES10 | ADDES2 | ADDES3 | ADDES4 | ADDES5 | ADDES6 | ADDE |
|---|---|---|---|---|---|---|---|---|---|---|---|---|---|
| 1 | 32001 | ABC 123 | | | | | | | | | | | |
| 2 | 32001 | ABC 123 | | | | | | | | | | | |

--- Destination Data: STDMLIB.AE ---
Subset by subjects: 32001 32002 32003

| Obs | domain | studyId | usubjId | aebodsys | aecat | aedecod | aeendtc | aemodify | aeout | aerel | aerelnst | aescat | aeseq |
|---|---|---|---|---|---|---|---|---|---|---|---|---|---|
| 1 | AE | ABC 123 | 32001 | On-Study Form 1559 (non-EPP) | | | | Hemoglobin | | | | Blood/bone marrow | 1 |
| 2 | AE | ABC 123 | 32001 | On-Study Form 1559 (non-EPP) | | | | Nausea | | | | Gastrointestinal | 2 |

cation is a "frequency review". This report will show the corresponding variables before and after the transformation is applied in aggregate form with a frequency count. This will confirm or point out deviations such as values being dropped. An example output is:

--- Source Frequency of source DATAWARE.AE ---

The FREQ Procedure

**Subject ID (Num)**

| PATNUM | Frequency | Percent | Cumulative Frequency | Cum. P. |
|--------|-----------|---------|----------------------|---------|
| 32001 | 7 | 0.13 | 7 | |
| 32002 | 1 | 0.02 | 8 | |
| 32003 | 5 | 0.09 | 13 | |
| 32004 | 4 | 0.07 | 17 | |
| 32005 | 1 | 0.02 | 18 | |
| 32006 | 3 | 0.05 | 21 | |
| 32007 | 6 | 0.11 | 27 | |
| 32008 | 6 | 0.11 | 33 | |
| 32009 | 1 | 0.02 | 34 | |
| 32010 | 11 | 0.20 | 45 | |
| 32011 | 3 | 0.05 | 48 | |
| 32012 | 6 | 0.11 | 54 | |
| 32013 | 17 | 0.31 | 71 | |

--- Destination Frequency of output STDMLIB.AE ---

The FREQ Procedure

**Domain Abbreviation**

| domain | Frequency | Percent | Cumulative Frequency | Cu |
|--------|-----------|---------|----------------------|----|
| AE | 5459 | 100.00 | 5459 | |

**Study Identifier**

| studyid | Frequency | Percent | Cumulative Frequency | Cu |
|---------|-----------|---------|----------------------|----|
| E3200 | 5459 | 100.00 | 5459 | |

**Unique Subject Identifier**

| usubjid | Frequency | Percent | Cumulative Frequency | Cu |
|---------|-----------|---------|----------------------|----|
| 32001 | 7 | 0.13 | 7 | |
| 32002 | 1 | 0.02 | 8 | |
| 32003 | 5 | 0.09 | 13 | |
| 32004 | 4 | 0.07 | 17 | |

Both these reports are shown in a format that is displayed in multiple framed windows. You can therefore scroll to view both the data before and after it has been transformed as a way of verifying that the transformation is according to the specifications. The verification reports are commonly applied during verification and can be automatically generated with Transdata. There is no need to write additional SAS code to generate the report in these instances. Other more detailed verification reports would be required but this gives you an example of the types of reports used in a validation effort.

## STEP 8: Special Purpose Domain

CDISC has several special purpose domains. Among these are three named SUPPQUAL, RELREC and CO.

1. **SUPPQUAL** - The Supplemental Qualifiers is used to capture non-standard variables and their association to parent records in domains, capturing values for variables not presently included in

the general observation-class models.

2. **RELREC** - The Related Records is used to describe relationships between records in two (or more) datasets. This includes such records as an "event" record, "intervention" record, or a "finding" record.

3. **CO** - The Comments special-purpose domain is a fixed domain that provides a solution for submitting free-text comments related to data in one or more domains which are collected on separate CRF pages dedicated to comments.

These three are similar in structure and capture values that are related to the associated domains.

## Supplemental Qualifiers

An example of the SUPPQUAL is shown here:

| | | | | | | | Preview of Dataset Name: SUPPQUAL | | |
| Obs | Study Identifier | Related Domain Abbreviation | Unique Subject Identifier | Identifier Variable | Identifier Variable Value | Qualifier Variable Name | Qualifier Variable Label | Data Value | Origin |
|---|---|---|---|---|---|---|---|---|---|
| 1 | 23423 | AE | 1803 | seqnum | 64001 | ae | ADVERSE EXPERIENCE | | derived |
| 2 | 23423 | AE | 101 | seqnum | 64007 | ae | ADVERSE EXPERIENCE | (R) PLEURAL EFFUSION | derived |
| 3 | 23423 | AE | 1102 | seqnum | 64003 | ae | ADVERSE EXPERIENCE | (SOB) SHORTNESS OF BREATH | derived |
| 4 | 23423 | AE | 1103 | seqnum | 64001 | ae | ADVERSE EXPERIENCE | ABDOMINAL CRAMPING | derived |
| 5 | 23423 | AE | 102 | seqnum | 64009 | ae | ADVERSE EXPERIENCE | ABDOMINAL DISTENTION | derived |
| 6 | 23423 | AE | 101 | seqnum | 64004 | Ae | ADVERSE EXPERIENCE | ABSCESS PARADONTAL | derived |

Most data used in clinical trials for the purpose of analysis and reporting are not stored in this manner. The data structure in this example is optimized for submission. The "qualifier variable name" is usually one of the columns found in the dataset. However, in this case, it is transposed and the column variable is stored in a separate column. This approach allows the structure to handle different variables and is more flexible. The flexibility is useful to allow the inclusion of non standard variables; however, this usually requires you to perform a transposition from your source data.

Since the destination value is a character field, the transformation may require additional conversions for numeric or date source variables. Here is an example code segment that performs this type of transformation.

```
*** Transpose the for variable TRTCYC ***;
data work.suppqual;
   set sourcelib.ae;

   *** Convert numeric idvar ***;
   idvar="aerbdt";
   idvarvan = aerbdt;
   idvarval = left(trim(put(idvarvan,DATE9.)));
   qvaln = trtcyc;
   qval = left(trim(put(qvaln,best.)));
   usubjidn = patnum;
   rdomain = "AE";
   qnam = "otherae";
   qlabel = "Other Specify Adverse Event";
run;

*** Append data to the final destination SUPPQUAL ***;
data SDTMLIB.suppqual (label =
   "Supplemental Qualifiers for Adverse Events");
   set SDTMLIB.suppqual_ae
      work.suppqua2;
   if compress(studyid) = '' and
   compress(usubjid) = '' then delete;
run;
```

This code segment only shows you part of what is happening. It does however illustrate the need to handle transformations one variable at a time and the need for handling different variable types. If there are many datasets with many variables, this type of transformation can cumulatively add up to be a big task. CDISC Builder™ contains tools to handle these transformations of structures including SUPPQUAL, RELREC and CO.

The following decisions need to be made when working with the SUPPQUAL dataset. They include:

1. **Input Dataset** - Select all the input datasets from the source location that need to contribute to the SUPPQUAL.

2. **Input Variables** - Select variables that are not part of the main domain but are considered supplemental. These are deemed important enough to be part of the final submission yet do not fit perfectly to the variables within the specified domain.

3. **Source Type** - Define the type of source of specified variables. This can have values such as CRF, Assigned, or Derived.

4. **Related Domain** - Determine which related domain this dataset is

pertaining to.

5. **Study Identifier** - Document what study or protocol name and number this belongs to.

6. **Identification Variable** - Identify what key fields can be used to uniquely identify the selected fields. This can be a sequence variable, group ID or unique date variable.

7. **Unique Subject ID** - Identify the variable which contains the unique subject identification value.

The selection of the above criteria can be made with the following interface.

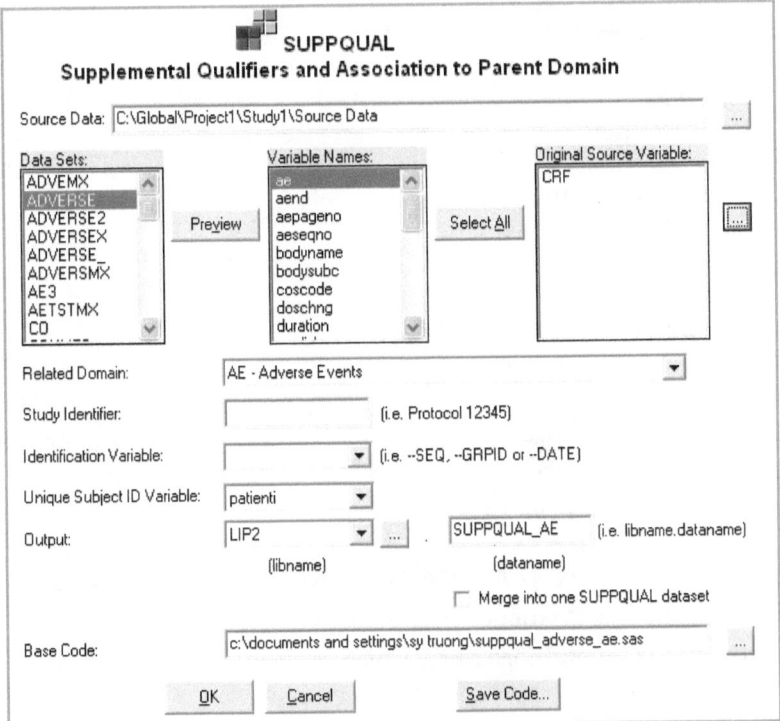

Parameters are selected, the user can decide upon the origins. The interface provides default values that can assist the user in making these decisions quickly. Once the user is proficient at making these types of selections, a macro interface is available for efficient production batch processing.

## Related Records

The related records data domain is similar in structure to the supplemental qualifier. These variables are found in events, findings or intervention records. The domains which are identified in these records include:

**Intervention**
Concomitant Medications
Exposure
Substance Use

**Events**
Adverse Events
Disposition
Medical History

**Findings**
ECG Test Results
Inclusion/Exclusion Exceptions
Laboratory Test Results
Physical Examinations
Questionnaires
Subject Characteristics
Vital Signs

This covers a wide range of fields. The types of fields selected to be related records can be very flexible, but the data structure which is used to store RELREC is strict. The following decisions therefore need to be made to transpose the data into a related record.

1. **Input Dataset** - Select all the input datasets from the source location that needs contribute to the RELREC.
2. **Related Domain** - Determine which related domain this dataset is pertaining to.
3. **Study Identifier** - Document what study or protocol name and number this belongs to.
4. **Identification Variable** - Identify what key fields can be used to uniquely identify the selected fields. This can be a sequence variable, group ID or unique date variable.
5. **Unique Subject ID** - Identify the variable which contains the

unique subject identification value.

A graphical user interface implemented by CDISC Builder is used to assist in selecting these decisions.

The interface also has a "find related" tool which assists you in identifying fields that are potentially considered to be a related record field. It searches through the variable names and labels for key words. A report is then generated showing the possible related field.

*Find Related Domain for: DEATH*

| Obs | Dataset and Variable | Data Table Name | Variable Name | Variable Length | Variable Label | Variable Type | Matched Criteria |
|-----|----------------------|-----------------|---------------|-----------------|----------------|---------------|------------------|
| 1 | death.event | Death | EVENT | 8 | EVENT LEADING TO DEATH | N | Variable label (to ) |

*Generated on: 02/12/2006, 5:03:10 pm, Sy Truong*
*Located at: C:\GLOBAL\PROJECT1\STUDY1\SOURCE DATA*

In this example, the key word it found was the word "to" in the label. This report is an example of how the tool can assist in expediting the selection and the creation of related record domain dataset.

## Comments

An analysis file or source data from an operational database usually has the comment fields stored in the same dataset which the comments pertains to. For example, if there is a comment captured on a CRF pertaining to adverse events; you would find this in the adverse event dataset. CDISC data structure is different in that all the comments from all different sources are gathered together and stored separately in its own dataset named CO. In doing so, you have to identify additional information such as which domain the comment is related to. The decision and selection process for the comment is similar to SUPPQUAL and RELREC. In the "find related", there is a tool named "find comment". This will search through variables and labels finding possible comment fields. This is usually pretty accurate since comment fields usually have labels that have key words such as "comment" in them.

The three special purpose domains defined by CDISC are very flexible. It is vertical in structure so it can handle just about any source data. It is however very unusual for data to be stored in this manner when being captured, entered or analyzed for clinical trials. It is therefore necessary to perform the transformation which is a time consuming task. Automated macros and tools can help expedite these types of transformations.

### STEP 9: Sequence, Order and Lengths

Data value sequence along with variable order and lengths needs to also follow standards. CDISC specify guidance for data sequences and variable order but it does not strictly define specific variable lengths. Even without specific variable length settings, it is still important to have these applied consistently.

## Sequence

Any dataset that contains more than one observation per subject requires a sequence variable. The sequence variable would then identify the order of the values for each subject. If your data does not contain this sequence variable, you would need to add it. Besides the subject ID, you would also need to identify a unique identifier variable that would distinguish between the observations within one subject. This can be another type of identification variable such as a form date.

CDISC Builder supplies a tool named ADDSEQ that would add this sequence based upon the choices you decide upon a specific dataset.

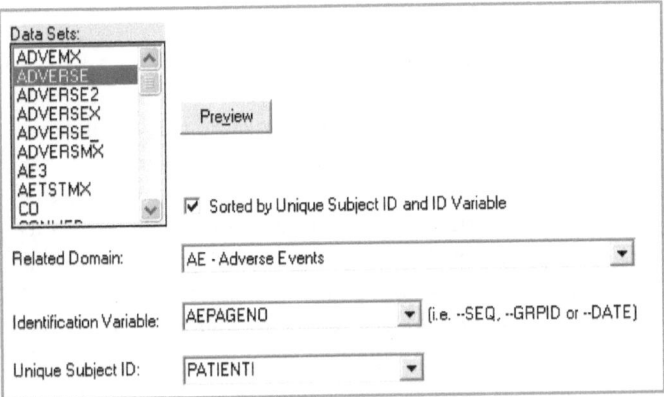

The ADDSEQ tool will then create a new sequence variable containing sequential values after it sorts the data by the subject ID and identification variable. In addition to creating the sequence variables, there is also a tool that tells you if the dataset requires a sequence variable or not. It essentially verifies if there is more than one observation per subject. This will then help prompt you to add sequence variables in case it is overlooked.

## Variable Order

The data that is delivered in CDISC format needs to be ordered in a standard manner. All the key fields need to be first. The rest of the variables are then shown in alphabetical order or in the order that is defined in the case report form. SAS datasets has its variables stored in a specified order and it is not necessary in this standard order. CDISC Builder will re-order the variables with the keys appearing first followed by the rest of the variables. The rest can be optionally alphabetized or left in their original order. This task may appear mundane but can be very helpful for the reviewer who is navigating through many datasets.

## Variable Lengths

Variable lengths are not strictly specified by CDISC guidelines. It is still however important to have variable lengths follow a standard for consistency. This includes:

- Consistent lengths between variables that are the same across different data domains
- Optimal lengths set to handle the data

In order to accomplish consistent lengths, if you were to assign a length of one variable such as USUBJID on one dataset; you would need to set the same length for all other variables that are the same across all datasets. The second rule suggests that if the contents of your variables for the same field have the largest text value of 9 characters. In this case, a better standard is to set the length to 10. It makes sense to round up to the nearest tenth to give it some buffer but not too much so that it would be wasteful. Datasets can be very bloated and oversized for the stored values. The following tool named VARLEN from CDISC Builder assigns the length optimally.

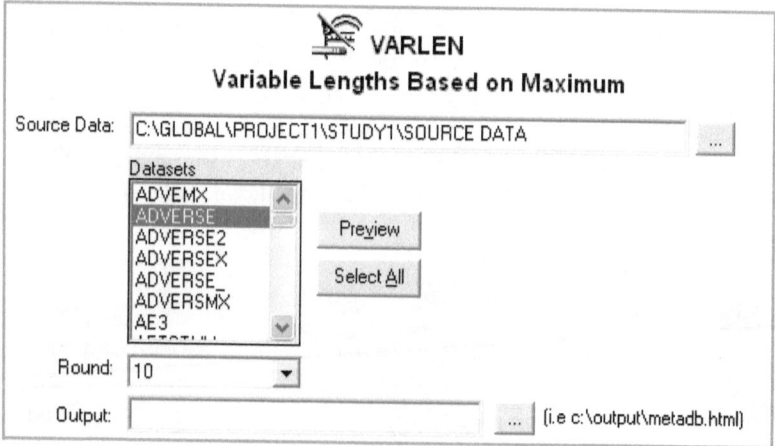

In this example, the rounding option can be set to 10, 20 or none. It can therefore assign the exact maximum length which the data value contains if that is what is required. This would create the proper length statement so that your data will have the optimal lengths used for the associated values stored in that data.

## STEP 10: Data Definition Documentation

When you plan for a road trip, you need a map. This is analogous to understanding the data that is going to be included as part of an electronic submission. The reviewer requires a road map in order to understand what all the variables are and how they are derived. It is within the interest of all team members involved to have the most accurate and concise documentation pertaining to the data. This can help your internal team work more effectively while also speeding up the review process which can really make or break an electronic submission to the FDA.

## Levels of Metadata

There are several steps towards documenting the data definition. The largest component in the process of documentation is capturing the metadata. The metadata is the contextual information about the data that provides essential details for the reviewer to gain greater understanding of what is being submitted. There are several layers to the metadata. These include:

1. **General Information** – High level descriptions and labels that affects the entire set of datasets that are to be included. It could be things such as the name of the study, the company name, or location of the data.
2. **Data Table** – Descriptive detailed information at the SAS dataset level. This includes things such as the dataset name and label.
3. **Variable** – This information pertains to attributes of the variables within a dataset. This includes such information as variable name, label and lengths.
4. **Value Level** – This is the metadata pertaining to the each value stored in the variables.

There is a top down relationship between these levels of information. The top level of general information is an umbrella over all information that spans all datasets. The data table level in turn spans over all the variables. The variable level is then contained in each specified dataset. It is therefore important to order for metadata displayed in the documentation in the same order as the layers from top to bottom.

## Capture General Information

The following lists the types of information you need to be included at the highest level for the General Information.

| Metadata | Description |
|---|---|
| Company Name | This is the name of the organization that is submitting the data to the FDA. |
| Product Name | The name of the drug that is being submitted. |
| Protocol | The name of the study on which the analysis is being performed which includes this set of data. |
| Layout | The company name, product name, and protocol are all going to be displayed on the final documentation. The layout information will describe if it will be in the footnote or title and how it is aligned. |

This level metadata will be used in the final documentation in the form of headers and footers on the final documentation.

## Dataset Level Information

Some of the dataset level information can be captured through the PROC CONTENTS but this only captures a subset of the information. Additional information needs to be defined when you are documenting your data definition. Some of the information needed to be documented for the data level includes:

| Metadata | Description |
|---|---|
| Data Library | Library name defines what physical path on which server and where the data is located. This can also be in the form of a SAS LIBNAME. |
| Key Fields | Keys usually correlate to the sort order of the data. These variables are usually used to merge the datasets together. |
| Format Library | This is where the SAS format catalog is stored. |
| Dataset Name | The name of the SAS dataset that is being captured. |
| Number of Variables | A count of the number of variables for each dataset. |
| Number of Records | Number of observations or rows within each dataset. |

| | |
|---|---|
| Dataset Comment | A descriptive text describing the dataset. This can contain the dataset label and other descriptive text explaining the data. |

SAS Tools such as PROC CONTENTS can contribute to most of these items. However, comments and key fields can be edited which may differ from what is stored in the dataset.

## Variable Level Information

The variable level to the data definition documentation captures the variable attributes. This includes the following:

| Metadata | Description |
|---|---|
| Variable Name | The name of the SAS variable. |
| Type | The variable type which includes values such as Character or Numeric. |
| Length | The variable length. |
| Label | The descriptive label of the variable. |
| Format | SAS formats used. If it is a user defined format, it would need to be decoded. |
| Origins | The document where the variable came from. Sample values include: Source or Derived. |
| Role | This defines what type of role the variable is being used for. Example values include: Key, Ad Hoc, Primary Safety, Secondary Efficacy |
| Comment | This is a descriptive text explaining the meaning of the variable or how it was derived. |

Similar to the data set level metadata, some of the variable level attributes can be captured through PROC CONTENTS. However, fields such as origins, role and comments need to be edited by someone who understands the meaning of the data.

## Generating Documentation

After the information has been captured; the process is to generate the documentation in either PDF or XML format. The challenge is that in order to make the documentation useful, it requires hyperlinks to link the information together. The manual method does allow you to format the information in Word and this can be converted into PDF format. Even though Word and Excel can generate XML, it does not have the proper schema so there is no manual way of generating the XML version of the report. Definedoc™ has the flexibility of generating the report in Excel, RTF, PDF and XML.

It utilizes ODS within SAS to produce the output to in all these formats. In addition to the XML file, Definedoc also produces the accompanying cascading style sheet and XSL file to format the XML so that you can view this within a web browser similar to an HTML file. An example DEFINE.XML output is shown below.

## CDISC Challenges

There are many challenges in working with the CDISC SDTM. The data structure that has been established is optimized and intended for the reviewer. The flexibility structure intended for submission can also create a structure that is very different from how users use it during the conduct of the clinical trials while performing analysis. The difference in the types of structure leads to the need to perform transformations. Since the transformations are handled differently for each variable, the accumulated amount of the work can be very resource intensive. It does require a substantial amount of organization before implementing the project. The techniques, methodologies and tools presented in this chapter demonstrate ways of optimizing and working with CDISC data which is based on real world experience. Armed with these approaches, you can avoid the pitfalls and mistakes leading to a successful implementation of CDISC models.

two

# The Past, Present, and Future of Clinical Data Standards

### Chris Decker

One of Albert Einstein' s many great quotes during his life included the following: "The distinction between past, present and future is only a stubbornly persistent illusion". This quote is a perfect microcosm for data standards in the clinical research industry.

Over the last decade the clinical research industry has attempted to work toward a common data standard with the goal of accelerating the drug development process by improving the data collection, transformation, analysis and submission process. The adoption of industry wide standards has been slow going and led to a wide range of challenges. Decades of legacy processes and non standard data have led to internal company data standards that are inconsistent and differ wildly from company to company. Within a company, there are a many levels of consistency depending on the enforcement of these standards. Across companies the exercise of trying to combine data becomes a bottomless pit of unusable data. Given the issues of drug safety over the last decade, both pharmaceutical companies and the FDA are accelerating the need for data standards across the industry. This chapter will provide a history of clinical data standards, the current state of the union, and one person's peek into how standards might evolve over the next decade. The chapter will also discuss the parallel role of SAS in these standards over time.

In the famous story, a Christmas Carol, Ebenezer Scrooge is visited by the ghost of Christmas past, present and future with the hope of showing him the error of his ways and positively changing his future. Using the Christmas Carol story, this chapter will describe how the Ghost of Clinical Standards past, present and future can help us change our ways and provide hope for the future.

## THE PAST

The Ghost of Christmas Past visited Ebenezer Scrooge to remind him of the simpler times, within his childhood. If the Ghost of Clinical Standards Past visited us today he would tell us a similar story. With the introduction of computers, the data collection process for clinical trials was a new fangled idea and the idea of data standards really did not cross many people's minds. Each study had their own unique set of data and the perception was that there was no way you could reuse information across studies. Clinical studies and the associated data were "special".

## IDENTIFYING CHALLENGES

As technology became more robust, clinical programmers started to realize the inefficiencies in recreating processes and metadata from scratch every time as well as the overlap in data elements across studies. They also saw the many inconsistent methods for collecting specific data elements that seem simple on the surface. The simplest examples that convey this challenge is the definition of gender of a subject (Male or Female) within a clinical study. At quick glance, this seems like a very a non ambiguous data point. However, as you can see from the figure below even something this simple can lead to challenges.

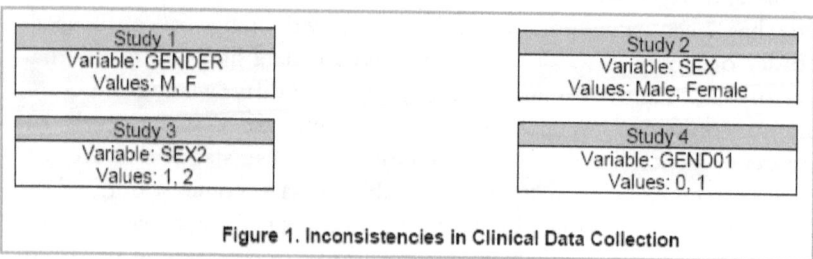

Figure 1. Inconsistencies in Clinical Data Collection

It's fairly obvious from this figure that the lack of data standards can lead to a myriad of issues when different people define codes, variables, and processes across studies. This led companies to begin defining data standards within their organizations.

## COMPANIES BEGIN TO STANDARDIZE

Clinical research companies began to define companywide data standards to improve efficiencies in both the reusability of tools as well as the ability to combine data across clinical studies. While this seems like it would be a fairly straightforward process, companies soon find themselves buried in discussions around the best way to accomplish this task.

Many of the data managers, clinical programmers, statisticians, and clinicians had different perspectives primarily due to their specific needs. These needs, while similar in some cases, differed more often than not. Data Managers were very focused on defining a data standard that optimized the data collection process and reduced the need to reconcile data issues. Clinical programmers and statisticians wanted data that was analysis ready to generate the tables, listing, and figures needed for submission to the FDA. The clinicians did not necessarily understand the need for standards, but just wanted as much information they could have within their data. These differences among users led to many late night discussions to hammer out standards.

In addition, there are a number of unique aspects of the clinical research process which make defining a rigid data standard complex. First, each disease studied within clinical research has its own methodology and testing associated with it. So the way you study heart disease is very different from how you study asthma. Therefore, the type of data, as well as the way you collect it, varies greatly. Second, advances in medical science occur very rapidly within a disease and thus lead to even more changes in how the data is collected, analyzed, and reported.

Finally, the clinical research industry is governed by rigorous regulation and the data collected in this process has many audiences. A drug development company uses the data in one way whereas regulatory agencies use it differently.

All of these differences lead to roadblocks in defining a common standard. These additional complexities create even more challenges with defining, using, and maintaining a data standard.

## CDISC IS BORN

Over the last 25 years, data standards have slowly been adopted for the collection and transfer of clinical data. In the beginning the focus was on real time data collected at hospitals, and the standard used for this exercise was Health Level 7 (HL7). However, this standard was more for the individual patient data points in the health care arena and could not easily be translated to the clinical research area.

In the late 90's a group of individuals decided to get together to see if they tackle the monumental challenge of defining a data standard across clinical research. The Clinical Data Interchange Standards Consortium (CDISC) was formed with the mission "to develop and support global, platform-independent data standards that enable information system interoperability to improve medical research". Over the last decade, a number of models have been developed within CDISC to support the needs of clinical trial data. The table below contains a list of the more critical models CDISC has developed over the years.

Table 1. Summary of Relevant CDISC models

| Model/Standard | Purpose |
| --- | --- |
| Operational Data Model (ODM) | XML specification supporting interchange of data, metadata or updates of both between clinical systems |
| Clinical Data Acquisition Standards Harmonization (CDASH) | Data model for a core set of global data collection fields (element name, definition, metadata) |
| Submissions Data Tabulation Model (SDTM) | Submissions Data Tabulation Model (SDTM) including standard domains, variables, and rules |
| Analysis Dataset Models (ADaM) | Data model closely related to SDTM to support the statistical reviewer |
| Define.xml | XML Specification to contain the metadata associated with a clinical study for submission |
| Standards for the Exchange of Non-clinical Data (SEND) | Data model extending SDTM to support the submission of animal toxicity studies |
| Protocol Representation Model (PRM) | Metadata model focused on the characteristics of a study and the definition and association of activities within the protocols, including "arms" and "epochs". |
| Terminology | Standard list of terms across all the CDISC data models. |

The standards described in this table have varying levels of maturity. The SDTM and define.xml are probably the most widely used CDISC components and has been referenced in various FDA documents. While CDISC has done an excellent job of laying the foundation for clinical data standards, changing the large and extremely lethargic clinical research industry is a daunting task. It has taken 10 years to get organization on board with this effort and moving in the same direction.

## ROLE OF SAS

SAS has always been a core component to the data processing and analysis of clinical data. In the early days of collecting data electronically, the clinical research industry, which consisted of predominantly non technical people needed a programming language that easy to use and could perform high end analytics. SAS was obviously a perfect fit, and this began a long and dominant use of SAS for processing clinical data. In 1999, the FDA identified the SAS V5 transport file as the mechanism for delivering data to the FDA. The FDA selected this format because it was an open format which means the structure was in the public domain and could be consumed by other technologies. By US law, the FDA must remain "vendor neutral" and cannot endorse or require use of any specific vendor's product.

In the mid 1990's, SAS began looking at building industry specific solutions and the pharmaceutical industry was an obvious target. SAS came out with two products to support data warehousing and clinical reporting. PH.DataWare was built on top of Warehouse Administrator and was SAS first attempt at building an ETL specific tool for data transformations. PH.Clinical (Figure 2) was built as a SAS report generation tool as well as a clinical tool for viewing and exploring clinical data. Both products had some success but were not widely adopted. The ETL solution was too rigid and did not provide enough flexibility for the uniqueness of clinical data; a challenge commonly seen in ETL solutions. The PH.Clinical solution took too much programming out of the hands of hard core SAS programmers and made them work with point and click interfaces. Both products were slowly phased out in the mid 2000's.

## Figure 2. Reporting Interface within PH.Clinical

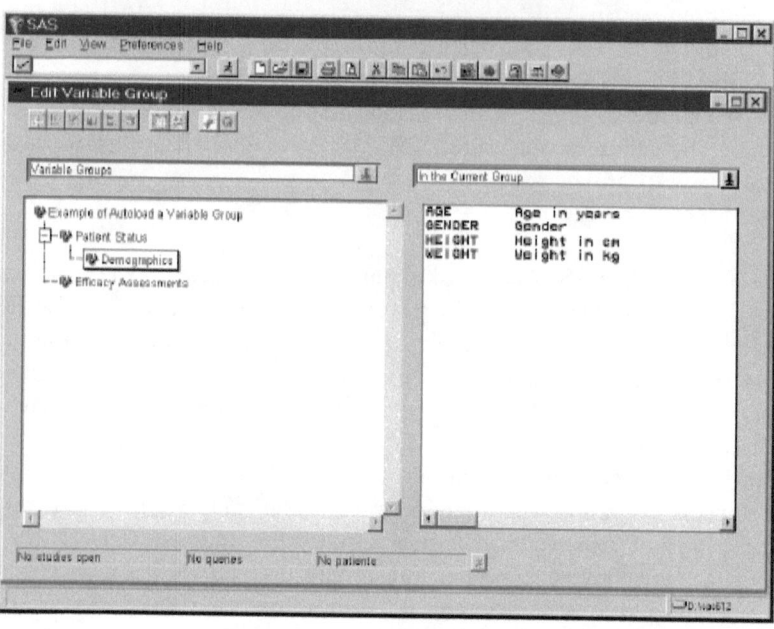

PROC CDISC was developed in the early 2000's to help support the new emerging CDISC standard. It attempted to support the ODM standard within CDISC and provide tools to move data back and forth between SAS and the ODM xml specification. While it provided some basic capabilities for SAS programmers, it was not fully supported by SAS and never had a production release. In addition, because the use of ODM was somewhat limited early on, there was no real demand for this capability.

The biggest challenge SAS faced in implementing solutions to support clinical data standards for the Clinical SAS programmers. Programmers within this industry have a long history of using BASE SAS for creating, in some cases, very elaborate SAS frameworks for dealing with clinical data standards. Replacing these home grown solutions that involved entrenched SAS programmers was sometimes difficult even though most of the time, the home grown systems were not very robust.

## THE PRESENT

In the Christmas Carol, the Ghost of Christmas Present visits Ebenezer Scrooge to show him a variety of scenes ranging from festive events to lonely orphans in an attempt to teach Mr. Scrooge a sense of responsibility for his fellow man. Again, this story provides a parallel analogy to the Clinical Standards process. The Ghost of Clinical Standards Present would tell us that industry wide standards have been adopted with mixed results and the technology to support those standards is all over the map. However, the same Ghost would tell us that we must all feel a sense of responsibility to our fellow industry colleagues to help make the drug development process more efficient.

## INEFFICIENCES OF THE REGULATORY REVIEW PROCESS

Probably the one issue that has ignited an aggressive movement towards data standards is the need to make drugs safer as major issues have surfaced regarding the safety of drugs over the last decade. In the past, most companies have submitted data in their own proprietary standards; making the need to combine data across therapeutic classes of drugs an impossible task. Therefore, the FDA and other regulatory agencies cannot look at integrated data to identify safety issues before they occur. In addition, without standardized data to use with standard review tools, the review cycle becomes slow and tedious. Figure 3 below from an FDA reviewer highlights the sophisticated review process. As you can tell, this is probably not the most efficient way to review data.

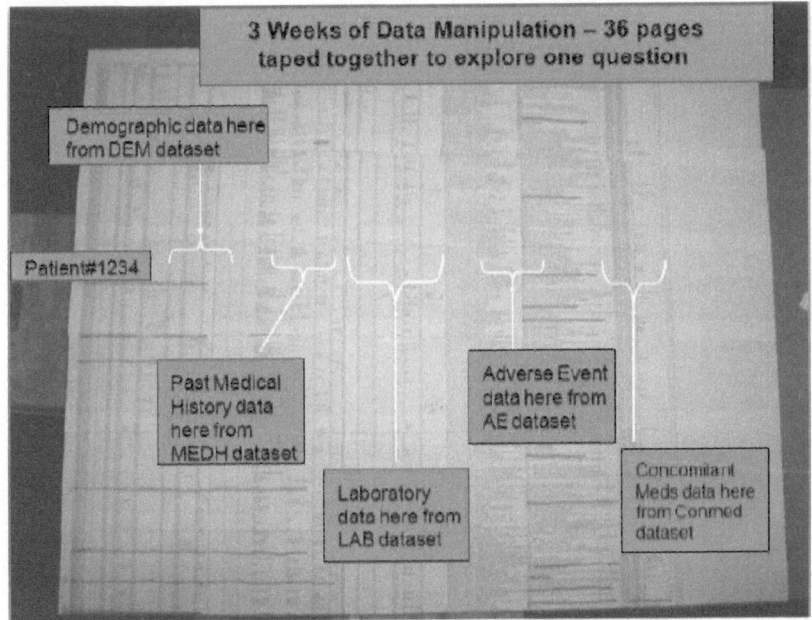

Figure 3. FDA Review Process[1]

These issues have led to increased funding at the FDA to support the implementation and use of data standards including training, pilots, and creating the Computational Sciences Center (CSC) to drive the direction within the agency. The mission of the CSC is to create an integrated review environment including an informatics platform allowing easy access to review tools, use of data standards, and support for data management and review tool development.

Recently, the FDA gave a clear message that they want data submitted in the CDISC SDTM, ADaM, and define.xml formats even if the standards do not currently meet all their needs. The CDISC standards should by every company' s baseline and it should begin during data collection. The FDA will continue to collaborate with industry and CDISC to refine the standards to meet their needs.

## BARRIERS TO ADOPTION

One of the biggest challenges in adopting standards and technology is the strong reluctance to change. "It it is not broken then do not fix it" is the comfortable cliché people use and reluctance to change is common behavior among most individuals.

Unfortunately, as companies begin to adopt data standards, they are not defining it as an integral part of their operational process but after the fact as a necessary evil of submitting the data to the FDA. This issue began due to the widespread adoption of CDISC SDTM, a model defined for the raw data in a submission format. By defining this model first, CDISC started their standards development smack dab in the middle of the process, the creation of study data for submission in the model. At the time this made sense because the most important customer of the data was the FDA. Unfortunately, this creates challenges because it is not the way data is collected or analyzed within the drug development process. As companies try to adopt the SDTM standard, they are very reluctant to change their processes and internal operational data standards. Therefore, if the standards are not integrated into their process and initiated much further upstream during study design and data collection, SDTM ends up being a very expensive and time consuming exercise at the end of a clinical trial.

However, companies are slowly starting to modify their internal processes to better support the standard. With the increased use of the ODM model for data transfer as well as the introduction and swift implementation of CDASH for data collection, the adoption of the standards should increase rapidly over the next decade. The data standards will now be used at beginning of the clinical trial, the data collection step, and more easily move through the data transformation and analysis steps.

Finally, the current standards do a very good job of defining the generic data structures because those data domains are very consistent across clinical studies. These include domains such as Demographics, Adverse Events, and Laboratory parameters, data usually categorized as safety data within a clinical trial. Figure 4 shows a sample of the standard SDTM domains.

## Figure 4. Summary of CDISC SDTM Domains

**Special-Purpose Domains (defined in Section 5):**
- Demographics — DM
- Subject Elements — SE
- Comments — CO
- Subject Visits — SV

**Interventions General Observation Class (defined in Section 6.1):**
- Concomitant Medications — CM
- Substance Use — SU
- Exposure — EX

**Events General Observation Class (defined in Section 6.2):**
- Adverse Events — AE
- Medical History — MH
- Clinical Events — CE
- Disposition — DS
- Protocol Deviations — DV

**Findings General Observation Class (defined in Section 6.3):**
- ECG Test Results — EG
- Laboratory Test Results — LB
- Questionnaires — QS
- Vital Signs — VS
- Microbiology Specimen — MB
- PK Concentrations — PC
- Inclusion/Exclusion Criterion Not Met — IE
- Physical Examination — PE
- Subject Characteristics — SC
- Drug Accountability — DA
- Microbiology Susceptibility Test — MS
- PK Parameters —PP

**Findings About (defined in Section 6.4)**
- Findings About — FA

**Trial Design Domains (defined in Section 7):**
- Trial Arms — TA
- Trial Visits — TV
- Trial Summary — TS
- Trial Elements — TE
- Trial Inclusion/Exclusion Criteria — TI

**Relationship Datasets (defined in Section 8):**
- Supplemental Qualifiers — SUPPQUAL or multiple SUPP-- datasets
- Related Records — RELREC

However, diseases have unique data elements that must be analyzed leading to different collection mechanisms and the need to define disease specific data standards. The question from users is always, "Where do I put this data?" and this challenge leads to inconsistency in these disease specific standards. While the FDA has stated their support for the current standards, they have asked CDISC to increase the speed at which they develop disease specific standards.

## NOT A TWO DIMENSIONAL WORLD

The most critical gap in the existing standards is the two dimensional world they live in. The standards define specific data domains with variable names, definitions, and rules but clinical research is much more complex than rows and columns in a SAS data set. Tabular data structures are very limited in the information they can convey. The CDISC models strongly encourage the use of metadata to help define the traceability and transparency of the data. The define.xml is an xml specification which captures the metadata about the data submitted to the FDA. However, the xml and the SAS data sets are technically disconnected from each other. Therefore, the process of defining and managing metadata is very manual and prone to errors and inconsistent information.

In addition to the need for more tightly connected metadata and data, the standards must provide a better mechanism for tying together data around a patient instead of data associated with a domain. For example, currently Adverse Events are collected in a single domain within SDTM. However, a clinician wants to understand the complex relationships across multiple clinical endpoints within a patient, with Adverse Event being just one endpoint. There needs to be a better way to define metadata about the data in a much more transparent and hierarchical way so more dynamic relationships can be described.

In recent years the FDA has discussed the idea of moving the clinical research data standards into a more robust HL7 xml standard which is currently used for health care systems and electronic health records. However, over the last year, large gaps have been identified in attempting to move the current standards to this model. While this will continue to be investigated, there is no timeline for an implementation. In lieu of a drastic shift to a standard such as HL7, the increased adoption of the ODM xml specification for transferring data between systems might provide a more realistic opportunity to shift towards a hierarchical data standard and tightly integrate metadata and data.

## ROLE OF SAS

At the beginning of 2009 SAS put a new focus on developing solutions to support clinical data standards and transformations.

After years of attempting to develop tools to support clinical data standards, SAS has developed what appears to be a robust framework within BASE SAS to support the management of clinical data standards. The SAS Clinical Standards Toolkit is a framework of SAS macros, metadata, and configuration files including a representation of the SDTM metadata (Figure 4), a large set of validation checks, and the ability to create define.xml for submissions.

### Figure 4. Study Metadata within Clinical Toolkit

VIEWTABLE: Source Table Metadata

| | Table Name | Table Label | Observation Class within Standard | Relative path to xpt file | Title for xpt file |
|---|---|---|---|---|---|
| 2 | DM | Demographics | Special Purpose | ..\cdisc-sdtm-3.1.1\sample\cdisc-sdtm-3.. | Demographics SAS transport |
| 3 | DS | Disposition | Events | ..\cdisc-sdtm-3.1.1\sample\cdisc-sdtm-3.. | Disposition SAS transport file |
| 4 | DV | Protocol Deviations | Events | ..\cdisc-sdtm-3.1.1\sample\cdisc-sdtm-3.. | Protocol Deviations SAS tran |
| 5 | IE | Inclusion/Exclusion Exceptions | Findings | ..\cdisc-sdtm-3.1.1\sample\cdisc-sdtm-3.. | Inclusion/Exclusion Exceptio transport file |
| 6 | LB | Laboratory Tests | Findings | ..\cdisc-sdtm-3.1.1\sample\cdisc-sdtm-3.. | Laboratory Tests SAS transp |
| 7 | MH | Medical History | Events | ..\cdisc-sdtm-3.1.1\sample\cdisc-sdtm-3.. | Medical History SAS transpo |
| 8 | PF | Pulmonary Function | Findings | ..\cdisc-sdtm-3.1.1\sample\cdisc-sdtm-3.. | Pulmonary Function SAS tran |
| 9 | RELREC | Related Records | Relates | ..\cdisc-sdtm-3.1.1\sample\cdisc-sdtm-3.. | Related Records SAS transp |
| 10 | SUPPAE | Supplemental Qualifiers - AE | Relates | ..\cdisc-sdtm-3.1.1\sample\cdisc-sdtm-3.. | Supplemental Qualifiers -AE transport file |
| 11 | SUPPALL | Supplemental Qualifiers - ALL | Relates | ..\cdisc-sdtm-3.1.1\sample\cdisc-sdtm-3.. | Supplemental Qualifiers - ALL transport file |

VIEWTABLE: Srcmeta.Source_columns

| | SAS reference sourcedata label | Table Name | Column Name | Column Description | Column Order | Column Type | Column Length | Column Required or Optional | Column Origin | Column Role |
|---|---|---|---|---|---|---|---|---|---|---|
| 1 | SRCDATA | AE | STUDYID | Study Identifier | 1 | C | 40 | Req | CRF | Identifier |
| 2 | SRCDATA | AE | DOMAIN | Domain Abbreviation | 2 | C | 6 | Req | Derived | Identifier |
| 3 | SRCDATA | AE | USUBJID | Unique Subject Identifier | 3 | C | 40 | Req | Sponsor Defined | Identifier |
| 4 | SRCDATA | AE | AESEQ | Sequence Number | 4 | N | 0 | Req | CRF or Derived | Identifier |
| 5 | SRCDATA | AE | AEGRPID | Group ID | 5 | C | 40 | Perm | Sponsor Defined | Identifier |
| 6 | SRCDATA | AE | AEREFID | Reference ID | 6 | C | 40 | Perm | Sponsor Defined | Identifier |
| 7 | SRCDATA | AE | AESPID | Sponsor-Defined Identifier | 7 | C | 40 | Perm | Sponsor Defined | Topic |
| 8 | SRCDATA | AE | AETERM | Reported Term for the Adverse Event | 8 | C | 200 | Req | CRF | Topic |
| 9 | SRCDATA | AE | AEMODIFY | Modified Reported Term | 9 | C | 200 | Perm | Sponsor Defined | Synonym Qualifier |
| 10 | SRCDATA | AE | AEDECOD | Dictionary-Derived Term | 10 | C | 200 | Req | Derived | Synonym Qualifier |
| 11 | SRCDATA | AE | AECAT | Category for Adverse Event | 11 | C | 40 | Perm | Sponsor Defined | Grouping Qualifier |
| 12 | SRCDATA | AE | AESCAT | Subcategory for Adverse Event | 12 | C | 40 | Perm | Sponsor Defined | Grouping Qualifier |
| 13 | SRCDATA | AE | AEOCCUR | Adverse Event Occurrence | 13 | C | 1 | Perm | CRF or Sponsor Defined | Record Qualifier |
| 14 | SRCDATA | AE | AEBODSYS | Body System or Organ Class | 14 | C | 200 | Exp | CRF or Derived | Record Qualifier |
| 15 | SRCDATA | AE | AELOC | Location of the Reaction | 15 | C | 40 | Perm | CRF or Derived | Record Qualifier |
| 16 | SRCDATA | AE | AESEV | Severity/Intensity | 16 | C | 40 | Perm | CRF | Record Qualifier |

The initial version of the Toolkit implements the standard JANUS and webSDM validation checks and provides the ability to generate the define.xml based on a SAS representation of the metadata necessary within this specification. By providing the Toolkit with a set of tools that are familiar to SAS programmers (e.g. macros and SAS data sets), SAS has finally delivered a viable solution for managing clinical standards.

Based on the traditional SAS tools for data integration, SAS has developed the Clinical Data Integration, a solution to support the management of standards as well as the transformation of clinical data to a standard. Clinical Data Integration is a set of plug-ins sitting on top of SAS Data Integration Studio (Figure 5) which is a traditional ETL solution. The added capabilities contain specific functionality relevant to the clinical transformation process including the management of versions of standards, creating study specific components, creating customer specific standards, building SDTM custom domains, and reporting of the standards used. In addition, the solution uses the Toolkit described above to run validation checks and create the define.xml.

**Figure 5. SAS Data Clinical Data Integration**

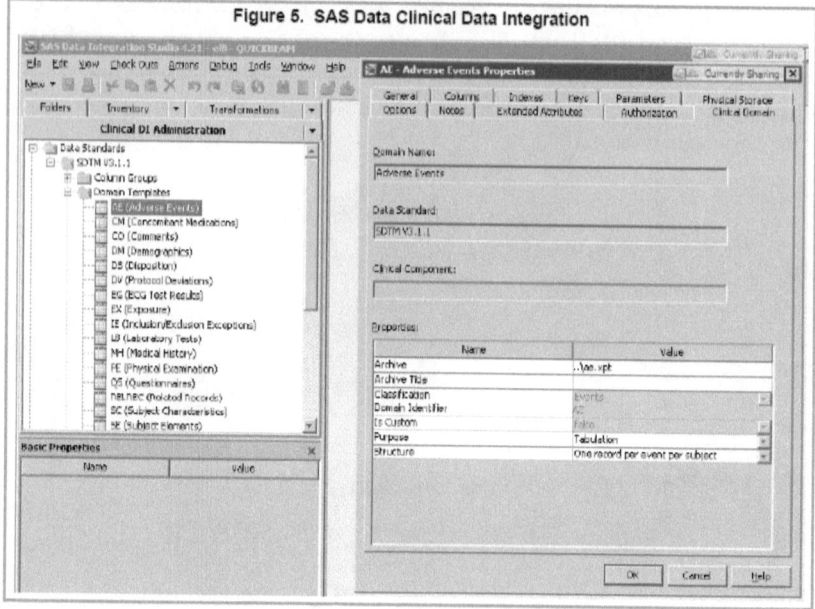

With the SAS Clinical Standards Toolkit and SAS Data Integration solutions, SAS appears to be headed in the right direction with supporting the needs within the industry. They still face the challenge of the traditional SAS programmer who just wants to write code, but the gap is closing as efficiencies become more apparent with the use of these tools.

## THE FUTURE

In recent years the FDA and other government organizations working with clinical data have seen the critical need for a more robust data standard which, in the long run, will lead to better and more efficient science. However, in order for this to be realized people have to adopt standards, use standards, and continue to evolve to make the standards better. The iterative process of changing can be very painful but innovation does not usually come without pain.

In the Christmas Carol, the Ghost of Christmas Future shows Ebenezer Scrooge what the future will hold if he does not change his ways – a quiet demise with nothing but a nonexistent legacy. The Ghost of Clinical Standards Future would provide us a similar message. We must continue to change and adopt to ensure we deliver data standards that leave a legacy of streamlining this process and bringing drugs to market in record time.

## MOVE TO A THREE DIMENSIONAL WORLD

There are limitations in defining data standards in a two dimensional world. The data and metadata must better define the complex interdependent relationships between clinical research data which cannot completely be captured in the existing data standards.

The FDA has indicated the need to move to a more robust XML standard such as HL7 that supposedly would provide the ability to define these complex relationships across data and metadata. However, the current HL7 model is designed to handle a single point in time and does not support either the relationships between different clinical trial domains within a patient as well as the need to capture the traceability of derived data. Recently, there has been a push to move in this direction with a deadline of 2013 for the adoption of an HL7 message and the elimination of the SAS transport file. However, because of the backlash from industry the FDA has backed off this message and has indicated there is no timeline for this implementation. They will take their time and develop an alternative that works and can be easily adopted by industry.

Even though the short term seems to support use of the standards as they exist today, the industry cannot deny the need to move to a three dimensional standard if they expect to realize rapid efficiencies. This leads to many challenges in the future as to how data standards will evolve to meet the needs of both clinical research and regulatory agencies.

## CONTINUED ADOPTION OF STANDARDS

While the current standards have limitations, the industry must continue to work towards adopting the standards in their process even if it does not lead to immediate efficiencies in the short term. By jumping full throttle into the standards, we can learn where the gaps are and work harder to close those gaps. This is easy to recommend in theory but leads to challenges as companies are under more pressure every day to get drugs submitted fast.

In the future, standards can be adopted more smoothly if the industry works harder at incorporating them earlier in the process. As CDASH matures, we can work on collecting the data in a standard and thus make everything else downstream much easier since the standards are aligned. The standards can even go back further to the development of the protocol with the CDISC release of the Protocol Representation 1.0 Model which not only provides a standard for collecting metadata about a Protocol but was also developed with a three dimensional world in mind. By iteratively following this lifecycle of clinical data standards in the future (Figure 6) and improving the steps as we go along; standards will become an integral part of the process instead of a necessary evil.

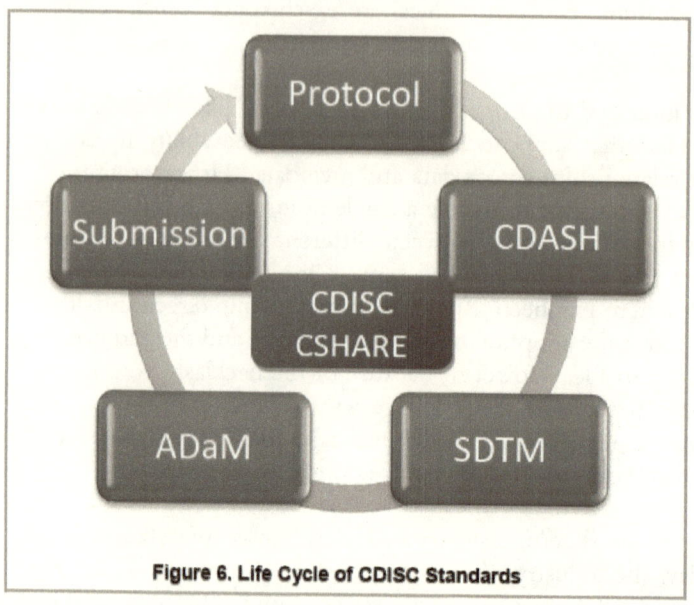

**Figure 6. Life Cycle of CDISC Standards**

In addition to the standards mentioned earlier, CDISC initiated the CSHARE project this year, a new and innovative project to improve the standards development process. In the past, each of the standards defined by CDISC were developed in a silo and communicated through word documents. This led to a lot of inconsistency and repetition across models and slowed down the development of new standards. The goal of CDISC SHARE is to create a global, accessible, electronic library, which through advanced technology, enables precise and standardized data element definitions that can be used within applications and across studies to improve biomedical research and its link with healthcare. This project has the potential to provide much needed consistency and more rapid standards development.

## CROSSROADS OF CLINICAL RESEARCH AND HEALTH RECORDS

Over the last decade clinical researchers have always had the dream to access data held within electronic health records (EHRs) at hospitals, doctors, and medical research centers. On the flip side, site clinicians who participate in clinical trials have to deal with the cumbersome process of entering data multiple times.

The CDISC Healthcare Link project began in 2005 and focused on the mission of interoperability between healthcare and clinical research. CDISC used a concept called Retrieve Form for Data-capture (RFD), which provides the ability for clinicians to access interfaces for entering their data into the electronic medical records (EMR) system and having the information populate the data elements required by clinical trials. This has many benefits including improvement in data quality, timeliness of data, and alleviating the pain researchers find when entering data multiple times.

This is an example of using the data standards to improve efficiencies and is yet another example of how these standards will be used in the future.

## ROLE OF SAS

SAS seems to be heading in the right direction with developing tools that support the needs of industry. However, they need to understand the complexities of the data collected so they do not become relegated to just analysis within the clinical research. They need to understand that clinical data and its associated metadata cannot be captured in rows and columns of the two dimensional world. As the standards continue to develop into something that is more dynamic and "three dimensional" SAS must build tools that leverage those new standards.

## GHOST OF CLINICAL STANDARDS

The Ghost of Clinical Standards past, present and future has provided you with a whirlwind journey through the history of clinical data standards including the challenges, progress, and future hopes.

The Ghost of Clinical Standards Past described the challenges of working with clinical data as technology was introduced into the drug development process. This included the inconsistency in the data across studies and the need to reinvent the wheel every time a new study was initiated. He gave us hope by discussing the birth of CDISC and its potential to solve all the pains of the clinical data world. Finally, he shared with us the previous history of SAS attempt at building solutions specific to clinical data standards and their mixed results.

The Ghost of Clinical Standards Present provided the current state of affairs. He described the gaps that still exist in the regulatory review process and how the FDA has not provided clear direction regarding their needs for reviewing submissions. He also explained that while the current standards are a step in the right direction, they still have adoption barriers including the challenge of using the standards in a company's day to day process as well as the disconnect between the data and metadata. Finally, he presented an overview of the promising new SAS solutions for working with clinical data standards including the SAS Clinical Standards Toolkit and SAS Clinical Data Integration.

The Ghost of Clinical Standards Future gave us a glimpse into what the future of clinical data standards might hold. The industry must continue to work harder at adopting the standards earlier in their process and seeing it through the entire workflow while the FDA must work harder at providing a clear direction for their expectations. He also explained the need to move towards a three dimensional world to better describe the complexities within clinical research and the eventual merging of electronic health records and clinical trial data. Finally, he provided a challenge for SAS to continue to adapt to the changing standards and realize rows and columns are not going to suffice in the long term.

At the end of the Christmas Carol, Ebenezer Scrooge realizes the error of his ways, and pleads to the Ghost of Christmas Future: "I will honor Christmas in my heart, and try to keep it all the year. I will live in the Past, the Present, and the Future. The Spirits of all Three shall strive within me. I will not shut out the lessons that they teach. Oh, tell me if I may sponge away the writing on this stone!" If the clinical research industry does not continue to adapt and change and get out of the world of rows and columns we will continue to repeat past history and not realize the efficiencies absolutely necessary to improve the drug development process and thus save more lives.

I will leave everyone with a question: "Are these the shadows of the things that Will be, or are they shadows of things that May be?"

## REFERENCES

Cooper, Chuck, M.D., Office of Translational Sciences, CDER, FDA. "Computational Science and Data Standards in CDER", 8th Annual DIA eCTD Conference, 2009.

## RECOMMENDED READING

CDISC Data Standards – http://www.cdisc.org

HL7 Data Standards – http://www.hl7.org
SAS Solutions for Life Sciences –
http://www.sas.com/industry/pharma/index.html

three

# Mapping CDISC Metadata Attributes: Using Data _Null_ and Proc Datasets in SAS

**Rita Tsang**

In the pharmaceutical environment, the CDISC Study Data Tabulation Model (SDTM) provides the framework for how clinical data should be submitted to the regulatory authority, such as the US Food and Drug Administration (FDA). Specific metadata attributes, such as variable type, length, control terminology, and variable label, are established to standardize the data format in the industry. The process of mapping these attributes can be tedious and time consuming. This chapter will walk you through how it can be made more automated by using Data _Null_ and Proc Datasets in a step-by-step approach. This automated process can help save time in manual programming and to ensure the accuracy of the updates.

## INTRODUCTION

The task here is to map our case report form (CRF) data to CDISC-standard SAS data sets based on the mapping specification in Microsoft Excel format. Individual domain programs will be set up for mapping purposes. Derived variables can be added in these individual domain programs. Data _Null_ will be used to create SAS programs for applying the metadata attributes to the CDISC domains using Proc Datasets.

## STEP 1 – From the Mapping Specification to SAS data:

We can import the Microsoft Excel mapping specification into a SAS data set (define.sas7bdat) using Proc Import or DDE. Here is an example of the CDISC standard mapping specification for the DM domain from CDISC.ORG:

The template from CDISC.ORG may be adapted for your protocol and sponsor needs. The key is to see the flow of data from the CRF source data to the final CDISC data. Here is an example of the DM domain in the mapping specification.

| | A | B | C | D | E | F | G | H | I |
|---|---|---|---|---|---|---|---|---|---|
| | J17 | ▼ | | fx | | | | | |
| 1 | Dataset: DM | | | | | | | | |
| 2 | Dataset Label: Demographics | | | | | | | | |
| 3 | Unique Key/Structure. USUBJID One record per subject | | | | | | | | |
| 4 | Source Dataset/Table | Source Variable Name | Domain | Variable Name | Variable Label | Type | Format | Comments | Origin |
| 5 | | | DM | STUDYID | Study Identifier | Char | $3. | | Derived |
| 6 | | | DM | DOMAIN | Domain Abbreviation | Char | $2. | equals 'DM' | Derived |
| 7 | demo | | DM | USUBJID | Unique Subject Identifier | Char | $20. | pending | CRF.Derived |
| 8 | demo | pt | DM | SUBJID | Subject Identifier for the Study | Char | $3. | take last 3 characters of pt | CRF.Derived |
| 9 | vis, drg | visdt, time1 | DM | RFSTDTC | Subject Reference Start Date/Time | Char | $18. | Day 1- visit 3 study drug administration - use vis visdt for date, and drg.time1 for time. Insert dashes to form expanded ISO 8601 date: YYYYMMDD becomes YYYY-MM-DD | CRF.Derived |
| 10 | vis, drg | visdt, time2 | DM | RFENDTC | Subject Reference End Date/Time | Char | $18. | Day 3 - visit 5 study drug administration - use vis visdt for date and drg time2 for time. If terminated early, use last visit date. Format date to ISO 8601 standard. | CRF.Derived |
| 11 | demo | invsite | DM | SITEID | Study Site Identifier | Char | $2. | take last 2 chardters of invsite | CRF.Derived |
| 12 | demo | dobdt | DM | BRTHDTC | Date/Time of Birth | Char | $10. | Insert dashes to form expanded ISO 8601 date: YYYYMMDD becomes YYYY-MM-DD | CRF.Derived |
| 13 | demo | dobdt | DM | AGE | Age in AGEU at RFSTDTC | Num | 8. | round numeric conversions of ( RFSTDTC - DOBDTC + 1 ) / 365.25 to 0.1 decimal places | CRF.Derived |
| 14 | | | DM | AGEU | Age Units | Char | $6. | equals YEARS | Derived |
| 15 | demo | sex | DM | SEX | Sex | Char | $1. | if demo.sex = 1 then "M", if demo.sex = 2 then "F", else "U" | CRF.Derived |
| 16 | demo | race | DM | RACE | Race | Char | $20. | upper case with possible decodes CAUCASIAN BLACK ASIAN HISPANIC OTHER | CRF.Derived |

The following SAS code reads in the Excel mapping specification into a SAS data set (DEFINE.SAS7BDAT) using PROC IMPORT.

```
* * * * * * * * * * * * * * * * * * * * * * * * * * * * * * * * * * * * * * * * *
Proc SQL is used to create macro variables for the CDISC do-
mains (&_dslist) and the number of domains (&_nds) in the RAW
library. There are two domains in the RAW library - DM and
SUPPDM. The macro variable _DSLIST resolves to DM SUPPDM, and
the macro variable _NDS resolves to 2.
* * * * * * * * * * * * * * * * * * * * * * * * * * * * * * * * * * * * * * * * ;
%let _dslist =;

proc sql noprint;
    select trim(left(memname)) into :_dslist separated by ' '
    from dictionary.tables
    where libname = 'RAW'
    order by memname;
quit;

%let _nds = &sqlobs;
%let _dslist = %upcase(&_dslist);
```

```
%put &_dslist;
```

```
*************************************************************
The following macro DEFINE uses a do-loop to read in the
attributes of each CDISC domain from the individual Excel
worksheet in the Excel workbook (define.xls). The attributes
that are kept in the SAS data EFINE.SAS7BDAT are domain name
(DOMAIN), variable name (VNAME), variable label (VLABEL), va-
riable type (VTYPE), and variable format (VFORMAT).
*************************************************************;
```

```
%macro define;

%do i = 1 %to &_nds;
   %let _cds = %scan(&_dslist,&i,%str( ));

   proc import out= work.&_cds (keep=f3-f7
      rename=(f3=domain f4=vname
      f5=vlabel f6=vtype f7=vformat) where=(domain>' ' and
      upcase(domain) ne
      'DOMAIN')) datafile = "C:\cdisc\define.xls"
      dbms=EXCEL replace;
      sheet="&_cds$";
   run;

   %if &i=1 %then %do;
      data cdisc.define;
         set &_cds;
      run;
   %end;
   %else %do;
      data cdisc.define;
         set cdisc.define &_cds;
      run;
   %end;
%end;

%mend define;
%define;
```

This is an example of the contents of DEFINE.SAS7BDAT. The SAS
data set will contain attributes of the metadata.

| Obs | domain | vname | vlabel | vtype | vformat |
|-----|--------|-------|--------|-------|---------|
| 1 | DM | STUDYID | Study Identifier | Char | $9 |
| 2 | DM | DOMAIN | Domain Abbreviation | Char | $2 |
| 3 | DM | USUBJID | Unique Subject Identifier | Char | $20 |
| 4 | DM | SUBJID | Subject Identifier for the Study | Char | $3 |
| 5 | DM | RFSTDTC | Subject Reference Start | Char | $16 |

| Obs | domain | vname | vlabel | vtype | vformat |
|-----|--------|-------|--------|-------|---------|
|     |        |       | Date/Time |     |         |
| 6   | DM     | RFENDTC | Subject Reference End Date/Time | Char | $16 |
| 7   | DM     | SITEID | Study Site Identifier | Char | $2 |
| 8   | DM     | BRTHDTC | Date/Time of Birth | Char | $10 |
| 9   | DM     | AGE | Age in AGEU at RFSTDTC | Num | 8 |
| 10  | DM     | AGEU | Age Units | Char | $6 |
| 11  | DM     | SEX | Sex | Char | $1 |
| 12  | DM     | RACE | Race | Char | $20 |
| 13  | DM     | ARMCD | Planned Arm Code | Char | $5 |
| 14  | DM     | ARM | Description of Planned Arm | Char | $50 |
| 15  | DM     | COUNTRY | Country | Char | $3 |
| 16  | DM     | DMDTC | Date/Time of Collection | Char | $16 |
| 17  | SUPPDM | STUDYID | Study Identifier | Char | $9 |
| 18  | SUPPDM | RDOMAIN | Related Domain Abbreviation | Char | $2 |
| 19  | SUPPDM | USUBJID | Unique Subject Identifier | Char | $20 |
| 20  | SUPPDM | IDVAR | Identifying Variable | Char | $8 |
| 21  | SUPPDM | IDVARVAL | Identifying Variable Value | Char | $200 |
| 22  | SUPPDM | QNAM | Variable Name | Char | $8 |
| 23  | SUPPDM | QLABEL | Variable Label | Char | $40 |
| 24  | SUPPDM | QVAL | Data Value | Char | $200 |
| 25  | SUPPDM | QORIGIN | Origin | Char | $40 |
| 26  | SUPPDM | QEVAL | Evaluator | Char | $40 |

## STEP 2 – Using Data _Null_ and the PUT statement to create SAS code:

With the Define SAS data set now created, we can use Data _Null_ and the PUT statement to create SAS code to apply the metadata attributes using Proc Datasets. The following code will create a program called LABEL.SAS for labeling variables based on the information in the De- fine data set (DEFINE.SAS7BDAT):

```
proc sort data=cdisc.define out=label;
by domain;
run;


****************************************************************
Data _null_ is just a simple SAS statement that asks SAS
not to create a data set when executing the DATA step,
since our main interest here is really to create a SAS
program. The FILE statement when used in conjunction with
the PUT statement, tells SAS to write lines of text to an
external location, a SAS program in this case.
****************************************************************;

data _null_;
set label end=eof;
by domain;
file "C:\cdisc\label.sas";


****************************************************************
By using the PUT statement, we write the Proc Datasets
syntax at the first few lines of the program. Note that there
are line pointer controls (/) in some of the PUT statements.
Each line pointer control instructs SAS to advance the pointer
to column 1 of the next line. As a result, blank lines can be
inserted into the program.
****************************************************************;

if (_n_ = 1) then do;
   put "proc datasets memtype=data;" ;
   put " copy in=raw out=cdisc;" ;
   put "run;" //;
   put "proc datasets library=cdisc memtype=data;" /;
end;


****************************************************************
In the following example, we are combining both the character
constant (e.g. " modify ") and a variable (e.g. DOMAIN), and
followed by another character constant (";") in the PUT state-
ment. When a variable (e.g. DOMAIN, VNAME, VLABEL) is being used
as an argument of the PUT statement, the value of the variable
will be written in the file.
Note that by using the format $8. after VNAME, the output style
is formatted. The value of the variable VNAME will have a width
of 8 characters in the SAS program.
Also note that the +(-1) is a pointer control that moves the
pointerbackward to remove the unwanted blank space that occurs
between the value of VLABEL and the double-quotes ('"').
****************************************************************;

if (first.domain) then do;
   put " modify " domain ";" ;
   put " label " vname $8. ' = "' vlabel +(-1) '"';
```

```
end;
else put " " vname $8. ' = "' vlabel +(-1) '"';
if (last.domain) then put " ;" /;
if eof then do;
   put "run;";
   put "quit;";
end;
run;
```

Similarly, Data _Null_ and the PUT statement can also be used to generate program code to format variables in the metadata.

## STEP 3 – Running Proc Datasets to apply the CDISC metadata attributes

The program LABEL.SAS generated by Data _Null_ and the PUT statement in Step 2 is shown below. Proc Datasets is a versatile procedure in SAS. It can be used for copying datasets from library to library, renaming and deleting data sets within a data library, as well as modifying the attributes (such as labels, formats, informats) in a data library.

```
proc datasets memtype=data;
   copy in=raw out=cdisc;
run;

proc datasets library=cdisc memtype=data;
   modify DM ;
   label STUDYID = "Study Identifier"
         DOMAIN = "Domain Abbreviation"
         USUBJID = "Unique Subject Identifier"
         SUBJID = "Subject Identifier for the Study"
         RFSTDTC = "Subject Reference Start Date/Time"
         RFENDTC = "Subject Reference End Date/Time"
         SITEID = "Study Site Identifier"
         BRTHDTC = "Date/Time of Birth"
         AGE = "Age in AGEU at RFSTDTC"
         AGEU = "Age Units"
         SEX = "Sex"
         RACE = "Race"
         ARMCD = "Planned Arm Code"
         ARM = "Description of Planned Arm"
         COUNTRY = "Country"
         DMDTC = "Date/Time of Collection"
         ;

   modify SUPPDM ;
   label STUDYID = "Study Identifier"
         RDOMAIN = "Related Domain Abbreviation"
         USUBJID = "Unique Subject Identifier"
         IDVAR = "Identifying Variable"
         IDVARVAL = "Identifying Variable Value"
         QNAM = "Variable Name"
         QLABEL = "Variable Label"
         QVAL = "Data Value"
         QORIGIN = "Origin"
```

```
        QEVAL = "Evaluator"
        ;
run;
quit;
```

## CONCLUSION

In the process of CDISC mapping, the CDISC mapping specifications document is a living document that may be updated based on project team discussion. This chapter has shown you an example of the automated process that can help save programming time and avoid manual errors. It can also help accommodate for numerous updates in the mapping specification. More importantly, the consistency between the mapping specifications and the final CDISC domains can be more assured.

## REFERENCES

Clinical Data Interchange Standards Consortium (CDISC) (2005), Study Data Tabulation Model Implementation
Guide: Human Clinical Trials, Austin, TX: CDISC Inc.

SAS Institute (2007), SAS Online Documentation for SAS 9.1.3 release, Cary, NC: SAS Institute Inc.

## ACKNOWLEDGEMENT

The author would like to express her appreciation to the following individual for her invaluable comments and suggestions in this chapter: Shannon Escalante, Ikaria

four

# Implementing CDISC When You Already Have Standards: A Case Study

### Sandra Minjoe

How you choose to implement CDISC will be based on current company standards and their robustness, the amount of control you have at each step of the data flow process, your time vs. resource needs, and your willingness to change. We began by implementing CDISC between data collection and analysis. That is, data will be collected in non-CDISC structures, but we will use SDTM and ADaM for analysis, reporting, and filing to FDA. This allows us to file the same data to FDA that we have used ourselves in analysis, without having to do extra work at the time the submission is being prepared. This chapter will describe what we have done and are still doing to implement CDISC.

## INTRODUCTION

A simplified view of CDISC, from data collection through reporting, can be thought of as shown here:

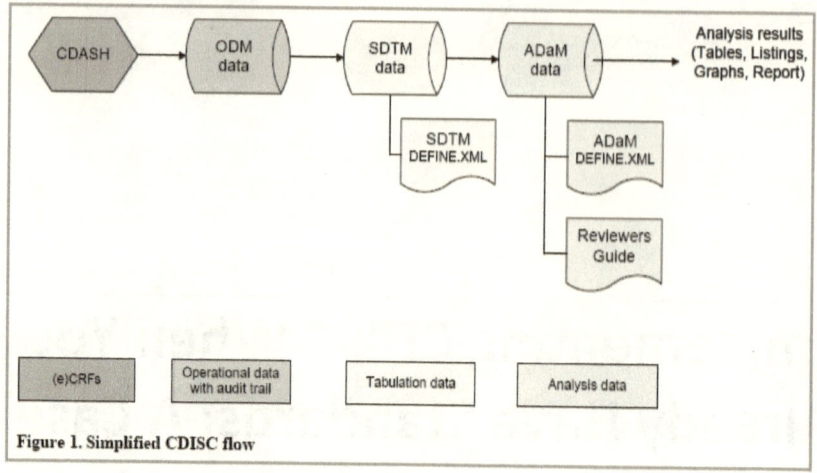

Figure 1. Simplified CDISC flow

The FDA has been threatening to require CDISC data for some time now, and we realized that we needed to start preparing for this eventuality. The CDISC organization has stressed that a greater overall savings can be gained from implementing CDISC as far up-stream as possible. As you can imagine, implementing CDISC from data collection through reporting requires agreement and support from many levels of management. In a larger company, it can be difficult to convince management to make such a big change.

## STEP 1: PILOTS
To allow us to best make any recommendations on CDISC implementation to the various levels of management, a few of us who were interested in and/or had some basic understanding of CDISC formed a cross-functional working group. The group included representatives from data management, statistical programming, biostatistics, electronic submissions, regulatory, and information technology. We set about trying to determine the "best" approach for CDISC adoption in our company.

Our first issue was to determine how much work it would be to convert a "typical" study to CDISC, so we would have an idea what we were dealing with. Our hope was that it would be a relatively simple and fast task tacked on at the end of the data stream, on the way out the door to FDA. In this way we would not need to change any of our current standards, processes or tools, and we could do this extra task only for the studies that need to be sent to FDA.

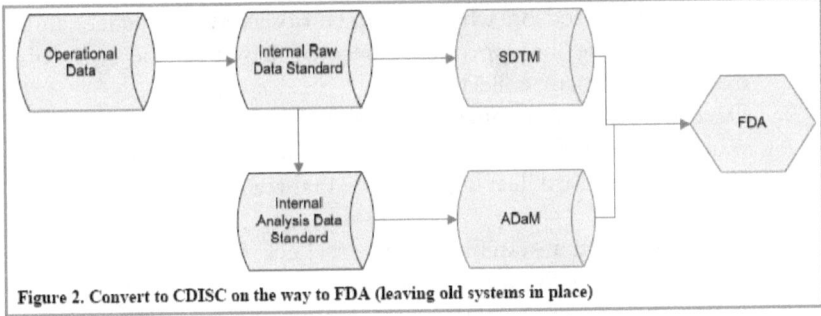

Figure 2. Convert to CDISC on the way to FDA (leaving old systems in place)

The alternative, to change our internal standards, processes, and tools, would result in a more streamlined process but require changes throughout the organization.

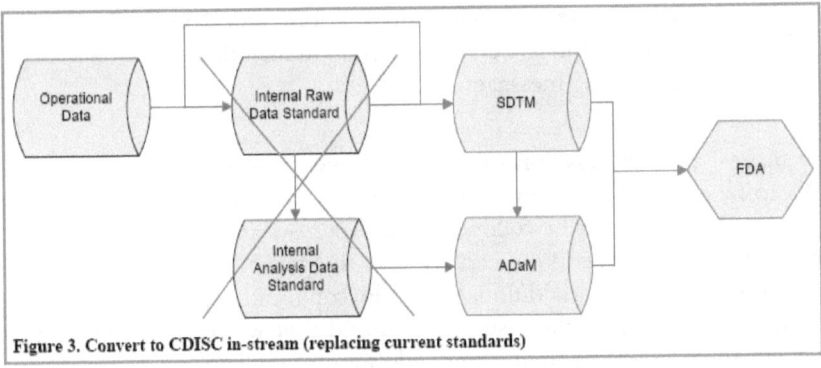

Figure 3. Convert to CDISC in-stream (replacing current standards)

To help us make our decision we decided to run pilots on some "typical" studies. We did not want to impact any filing teams, so a team member with experience in that indication was the only study expertise we used. Since we did not have a lot of extra resources to give, we contracted out the bulk of the work. We used two different companies, each to perform the data mapping and conversion for one or two pilots. These companies mapped and converted our operational data into SDTM, derived a handful of ADaM datasets, and created the supporting define documents. We used internal employees to answer contractor questions and QC their work.

We learned a lot from these pilots, including:

1. SDTM leaves a lot open to interpretation. Companies choose to map the same type of information in different ways. Contractors who understand this will lay out the options, make some recom-

mendations based on what they have observed in practice, and have you make the appropriate decision based on the types of data your company collects.

2. Data mapping and conversion appeared to be pretty straightforward to standardize. We estimated at least 80% of any study should be standard, leaving less 20% that really needs more oversight.

3. You must have a systematic way to check that your data conforms to SDTM. Manual checks are not sufficient.

4. It was a lot of work to convert our specs from:
   a. operational data -> internal raw data standard -> internal analysis data standard
   b. into a define document that read as if we went from internal raw data standard -> SDTM -> ADaM

5. You can submit pilot data to FDA. They will attempt to load it into the pilot area of their system and provide you feedback on whether or not they were able to load it, including lists of any error and warning messages.

Our biggest concern was bullet point #4 above. This step is required for FDA to be able to trace analysis results to analysis data to tabulation data to CRF. We knew that by following the data flow as shown in Figure 2 (above) we would have to convert data on the way out the door, but we had not considered the additional work in converting specs to a define document. Because of this issue, we realized that we might have to indeed tackle some sort of an in stream adoption of CDISC.

We found our pilots to be very useful in helping us determine the volume of work to be done. In retrospect, it might have been even better to have used more of our internal resources in generating the pilot deliverables, rather than outsourcing so much of the effort.

## STEP 2: CREATING AN ADOPTION STRATEGY
We now had the information from our pilot, but wanted to supplement it with some additional industry research. We spoke to colleagues at various meetings, talked with many vendors, and read through official materials from both the FDA[1] and CDISC[2] websites. We formed the cross-functional team again and set about developing a CDISC adoption strategy recommendation.

## CHOOSING AN ADOPTION SCENARIO

We considered several different scenarios and weighed the pros and cons of each:

1. Leave all tools and processes in place and convert to CDISC on the way to FDA
   a. Pros: No change to current standards, tools, or processes. No need to convert studies that would not be filed to FDA.
   b. Cons: Time consuming effort to wait until ready to file. Two versions of specs and annotated CRFs would be needed. The data used for in-house analysis would be different than that used by FDA, which would probably make it more difficult to answer their questions during a review.
2. Leave data collection and operational data in place and convert to CDISC before analysis
   a. Pros: No changes to data collection tools and processes or to operational data structure. Works for both internal data and data we receive from partners. Data used for in-house analysis is the same as that used by FDA, so answering questions would be straight forward.
   b. Cons: Changes to analysis tools and processes would be needed. Two versions of annotated CRFs would be needed. The decision to convert a study would have to happen before determining if we would use it in a filing.
3. Pull data as ODM from our operational system and use CDISC from there through reporting
   a. Pros: No change to data collection tools and processes. The conversion of operational data to SDTM becomes trivial. Only one version of specs is needed. Data used for in-house analysis is the same as that used by FDA, so answering questions would be straightforward.
   b. Cons: Changes to operational system and analysis tools would be needed. Two versions of annotated CRFs would be needed. Data from external sources would still to go through some sort of conversion before analysis. The decision to convert a study would have to happen before determining if we would use it in a filing.
4. Change CRFs to collect CDASH data, pull data as ODM from our operational system, and use CDISC through reporting
   a. Pros: The conversion of operational data to SDTM be-

comes trivial. Only one version of annotated CRFs and specs are needed. Data used for in-house analysis is the same as that used by FDA, so answering questions would be straightforward.

b. Cons: Changes to data collection tools, operational system and analysis tools and processes would be needed. Data from external sources would still to go through some sort of conversion before analysis. The decision to convert a study would have to happen before determining if we would use it in a filing.

We realized that making this decision was not trivial: There seemed to be valid pros and cons for each scenario and we needed to somehow prioritize them to choose the right solution for our needs.

We used some parts of a tool from Kepner Tregoe[3] to quantify these pros and cons for us. This allowed us to identify our objectives, determine "must haves" vs. "wants", and weigh each of the different scenarios against our objectives. And it was a fast process: the cross functional team, led by an outside facilitator, did this in a single 2-hour session. Even though we learned a little more and made a few minor tweaks after that 2-hour session, the ultimate ranking of the scenarios and thus our overall selection did not change.

Basically, the work was captured in a decision-making chart that looked like the following:

| Must/ Want Weight | Objectives | Scenario A: | Scenario B: Rating | Product of Weight and Rating | Scenario C: | | Scenario D: | |
|---|---|---|---|---|---|---|---|---|
| M | Meet FDA requirements and timelines | Y | Y | | Y | | Y | |
| M | Increase efficiency of internal processes | N | Y | | Y | | Y | |
| 7 | Facilitate sharing data with business partners | | 8 | 56 | 9 | 63 | 9 | 63 |
| 5 | Ensure smooth integration with current Dev processes and tools | | 8 | 40 | 3 | 15 | 1 | 5 |
| 10 | Common data model across study teams (molecules, functions, phases) | | 3 | 30 | 6 | 60 | 8 | 80 |
| ... | ... | | | | | | | |
| | TOTAL | | | XXX | | XXX | | XXX |

Figure 4. Decision-making chart

We outlined 4 different scenarios, as described above. Then we described our company objectives, some of which I included above. Once those objectives were all listed, we determined which ones were "must-haves". Everything that was not a "must have" was then assigned a 1-10 weight. Each scenario was evaluated against each objective to determine how well it would be met. All "must haves" were evaluated as a "Yes/No", and the rest were given a 0-10 rating. (Note: a "No" for a "must have" was found in scenario A, so that scenario was quickly eliminated.) Then it was just a matter of multiplying the weight by the rating and totaling up each column. The column with the highest total value was the one that best met our objectives.

## CREATING A TIMELINE

Once we decided on the adoption scenario, we needed to figure out the timeline. As the team leader, I reviewed the status of all the CDISC standards we were looking to adopt and made an initial estimate of when each would be ready for our adoption and how long it would take us.

I put it into the following layout:

| | | Resources (estimated Full Time Staff, $ Purchase) | | | | | | | | | | | | | | |
| | | Year 1 | | | | | Year 2 | | | | | Year 3 | | | | |
| Function | Task | Q1 | Q2 | Q3 | Q4 | $ | Q1 | Q2 | Q3 | Q4 | $ | Q1 | Q2 | Q3 | Q4 | $ |
| | | | | | | | | | | | | | | | | |
| | | | | | | | | | | | | | | | | |

Figure 5. Resource estimate chart for each function and task over time

Once I had this drafted, I then met with the team representatives from each function to review the parts of the table that applied to their function. They provided guidance as to when their function would be able to work on specific deliverables and how long they thought their parts of the adoption would take. There were some specific advantages of putting in this little work up front:

- It allowed me to identify the scope so that each function new what they were dealing with
- It seemed to help the functional representatives to see the big picture and where their pieces would fit in
- It was quick to do, since multiple people reviewing a single document takes much less time than creating multiple documents and then combining them together

## GAINING APPROVAL

The final document we prepared for senior management contained the following sections:

- **Executive Summary**: a couple paragraph overview outlining the basic adoption proposal, including that the company keeps up with the changing standards and modify the plan as appropriate
- **Scope**: de scribing what the adoption plan covers and what it does not
- **Recommendation**: a short bullet list of the specific CDISC standards to be adopted by which functions
- **Pre-Requisites to Success**: included things like a tight adherence to standards and ability to implement appropriate tools
- **Benefits**: the list of objectives from Figure 4 that would be met with the scenario we chose
- **Investment**: a summary of the resource estimates from Figure 5, followed by the full chart itself (Figure 5)
- **Current Issues**: the list of issues that drove the creating of Figure 4
- **Alternatives**: a 1-paragraph description of each scenario from Figure 4
- **Alternative Discussion**: a summary of the alternative chosen and the reasons why the other alternatives were not chosen
- **Decision Process**: a description of the method we used to make our decision (Kepner Tregoe) followed by the worksheet itself (Figure 4)
- **Team Representatives**: list of all contributors by function
- **Glossary of Acronyms**: because many reviewers would not be familiar with CDISC or potentially even acronyms common in one function but not another
- **Reference Documents**: Copies of documents or partial text from large documents that support the need to adopt CDISC, found mostly on the CDISC and FDA websites

As you can imagine, this ended up to be quite a large document! Ours was 8 pages for the recommendation itself, plus another 11 for the references.

The document was sent around for buy-in from functional heads. The next step was to get on a senior management agenda and present this information in 10-15 minutes.

Our slides were developed to summarize a lot of the information in the recommendation document. Because there was the potential that not everyone in the room would understand CDISC, we spent a couple slides giving the basic overview, including a chart similar to Figure 1. Instead of the Figure 5 resource estimates with more than 20 specific tasks listed, we condensed it down to the following:

| Activity | Functions | | | | | Timing | | |
|---|---|---|---|---|---|---|---|---|
| | A | B | C | D | E | 2008 | 2009 | 2010 |
| | S | P | | | | X | X | |
| | S | | | | S | | | X |
| | P | S | | S | | | X | X |

P = Primary, S = Supportive

Figure 6. Rolled up resource estimate chart for use in slide deck

We closed the slide deck by also recommending that one person take on the role to drive the CDISC adoption across all functions and ensure that all the functional deliverables would mesh together in the end.

## STEP 3: IMPLEMENTATION

Even while all this cross-functional work was going on, we in the statistical programming and analysis function had already been investigating CDISC as a new standard. We receive data in many forms, from paper CRFs, an EDC system, partners in their native structure, and outside vendors in previously-agreed-upon standards. Although we are unable to control the structure of the data we receive, once it is brought in-house, we could convert it into a single standard structure before analysis. Not surprisingly, the structures we selected were CDISC SDTM for tabulation data and CDISC ADaM for analysis data.

Looking back at Figure 1, this meant the initial focus of implementation was on the right half of that picture:

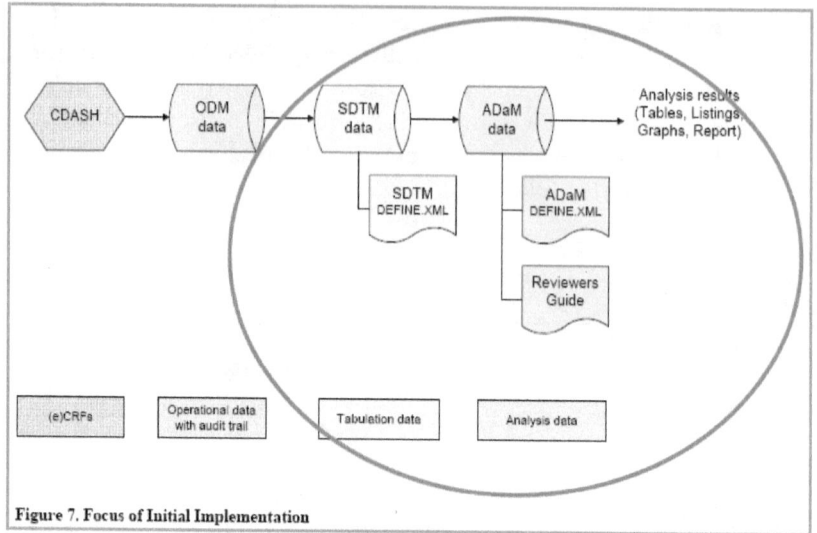

Figure 7. Focus of Initial Implementation

Because the initial focus of our CDISC implementation was after data had already been collected in non-CDISC structures, for our implementation we started by developing:

1. A process and tool for mapping and converting collected data into SDTM
2. New standard analysis dataset structures (including ADaM) and programs, building from SDTM
3. Revised standard reporting macros, based on new data structure and variable names
4. Simple SAS macros to help us work with data in the new structure

Additionally, we also began looking at our filing needs, including define.xml instead of define.pdf that would allow us to submit a true CDISC filing.

Below is a simple diagram showing initial basic steps from the data conversion tool through production of TLGs.

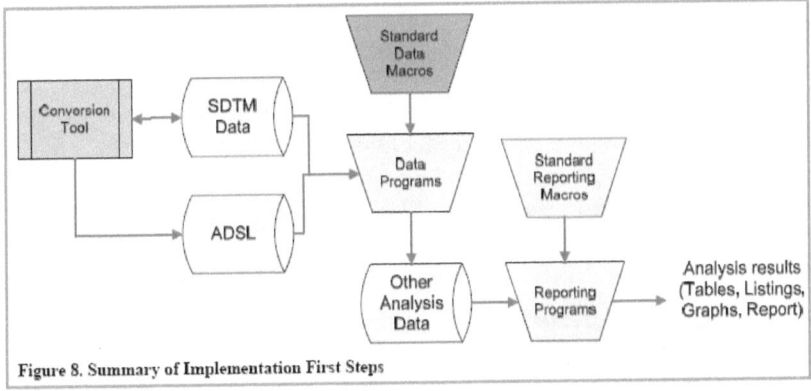

Figure 8. Summary of Implementation First Steps

# IMPLEMENTATION DECISION #1: USE TRUE SDTM OR SDTM-PLUS?

In listening to how other companies have implemented SDTM, we have heard again and again about "SDTM-Plus". This term basically means data in the general SDTM structure, with some extra columns to make it more human workable and analysis-friendly. We needed to decide whether we wanted to use this type of modification to SDTM as our instream standard, or if we should go with true SDTM structured data.

Choice#1: Use True SDTM

- Pro: We would be working with exactly what FDA would be using, thus allowing us to easily provide any analysis programs and answer their questions.
- Con: The SDTM structure is much more vertical than our current standard and requires that many variables be put in SUPPQUAL, a potentially difficult transition for many employees.

Choice#2: Create an SDTM-Plus

- Pro: It allows you to use some of the features of SDTM without being held to all the constraints. For example, you might include age, sex, race, and treatment group and convert character dates to numeric ones to make SDTM data into SDTM-Plus.
- Con: It would require modifications to specs to create DEFINE.XML and to any programs that need to be sent to FDA, and it would make it more difficult to answer FDA questions.

## DECISION

We decided that the benefit of working with the same data structure as FDA was the most important need to address. And because we are, after all, SAS programmers, we developed a few SAS macros that would allow us to do some standard things to an SDTM dataset to make it easier to use for both us and our friends in Biostatistics.

One of these macros creates numeric dates and times from the character version in SDTM. All these SDTM variable names end in "DTC", so they were easy to locate. The conversion piece of the program was a matter of string manipulation to parse the character dates and times, decision steps for imputing values as needed, and pushing that into SAS date and time functions to create resulting numeric dates and times. Kind of fun to write, actually!

Another macro first transposes and then merges all the corresponding SUPPQUAL data onto the relevant domain. SUPPQUAL is set up to make this fairly straightforward, since variable QNAM becomes the transposed variable name, QLABEL becomes the transposed variable label, and QORIG becomes the transposed value.

For us, this combination of true SDTM plus a suite of standard macros allowed us to meet both criteria – using exactly what we send FDA and making SDTM a little easier for us to work with.

## IMPLEMENTATION DECISION #2: WHAT TOOL TO USE FOR CONVERSION?

Once we decided what our SDTM model would look like, we needed to figure out how to get all of our data there. Some of the options we considered for data conversion were to purchase an off-the-shelf ETL (Extract-Transform-Load) tool, create a home-grown SAS tool, or farm the work out.

At the time our tool development programmers were busy with other projects, so building our own system would not happen quickly. We determined that SAS Data Integration (DI) Studio was not the best fit for us, especially since there would be a steep learning curve and we would have trouble finding contractors experienced with SAS DI Studio contractor who could do the data conversion for us.

In working with our IT department, we discovered that the company was already licensing an ETL tool, and to use it we would not have to pay for any additional users. We learned that a large Pharmaceutical company was already using this same ETL tool for their data conversion into SDTM. Additionally, our in-house pre-clinical group had recently begun using the tool for conversion to their data warehouse (and, as we described it, lab data is lab data, be it mouse or human). Finally, contractors familiar with this more common ETL tool were relatively easy to find, so we could get started right away.

As it turned out, this ETL tool we used did not meet our needs. While we could easily talk with the contract programmers in a common language (SQL), they were not able to develop a system that worked across multiple studies with even slightly different incoming data structures. It took more than 6 months just to convert 2 studies, and we had no expectations of any dramatic time savings for future studies.

In the end, we dropped the ETL tool in favor of developing our own SAS based tool. We learned a lot about data conversion during this process, and developed re-usable standard data maps; so it was not a total loss.

## IMPLEMENTATION DECISION #3: HOW MUCH ADAM SHOULD WE USE?

ADSL (Subject-Level Analysis Dataset) is very well-defined in the CDISC ADaM documentation. That documentation describes the structure (one record per subject) and gives examples of many variable names. FDA seems excited about including the ADSL domain in their Janus database. Conveniently, we were already creating a dataset that contained much of the same information as ADSL and in the same one-record-per-subject format. Implementing ADSL was an easy decision to make, since it basically involved changing a few variable names.

Other ADaM structures have been less well-described in the CDISC ADaM documents. In the past ADaM had defined a set of structures for different types of analyses, such as time to event or categorical, though in the current ADaM release these have been removed. Much of our analyses, such as adverse event and lab summaries, could actually be done with SDTM-plus style data, so we did not see a huge need for other "true" ADaM data structures.

We have decided to use a combination of ADSL and SDTM-plus for most of our analyses, and short-term we will continue to use our old standard analysis file structures for everything else. As ADaM delivers more specific direction on data structures, we will add them to our implementation.

## CDISC IMPLEMENTATION TIPS

I'm generally happy with how things have been developing in our CDISC adoption, though there are a few things I would have done differently if I were to start all over again. Combining it all together, I would recommend the following tips:

- Form a group of CDISC-interested parties across your company, and do a pilot or two to get a feel for the CDISC data structures before making any bold moves
- Form a small cross-functional team of highly placed functional reps and standards representatives and develop a well-thought-out adoption strategy recommendation to senior management, including both functional and cross-functional oversight
- Convince at least one high-level person that this is the right thing to do, and have them act as a CDISC champion
- Become a CDISC member organization and have at least one person from your company get involved in some part of the industry work they do, and you will get access to all sorts of information not available to the general public
- Hire consultants and contractors sparingly so that, as much as possible, CDISC knowledge is learned by and kept in the organization
- Make decisions based on current resources, including short-term gap solutions when necessary
- Revisit short-term gap decisions frequently and move to a longer-term solution as soon as possible
- Provide CDISC communication regularly to instill a sense of anticipation and a desire at all levels to make the move

## CONCLUSION

Working in a company with established standards can both help and hinder CDISC adoption. Because you have standards in place that so many people are used to working with, it can be quite a hurdle to replace them with the CDISC standards. And depending on the structure of the current standards, they may look vastly different than CDISC. However working within a larger organization also means you have people in place whose job it is to manage those standards, and getting those folks to embrace the CDISC standard can really drive it forward.

Keep in mind that adopting CDISC across a larger company will take awhile, and you are likely to have a few setbacks along the way. It's not a race against other companies, since each has their own issues to deal with. Our goal should be to ensure our own company will be ready to deliver our data to FDA in the way they will soon be mandating.

Also realize that by adopting CDISC you may also see other benefits, such as streamlined work processes, a better ability to share data with our partners, and less time spent defining data structures between vendors and clients.

Finally, consider the implementation of each standard as a milestone to the overall CDISC adoption plan, and you will be rewarded with many successes along the way.

## ACKNOWLEDGMENTS

Thanks must go out to Genentech's CDISC Working Group and Data Model Standards team, who did the bulk of the work described in this chapter. Thanks also to the many members of CDISC who have so generously answered our questions as we attempted to implement these standards.

## REFERENCES

1. See http://www.fda.gov/ for official FDA statements. Note that a search of FDA's website on "cdisc" will give you over 1000 hits. The specific FDA document that mentions CDISC is The PDUFA IV Technology Plan is at http://www.fda.gov/OHRMS/DOCKETS/98fr/FDA-2008-N-0352-bkg.pdf. CDISC also collects references from FDA on their website (see reference 2 below).
2. See http://www.cdisc.org/, specifically the tab for Publications and Presentations, for more CDISC information. Two publications outlining the business case for implementing upstream can be found at http://www.cdisc.org/news/PR31CDISCBusinessCaseApr2007final.pdf and http://www.cdisc.org/pdf/Interchange2005/01-

Business case for standardsV6 (2).pdf. The area where you can find FDA-related articles is at http://www.cdisc.org/publications/regdoc.html.

3. To learn more about Kepner Tregoe and their decision-making workshops, see http://www.kepnertregoe.com/.

## RECOMMENDED READING

It probably goes without saying that a thorough review of the CDISC standards themselves is recommended. Those standards can be found at http://www.cdisc.org/standards/index.html. Note that the documents in the first section of this web page are the most current production versions, though you can find versions in development further down the web page.

# five

# Practical Methods for Creating CDISC SDTM Domain Data Sets from Existing Data

**Robert W. Graebner**

Creating CDISC SDTM domain data sets from existing clinical trial data can be a challenging task, particularly if the database was not designed with the SDTM standards in mind. A key step in the process involves determining which of the STDM domain datasets need to be produced for submission and then determining what conversion process will be necessary to produce them from the existing data. Adequate planning and documentation of the conversion process is an essential first step before programming begins. The basic component of the planning phase involves metadata mapping – determining how each of the variables in the existing data will relate to the variables contained in the SDTM domains to be produced. The documentation of the conversion process should be recorded in a format that facilitates efficient access by those involved in the planning, programming and validation phases of the conversion. Tools suited to the task of complex data mapping and data manipulation can significantly reduce cost and improve quality. This chapter presents an example of a simple metadata mapping tool developed using SAS, Microsoft Excel and Visual Basic. The examples in this chapter are based on the CDISC SDTM version 1.1, the SDTM Implementation Guide version 3.1.1 and SAS version 9.1.3.

## INTRODUCTION

In order to increase the efficiency of the drug development process, the Clinical Data Interchange Standards Consortium (CDISC) has developed a series of clinical study data standards to facilitate efficient transfer, access and review of clinical trial data. These standards include the Operational Data Model (ODM), the Study Data Tabulation Model (SDTM) and the Analysis Data Model (ADaM). This chapter presents basic strategies and practical methods for creating SDTM domain data sets from clinical data management (CDM) system files. Before initiating the data mapping and conversion process it is crucial to have a basic understanding of the SDTM specifications. CDISC provides implementation guides for all of the CDISC data standards on their Website (www.cdisc.org). The SDTM Implementation Guide (SDTMIG) is an essential tool for anyone involved with the metadata mapping or programming associated with the creation of SDTM data sets. The SDTM Implementation Guide contains the specifications and metadata for all of the SDTM data domains and guidance for producing SDTM domain files. The SDTM is an evolving standard and it is important to ensure that everyone involved in the conversion process is adhering to the same version of the SDTM. It is also important to understand the difference in the version numbers for the SDTM standard and the associated implementation guide. The most recent versions in production are SDTM 1.1 and SDTMIG 3.1.1, which were released in 2005.

## CDISC SDTM OVERVIEW

The purpose of creating CDISC SDTM domain data sets is to provide Case Report Tabulation (CRT) data to a regulatory agency, such as the FDA, in a standardized format that is compatible with available software tools that allow efficient access and correct interpretation of the data submitted. The SDTMIG provides documentation on metadata for the domain data sets that includes the file name, variable names, types, labels, formats, roles and controlled terminology. While most of the SDTM domain data sets have a normalized (vertical) structure; they were not designed for use in a clinical data management (CDM) system. It is highly desirable to incorporate CDISC standards to the extent practical when designing CDM data structures. Proper adherence to the standards can greatly reduce the effort necessary for data mapping. Important standards to adhere to are domain name, variable name, variable type and format. Matching the SDTM variable labels is not important. The SDTM standard labels are available in the standard metadata and the labels are not used for match merging in the mapping process. While the SDTM documentation does not specify variable lengths, it is highly desirable to maintain consistency in length among variables with the same name across domains and between studies.

While the SDTM data sets do contain some derived variables, they are not designed for use as analysis data sets. Adherence to the "one proc away" philosophy for analysis files dictates the addition of additional derived variables and conversion to a horizontal structure. The SDTM data sets can however, be used in the creation of analysis files. The creation of standardized STDM data sets will aid in the creation of analysis files for each individual study, and the future task of integrating data from multiple studies will be accomplished with greater efficiency and quality. The ability to submit SDTM data sets in place of listings or patient profiles, resulting in additional cost reductions.

## DEFINING A PROCESS

The degree to which you can define a standard process for converting clinical study data to SDTM domains depends on the environment in which you are working. In an ideal situation, the CDM data structures would be designed to be as compatible as possible with the SDTM specifications. An SDTM annotated CRF is a valuable tool to aid in the mapping process. Creating a standard metadata library would allow you to maximize the consistency within and between studies. This level of consistency would allow you to develop a library of standard annotated CRF pages and a library of SAS macros for creating SDTM domain files with a minimum amount of metadata mapping and additional programming at the study level. This level of standardization would also reduce the cost of consolidating data for integrated studies. In such an environment a very detailed and specific SDTM conversion process can be defined.

In many current situations, existing data does not contain this level of standardization or compatibility with the SDTM standards. In such cases the conversion process must be very flexible and it can only be defined in general terms. Even though the process must be designed with considerable flexibility to accommodate different CDM data structures, it is still important to have a process in place to serve as a general frame work to promote consistency in SDTM domain creation, promote the use of standard terms to enhance communication, and provide guidance to those new to SDTM. Establishing a process will also facilitate the use of standard tools for metadata mapping and documentation, SDTM file creation and SDTM file validation. The focus of this chapter is on this second situation, where significant metadata mapping and programming will be necessary.

If a standard process for SDTM conversion does not currently exist, it is important to define one, at least in general terms, prior to starting the conversion. The process definition is a large-scale map that defines the major steps necessary to create the desired SDTM domains from the existing data. Once the major steps are defined, the components of each step can be determined. This will allow you to define dependencies between tasks, determine where there are possibilities for performing steps in parallel, and define the types of tools that will be necessary. The steps listed below outline a basic process for SDTM conversion. Starting with the end in mind, the goal is defined, the current situation is assessed, and a path is defined between the two.

1. Determine which SDTM domains will be created
2. Determine the extent of SDTM compliance in the existing data
3. Implement automatic direct mapping where possible
4. Map remaining source data sets to SDTM domains
5. Map variables in source data sets to SDTM domain variables
6. Determine if SUPPQUAL domain or custom domains will be required
7. Generate SAS programs to perform the data conversion
8. Validate the SDTM data sets
9. Generate DEFINE.XML
10. Validate DEFINE.XML

It is important to adequately document the general process and the specific steps requires for a particular study. This includes revising the documentation if it becomes necessary to modify the process. The documentation will play a critical role in validating the process and will be very useful as a guide during future SDTM conversion projects.

## SDTM DOMAINS

A basic understanding of the SDTM domains, their structure and their interrelations is vital to determining which domains you need to create and in assessing the level to which your existing data is compliant. The SDTM consists of a set of clinical data file specifications and underlying guidelines. These different file structures are referred to as domains. Each domain is designed to contain a particular type of data associated with clinical trials, such as demographics, vital signs or adverse events. In the current specification, each of these domains will be contained in a separate XPORT data file, based on the SAS version 5 data set file format, which is in the public domain. Future versions will support the use of XML files.

The CDISC SDTM Implementation Guide provides specifications for 30 domains and new domains are being developed. It is important to check the CDISK website for the latest updates before you begin a new conversion project. The SDTM domains are divided into six classes. The 21 clinical data domains are contained in three of these classes: Interventions, Events and Findings. The trial design class contains seven domains and the special-purpose class contains two domains (Demographics and Comments). The trial design domains provide the reviewer with information on the criteria, structure and scheduled events of a clinical trial. By placing key trial design information in a concise and standard data structure, the reviewer can have ready access to details of the trial design that allow them to view the clinical data in the proper context. The focus of this chapter is on creating clinical data domains from CDM system data files. A list of the SDTM clinical data domains is given below in Figure 1. Only the domains that are pertinent to a particular study need to be created. The only required domain is demographics. Demographics also differ from the other domains in the fact that it has a horizontal structure, with a single row per subject.

There are two other special purpose relationship data sets, the Supplemental Qualifiers (SUPPQUAL) data set and the Relate Records (RELREC) data set. SUPPQUAL is a highly normalized data set that allows you to store virtually any type of information related to one of the domain data sets. The initial specification for SUPPQUAL indicates that a single file should be used for all domains. The current trend, and possibly the requirement for the next version of SDTM, is to use a separate file for each domain named SUPP--, where the hyphens are replaced with the two-letter designation for each domain.

In general, the use of SUPPQUAL should be minimized. Its purpose is to provide a means of adding variables which are critical to a study, but which are not included in the specifications of the pertinent domain and are not suitable as an additional identifier, topic or timing variable. If the number of additional variables is large or if they are not pertinent to an existing domain, then the creation of a custom domain should be considered. Before considering the creation of a custom domain, you should review the latest information on the CDISC Web site, it is possible that a new domain has been defined that will suite your needs. Guidelines for creating custom domains are included in the SDTM Implementation Guide. Information on RELREC is provided in the section below on key variables and relating records.

CDISC SDTM DOMAINS

| CLASS | DOMAIN NAME | DOMAIN DESCRIPTION |
|---|---|---|
| Special Purpose | DM | Demographics |
| | CO | Comments |
| Interventions | CM | Concomitant Medications |
| | EX | Exposure |
| | SU | Substance Use |
| Events | AE | Adverse Events |
| | DS | Disposition |
| | DV | Protocol Deviations |
| | MH | Medical History |
| Findings | DA | Drug Accountability |
| | EG | ECG |
| | IE | Inclusion / Exclusion Criteria Exceptions |
| | LB | Laboratory Results |
| | MB | Microbiology Specimens |
| | MS | Microbiology Susceptibility |
| | PC | Pharmacokinetic Concentrations |
| | PP | Pharmacokinetic Parameters |
| | PE | Physical Exam |
| | QS | Questionnaires |
| | SC | Subject Characteristics |
| | VS | Vital Signs |
| Trial Design | TE | Trial Elements |
| | TA | Trial Arms |
| | TV | Trial Visits |
| | SE | Subject Elements |
| | SV | Subject Visits |
| | TI | Trial Inclusion/Exclusion Criteria |
| | TS | Trial Summary |
| Relationship Data Sets | SUPPQUAL | Supplemental Qualifiers |
| | RELREC | Relate Records |

Figure 1. CDISC SDTM Domains

## GENERAL GUIDELINES ON SDTM VARIABLES

Each of the SDTM domains has a collection of variables associated with it. There are five roles that a variable can have: Identifier, Topic, Timing, Qualifier, and for trial design domains, Rule. Using lab data as an example, the subject ID, domain ID and sequence (e.g. visit) are identifiers. The name of the lab parameter is the topic, the date and time of sample collection are timing variables, the result is a result qualifier and the variable containing the units is a variable qualifier. The SDTM guidelines contain a section on the fundamentals of the SDTM that cover this topic in detail. The SDTM fundamentals are important to understand before you begin the process of metadata mapping, particularly if you need to create custom domains.

Variables that are common across domains include the basic identifiers study ID (STUDYID), a two-character domain ID (DOMAIN) and unique subject ID (USUBJID). In studies with multiple sites that are allowed to assign their own subject identifiers, the site ID and the subject

ID must be combined to form USUBJID. All other variable names are generally formed by prefixing a standard variable name fragment with the two-character domain ID.

It is also important to understand which variables should be included in each domain to which you will be mapping study metadata. The SDTM specifications do not require all of the variables associated with a domain to be included in a submission. The SDTM is a standard designed to accommodate the wide range of trials that are conducted in the Pharmaceutical and Biotechnology industries, and some variables may not be necessary for a particular trial. Your metadata mapping will not necessarily include all of the variables associated with the domains you are creating nor will it necessarily include all of the variables contained in the CDM database. Any questions regarding which variables to submit should be addressed with your reviewer. In regard to complying with the SDTM standards, the implementation guide specifies each variable as being included in one of three categories: Required, Expected, and Permitted. An explanation of each is given below.

- **REQUIRED** – These variables are necessary for the proper functioning of standard software tools used by reviewers. They must be included in the data set structure and should not have a missing value for any observation.
- **EXPECTED** – These variables form the fundamental core of information within a domain. They must be included in the data set structure; however it is permissible to have missing values.
- **PERMISSIBLE** – These variables are not a required part of the domain and they should not be included in the data set structure if the information they were designed to contain was not collected.

The implementation guide provides information on the expected structure of each domain data set. For each variable, a name, label and type are provided. The length of the variables is not specified. The file structure is designed to comply with the XPORT file format, which is based on the SAS version 5 data set specifications. Variable names have a maximum length of 8, labels a maximum length of 40 and character variables a maximum length of 200. These restrictions may change in the future as the use of XML becomes standard.

To accommodate character variables longer than 200, the first 200 characters should be stored in the domain variable and the remaining text should be stored in the SUPPQUAL domain. For the sake of readability, the text from the source variable should be split between words, into sub-strings of length 200 or less. The first substring is stored in the appropriate variable in the parent domain. Each of the remaining sub-strings should then be stored in the variable QVAL in an observation within SUPPQUAL. In SUPPQUAL, the variable QLABEL should contain the same label as the domain variable and the variable QNAM should contain the name of the variable in the parent domain with a sequential integer from 1 to 9 appended. If the name of the parent domain variable has a length of 8 then the sequential number replaces the last character of the name. The variable IDVAR and IDVARVAL are used to relate the records in SUPPQUAL back to the appropriate record in the parent domain.

In addition, some variables require the specification for a controlled terminology or format. In such cases, the implementation guide specifies whether the controlled terminology is provided by an external source (e.g. MedDRA) or by the investigator. It is generally recommended that the text used in defining controlled terminology be placed in all uppercase. Exceptions to this rule are controlled terminology from external sources or designations such as units, which employ a generally accepted use of mixed case text. When defining controlled terminology, it is important to prevent ambiguity.

## MAPPING EXISTING DATA TO SDTM DOMAINS

Before beginning the task of developing programs to create SDTM domain data sets from your existing data, it is important to have a "road map" to design and document the process. As with planning any journey, the first step is to specify your current location and the location of your destination. By comparing alternate routes before starting the actual trip, you can avoid getting lost or needing to back track.

The first step in the mapping process involves the comparison of the study metadata with the SDTM domain metadata. If the CDM metadata is compliant to a significant extent with the SDTM metadata, it is possible to use automated mapping as a first pass. If CDISC standard data set and variable names were properly used in the CDM data sets, it is possible to use a DATA step merge or SQL join to combine rows of study metadata with matching rows of SDTM metadata based on variable name, type and format. Note that the SDTM standards do not specify variable length. They do provide the standard variable label, so it is important to make sure you are keeping the SDTM label rather than your CDM data label. Automatic mapping can potentially results in a significant reduction in cost, however it is important to check the validity of the mappings. This process only serves as a first pass of metadata mapping, in most cases some manual mapping will be necessary. If the CDM metadata is not compliant with the SDTM or worse yet, if SDTM specifications were improperly used, then auto mapping should be avoided.

The next step involves manually mapping the study data sets to the domain data sets and then mapping each individual variable to the appropriate domain. Depending on how the CDM data sets are structured, you may map each CDM file to a single domain, split its variables among multiple domains, or combine variables from multiple CDM files into a single domain. There are several possible types of variable mappings. In some cases it may be necessary to use more than one method in order to create the desired SDTM variable from the existing data. A list of basic variable mappings is given below.

- **DIRECT** – a CDM variable is copied directly to a domain variable without any changes other than assigning the CDISC standard label
- **RENAME** – only the variable name and label may change but the contents remain the same
- **STANDARDIZE** – mapping reported values to standard units or standard terminology
- **REFORMAT** – the actual value being represented does not change, only the format in which is stored changes, such as converting a SAS date to an ISO8601 format character string
- **COMBINING** – directly combining two or more CDM variables to form a single SDTM variable
- **SPLITTING** – a CDM variable is divided into two or more SDTM variables
- **DERIVATION** – creating a domain variable based on a computation, algorithm, series of logic rules or decoding using one or more CDM variables

While any mapping that involves changing or combining CDM variables to form a domain variable could be referred to as a derivation, further categorizing the type of mapping facilitates assigning a standard process (e.g. a SAS macro or block of SAS source code) to perform the mapping operation.

Effective manual mapping requires a method of managing and accessing the metadata for both your existing data and the SDTM domains. If your study data resides in SAS data sets, and you define a SAS library for their location, SAS will automatically provide a view to an internal table that contains the structure information for all data sets in any defined library. This metadata can be easily accessed by either specifying SASHELP.VCOLUMN as an input data set in a DATA step, or by selecting rows and columns from the table DICTIONARY.COLUMNS using PROC SQL. This file contains the library name, data set name, variable name, type, length, label, format and more for every variable in every data set in every currently defined library. The amount of information in this view can be overwhelming and it is usually necessary to use a where clause to obtain only the specific information needed. The fact that it contains metadata for all currently accessible data sets facilitates easy metadata comparisons across data sets or across studies, such as determining which variables have identical or similar names.

## KEY VARIABLES AND METHODS OF RELATING RECORDS

Every domain contains a required set of variables that form a unique key for that record. These include STUDYID, DOMAIN and USUBJID. DOMAIN contains the two-character domain name and is hard-coded into each record. USUBJID is a unique subject identifier within a study. Therefore, if multiple sites are used and subject numbers overlap between sites, then USUBJID must combine the initial site and subject numbers. An additional required key variable is –SEQ, where the two hyphens represent the domain name. When a subject has more than one record in a domain, then –SEQ is used to form a unique key. An additional, sponsor-defined key is –SPID. This variable is typically used for external identifiers, such as a sample number assigned by a lab.

The SDTM design provides several ways to relate records within and between domains. Records within a domain can be related by assigning them the same value for –GRPID. The RELREC data set can be used to relate multiple records in multiple domains. Each record in RELREC with the same value of RELID defines a relation. Each record also contains the key variables necessary to point to a record or group of records in a domain.

## CDISC SDTM METADATA MAPPING TOOLS

The use of software tools is essential to the efficient creation of SDTM data sets. The process of mapping study data to the SDTM domains can be complex. The large number of variables involved and the many different transformations required make mapping without a tool tedious and error prone. When decisions are made regarding process steps, it is important that the process be documented for consistency and repeatability. Direct electronic access to metadata for both the study data and the SDTM domains facilitates an efficient mapping process. Automation of basic processes can save significant amounts of time. Metadata about the mapping process can be used to generate documentation of the process and to generate the SAS source code to perform the derivation of domain data sets. Once the domain data sets have been produced, software tools documenting the metadata mapping can improve the efficiency of validating the domain data sets and producing the define.xml file.

The use of a metadata mapping tool can also be extended to the creation of ADaM analysis data sets from the SDTM data sets. A typical ADaM data set is created by merging data from two or more SDTM data sets, restructuring the data to a form convenient for analysis and creating derived variables. The use of a metadata mapping tool for creating ADaM data sets will provide similar advantages to those for producing SDTM data sets. Including metadata on both transformations in one system will provide complete documentation of the creation of the analysis data sets. The process by which each variable was created can be traced back to the original source. This approach will also simplify maintaining consistency between the SDTM and ADaM data sets. The CDISC specifications state that any variables copied from an SDTM domain into an ADaM data set must retain all of the attributes found in the SDTM domain. By storing the metadata for SDTM and ADaM in the same system and form it is easy to ensure that this condition will be met.

The SAS Metadata Server and the SAS Data Integration Studio provide a very powerful environment for mapping study data and producing domain data sets. This environment provides direct access to study metadata and CDISC SDTM domain metadata. The visual interface allows you to define data transformation and mapping steps using icons that represent predefined process steps. The system is extensible, allowing you to add new capabilities and the sequence of steps used in your process is stored in metadata.

## DEVELOPING A SDTM METADATA MAPPING TOOL

It is possible to create your own simple, but effective tools to aid in the metadata mapping process. Leveraging the power of SAS and Microsoft Excel together allows you to create a practical metadata mapping tool with relatively little programming. The combination of SAS and Excel allows you to combine a user interface with the familiarity of an Excel workbook with the power of SAS to access and manipulate data in a variety of forms. Important skills needed to develop such a tool includes a solid understanding of SAS DATA step programming, basic SAS Macro programming skills, and a working knowledge of Visual Basic and the Excel object model.

A key reason for the power of pairing SAS with Excel is the flexibility SAS provides for exchanging data with Excel. The SAS Excel libname engine allows you to read and write from Excel worksheets as though they were a SAS data set. The IMPORT and EXPORT procedures allow you exchange data for an entire data set as a stand-alone process or from within a SAS program. Dynamic data exchange (DDE) allows you to define a DDE triplet that defines a range of cells in Excel to be treated as a flat file in SAS. The SAS Add-In for Microsoft Office allows you to use SAS as a powerful data access, manipulation and analysis back end for Excel applications. SAS also provides the XML libname engine to facilitate reading and writing XML files. In version 9, SAS added ODM native mode support (xmltype = CDISCODM) to the XML engine. The SAS CDISC procedure currently provides read and write capability for ODM, and content and structure validation for SDTM.

The example presented here is a simple tool developed using Microsoft Excel, Visual Basic and SAS. The SDTM metadata mapping tool allows users to manage and document the mapping of study data to SDTM domains and it can produce text files containing SAS source code to be used as a starting point for programs to generate SDTM domain data sets from the study data sets. The tool consists of an Excel workbook with three main worksheets: an SDTM domain metadata dictionary, a study metadata dictionary with CDM data set specifications imported from the SAS view SASHELP.VCOLUMN, and a SDTM mapping sheet containing variable mapping and derivation information.

An advantage of using Excel is that there is a great deal of functionality available without any programming. One example of this is the Excel auto filter. When an auto filter is set for a column, a selection button appears in the label cell. Clicking on it displays a pick list containing all of the unique items in that column. If an item is selected, the sheet will then only display rows that contain that value in that column. This feature makes it easy to view subsets of the metadata. For example, you can view all of the variables in a particular data set or domain, or you can view all of the occurrences of a given variable name across all domains. The sheet containing the SDTM metadata dictionary is shown in Figure 2, the study metadata sheet is shown in Figure 3.

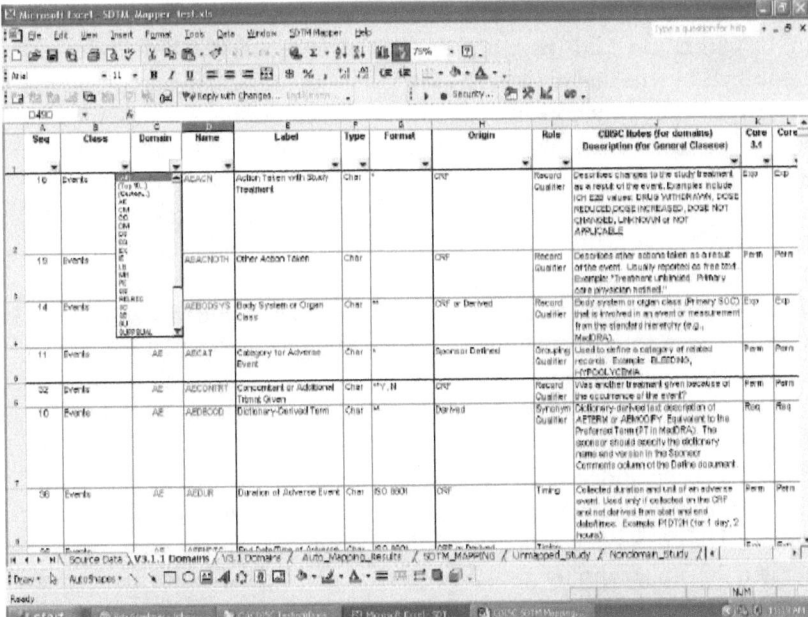

**Figure 2. SDTM Metadata dictionary with auto filter selection list**

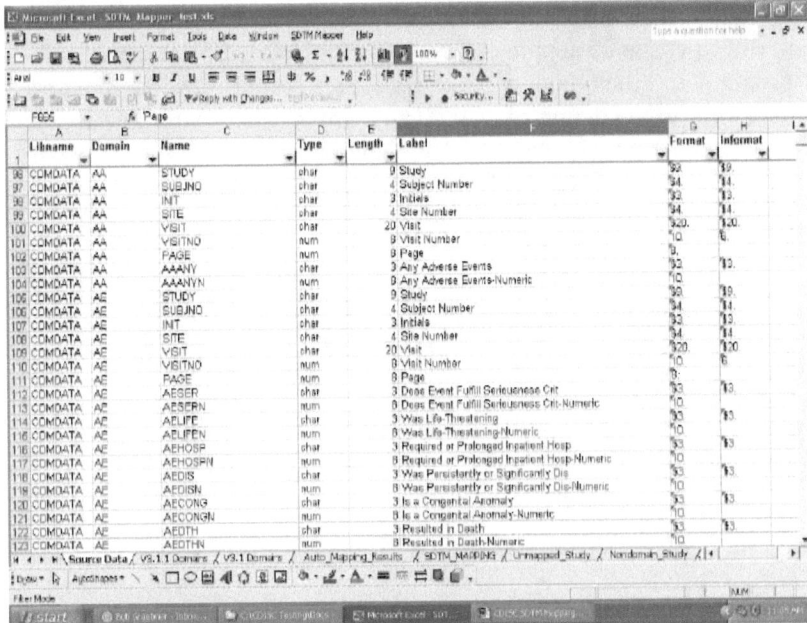

**Figure 3. Study Metadata Sheet**

The user interface includes a new main item called SDTM Mapper that is temporarily added to the Excel main menu just before the Help menu item, or within the Add-Ins tab if you are using Excel 2007. Current active submenu items include Map Study Variables and Generate SAS Code for Domain. The functionality behind these menu options is provided by a series of Visual Basic modules containing subroutines and functions stored within the workbook. Mapping study variables involves selecting the row corresponding to a given SDTM domain variable in the SDTM_MAPPING sheet, then selecting the desired study variable from a pick list that uses the study metadata dictionary as its row source. Once a variable is selected, the metadata for that variable is added to the same row in the appropriate columns of the SDTM_MAPPING sheet. The names of the study data metadata columns all begin with "s_" to differentiate them from the columns containing metadata for the STDM domain. If additional study variables are required to derive an SDTM domain variable, they can be added to the s_addvars column. Blocks of executable SAS source code or a SAS macro call can be entered into the SAS_code column. The SAS code is included the SAS program text files that are generated by the mapping tool and it also provides documentation on how the variable was created. If only basic instructions or pseudo code are available, they can be entered as a SAS comment statement. A valuable addition to this sheet would be a column to containing the derivation or imputation description or algorithm. This would ensure that the method used to create a variable can be easily understood by those who do not program and the contents could serve as a source for Computation-Method items in the define.xml file. The mapping sheet with the variable selection user form is shown in Figures 4 and 5.

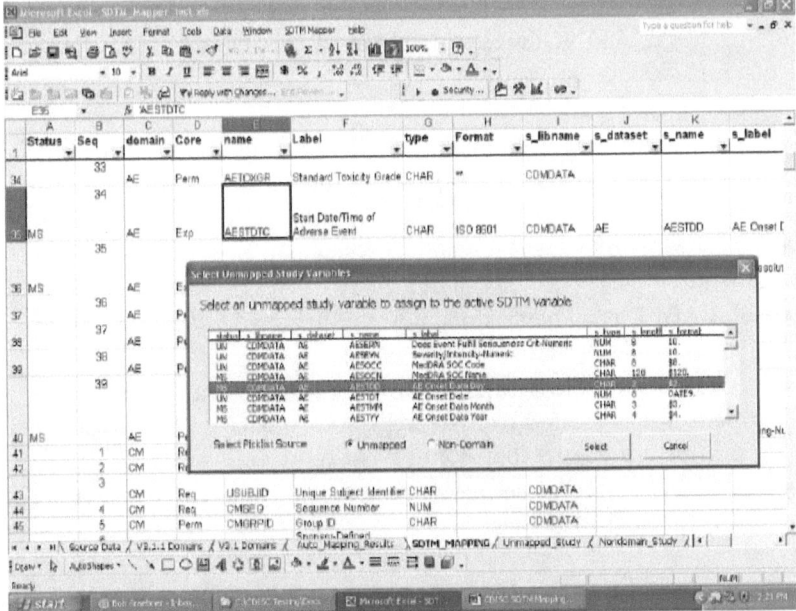

**Figure 4. Metadata mapping sheet showing the study variable pick list**

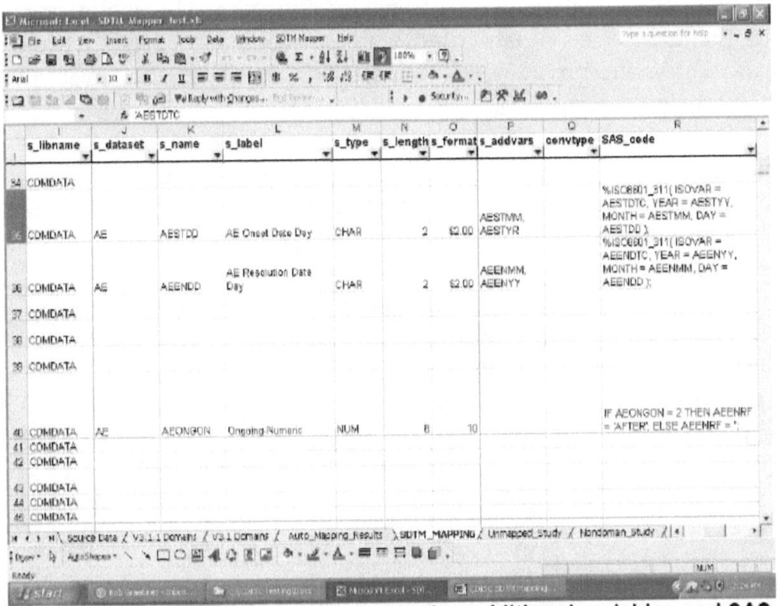

**Figure 5. Metadata mapping sheet showing additional variables and SAS code**

To generate a text file containing SAS source code, the user selects Generate SAS Code for Domain from the SDTM Mapper menu and then selects the desired domain. A Visual Basic module utilizes the metadata in the SDTM_MAPPING sheet to generate a text file with SAS source code that includes:

- A program header comment block which indicates the name of the SDTM domain is produced and the names of the source data sets
- RETAIN and KEEP statements containing all of the selected variable names
- A LABEL statement containing the name and standard CDISC label for all selected variables
- A DATA step to create the domain data set with a SET statement if it is created from a single source data set or a MERGE statement if it is created from two or more data sets
- All blocks of SAS source code from the relevant rows of the SDTM_MAPPER sheet

Because the metadata is used to generate the SAS source code you will end up with code that includes all of the necessary variables, with correct names, labels and types. While the text file is not meant to be a read-to-run program, it helps increase efficiency and consistency by eliminating most of the tedious tasks associated with developing conversion programs and allows the programmer to focus on the challenging issues of data mapping and derivation.

A simple application like this can be useful in situations where timelines are tight and do not afford the opportunity to develop a full-scale application. It is designed as a flexible, "in the trenches" tool. In addition to filling immediate project needs, such an application can serve as a prototype for testing new ideas and as a focal point while defining and refining the user requirements for a more robust, enterprise-level application. When using an Excel application of this type, it is important to limit the extent to which users and modify the functionality. The most critical safeguard is to password protect the Visual Basic source code modules so that only those with sufficient skill and adequate knowledge of the application can modify them.

## DOMAIN DATA SET VALIDATION

The SAS CDISC procedure is a very valuable tool for validating SDTM domain data sets is. With SAS version 9.1.3, Proc CDISC can be used to validate domain data sets. Future version will provide additional functionality. For validating STDM domain data sets, I developed a SAS macro that utilizes PROC CDISC. The macro has three parameters:

- **DOMAIN** - The two-letter of the SDTM domain to validate
- **SUPPQUAL** - If this parameter is not missing, the SUPPQUAL data set is validated
- **COMM** - If this parameter is not missing, the comments (CO) data set is validated

Only the domain name is required. The category parameter of PROC CDISC is automatically set by the macro. If the SUPPQUAL parameter is not missing, then the rows in SUPPQUAL that pertain to the specified domain are test merged with the domain data set. An error statement is generated in the SAS log for any SUPPQUAL rows that do not have a match in the domain data set. The same process is done with the comments data set if the COMM parameter is not missing. Any findings from PROC CDISC are also included in the log. This can include:

- An ERROR for any required variable that is not found or has a missing value, or any expected variable that is not found
- A WARNING for any expected variable that has a missing value
- A NOTE for any permissible variable that is not found

Note that unless you have the Beta patch for PROC CDISC, the SDTM 3.1.1 ISO8601 format is not supported and dates with missing components will generate an error in the log.

## DATES, TIMES AND THE ISO8601 FORMAT

The CDISC standard uses the nonproprietary ISO8601 format to represent date and time values. This standard expresses dates and times with character strings in a format that can readily be understood by humans and interpreted by software. A full representation of a date and time value would be of the form YYYY-MMDDThh:mm:ss. Years are represented using four digits, the remaining date and time components are all two digits with leading zeros if necessary. The date components are separated by a hyphen and the time components are separated by a colon. For values containing date and time, an upper case letter "T" is used to separate the date and time. There are no spaces between components and delimiters. The ISO8601 standard allows for the use of either the basic format, without delimiters, or the extended format described above. The SAS XML libname engine provides both basic and extended formats and informats. The CDISC specification requires the use of the extended format with delimiters.

Partial dates and times can be stored in this format, however the ISO8601 standard of handling partial dates was modified. In the original standard, the representation would start with the largest scale component (e.g. year) and continue until a missing component occurred. The representation would end at that point, resulting in a reduced precision representation. For example, if a date was recorded with a year and day, but missing month, it would only be stored in ISO8601 format as a year. With the new standard, hyphens could be inserted for the two missing month digits, resulting in a missing component representation. The SDTM 3.1 standard utilizes the reduced precision method, the 3.1.1 standard uses the missing component standard. The current version of SAS 9 was developed based on the SDTM 3.1 implementation guide however there are updates available to comply with the SDTM 3.1.1 implementation of the ISO8601 date and time formats. The examples below show the full representation of 10:30 AM on March 3, 2008, and the partial representations if the day was missing.

```
Full Datetime Representation:                      2008-03-18T10:30:00
Reduced Precision Representation (SDTM 3.1)    2008-03
Missing Component Representation (SDTM 3.1.1) 2008-03-T10:30:00
```

There are many features in SAS that facilitate reading and writing dates and times in the ISO8601 format. SAS provides a wide range of ISO8601 date and time formats and informats with the XML libname engine. When working with SAS data sets there are several informats that can be used to read ISO8601 text strings in as a SAS date. This might be necessary if the ISO8601 formats were used in creating the source data sets and you need to perform computations or comparisons of dates to create your SDTM domains. Partial dates or times will result in a missing value for the SAS date or time variable. The applicable SAS informats are listed below.

```
Reading ISO8601 Dates:     ANYDTDTE10. or YYMMDD10.
               Times:     ANYDTTME8. or TIME8.
               Datetime: ANYDTDTM19.
```

SAS provides many functions that are useful in creating dates and times in the ISO8601 format. The individual date and time components can be extracted, formatted and combined with the appropriate delimiter characters to form the equivalent ISO8601 representation.

## DEFINE.XML

FDA guidance for electronic submissions specifies that all electronic submissions include a Data Definition Document that describes the structure and content of the data included in the submission. In 1999 the FDA standardized on the use of SAS version 5 XPORT (.XPT) files for study data, and Portable Document Format (.PDF) files for metadata. In 2003 the FDA expanded the list of acceptable file types to include Extensible Markup Language (.XML) files. By transitioning from the use of define.pdf to define.xml, the metadata for the submission will be in a machine-readable form that can be used by standard data review tools. Placing both study data and metadata in a standard XML schema will facilitate validation and transfer into a data warehouse. The schema for the SDTM define.xml is based on an extension of the CDSIC ODM, which is a specification of a standard XML schema designed to facilitate efficient and robust storage and interchange of clinical trial data and associated metadata. Details on define.xml are published in the Case Report Tabulation Data Definition Specification (CRT-DDS) document available at the CDISC website listed at the beginning of this chapter. CDISC also provides standard style sheets that can be used to render the define.xml file into a readable form. The United States Food and Drug Administration (FDA) also provide guidance on preparing files for electronic submission.

The creation of the define.xml file must conform to the CDISC standards. The XML must be well-formed, standard XML without any proprietary XML tags, such as you can find in an Excel file saved as XML. The XML specification does not define a single file structure definition as is common with proprietary file formats such as SAS data sets or Excel spreadsheets. The "X" stands for extensible. Within the XML specification, matching tags are used to delimit items. In XML however, it is possible to define new tags to meet specific needs. It is essential that the tags used conform to the CDISC ODM standard.

The define.xml file is comprised of several sections. The file header contains information that identifies the file as XML and specifies the XML version used. The file also contains SDTM study-level metadata. The table of contents section contains domain-level metadata including the data set name for each domain, a description, structure description (e.g. one record per subject per event), the purpose, a list of the variables that form the key and a link to the actual data set. Another section is the Data Definition Table (DDT) that contains the variable-level metadata. Validation of the define.xml must be done on several levels including checks for conformance with the define.xml specification, checks for internal integrity between elements and checks for external integrity with other files referenced in define.xml such as domain data files and an annotated CRF in PDF format.

## CONCLUSION

The mapping of existing study data to CDISC SDTM domain data sets can be a daunting task. Developing an adequate understanding of the SDTM standard is an important first step. Proper planning and the use of metadata mapping tools can increase both the efficiency of the process and the quality of the resulting data sets. The use of standard processes and tools will increase the return on your development investment if they are flexible enough to be used on future conversion projects. If you are allowed to submit SDTM domain data sets in lieu of study report listings, patient profiles or monitoring board report listings, the cost of creating the STDM domain data sets can be offset. The ability of reviewers to readily access tabulation data can potentially eliminate some of the costs associated with ad-hoc requests. Having you study data in a standardized format can facilitate significant gains in efficiencies when creating analysis file data sets or when combining data from different trials for an integrated study.

# six

# XML in the DATA Step

**Michael Palmer**

SAS Institute's (SI) XMLMAP imports XML via the LIBNAME XML engine and a mapping file, by-passing the DATA step. For export of XML, SI offers custom tagsets and the Output Delivery System (ODS). Custom tagsets are built with PROC TEMPLATE, by-passing the DATA-step. By contrast, the DATA-step method discussed in this chapter uses a single, uniform methodology to import, export, and transform user-defined XML vocabularies in the familiar DATA-step. With XMLMAP, all of the information about the original XML hierarchical structure is lost and export back to XML is not readily available except for several XML formats built into the XML engine. For XML export, one has to use arcane customized tagsets and ODS. Nevertheless, SI's toolbox does work and has reportedly scaled to large, real life uses. The DATA-step method, on the other hand, indexes an XML hierarchy and uses these indexes to flatten the XML hierarchy and to preserve the information about the hierarchy in a DATA-step friendly format. The method has been in use successfully and supports complex XML vocabularies such as the pharmaceutical industry's CDISC XML standard for clinical data and proprietary XML schemas in the financial industry. It has scaled to XML files of over one million records.

## INTRODUCTION

XML is a format for data that is hierarchical, text-based, and consists of named content. These three characteristics make XML difficult to work within the row-and-column-oriented DATA-step and file structure in SAS. This chapter contrasts the SAS Institute's (SI) XML tools with a DATA-step friendly way to work with XML vocabularies. Both methods support the import of XML into SAS, the export of XML from SAS, and the processing and transformation of XML in the DATA-step.

A toolkit for working with XML in SAS should have the properties listed below because they bring true XML capability to the SAS workplace while preserving established ways of working in SAS.

1. The toolkit works with a very broad class of user-defined XML vocabularies.
2. The toolkit uses one uniform methodology for the import, export, and transformation of any instance of any data centric XML vocabulary.
3. XML work all takes place in the base SAS DATA-step. The programming techniques necessary to implement the method are familiar to even beginning SAS programmers.

SAS Institute offerings for working with XML include a LIBNAME engine for importing and exporting some fairly simple types of XML, including some common industry forms. The XMLMAP option of the LIBNAME Engine can import a broader class of XML directly to SAS datasets. A graphical user interface tool is also available for assisting in the creation of XML mapping files using a familiar drag-and-drop motif. The XML LIBNAME engine can automatically export a SAS-defined type of XML and some common industry forms. With customized tagset extension programming, ODS may export some user-defined types of XML. Version 9 also contains broader support for parsing XML in the DATA-step.

## WHAT'S THE PROBLEM WITH XML AND SAS?

XML is hierarchical, unlike the typical SAS dataset. In the typical SAS setting, data exist in fields on records in datasets. In a given dataset, every record has precisely the same fields with precisely the same attributes. One relates a data item to another data item by the fact that they share, or do not share, key variables and key variable values. In XML, a data item relates to other data items by the ancestors, descendants, and siblings that they share. XML is hierarchical so a data item inherits identity from its ancestors, shares identity with its siblings, and passes on identity to its descendents. To identify a data item, one has to literally traverse all of its ancestors. This traversal creates a path through the XML file. By contrast, in the typical SAS dataset, one identifies a data item by looking at key fields on the same record.

XML is text. All XML is text, accessible with a simple text editor. In

SAS datasets, by contrast, fields can be text or numeric and, despite the rich set of text-processing functions in SAS, numeric data is easier to process than text data. In addition, proprietary tools such as SAS Viewer or the base SAS product are necessary to access data and attribute information in a SAS dataset.

XML consists of named content. The name of each item in an XML file is written completely in text when that element's scope begins and written out again completely when that element's scope ends. The sequence of items in that scope is predictable to some extent, but not fixed like it is for a typical SAS dataset. In addition, field attributes, such as field name, are not explicit in SAS but are stored separately from the data itself.

From the point of view of a SAS user, XML is trouble for these three reasons: it's hierarchical, it's all text, and all content is explicitly named.

Despite these complications, SAS users would like to be able to import XML, export XML, and work with XML in the DATA-step as easily as they work with other data originating in other formats.

## A WISH LIST FOR A SUCCESSFUL METHODOLOGY

A successful methodology for working with XML in the DATA-step would include the following three features.

- One, the methodology should flatten the hierarchical XML structure into the row-and-column structure of SAS datasets but without losing the information needed to recreate the hierarchy. That is, the ancestor-sibling-descendent structure in native XML should be indexed into a flat representation.
- Two, the methodology should replace the unpredictably long and complex text strings that describe paths to data items in XML with numbers. Long and complex text strings are cumbersome to work within the SAS DATA-step. Numbers are relatively easy to work with.
- Three, the methodology should fit the numerically indexed content into a regular row-and-column SAS dataset.

A toolkit that has these characteristics along with the capability to support general data-centric XML import, export, and transformation would go a long way towards meeting the need for a familiar DATA-step way to work with XML.

## SAS INSTITUTE'S XML METHODOLOGY

Starting with SAS version 8.2, SAS has included production-level tools for working with user-specified XML. The tools have evolved and been refined with each new SAS version, but the basic approach has stayed the same. Import from XML is controlled by a mapping file that identifies paths in the XML and, for each path, defines a destination SAS dataset and destination field in that dataset. This is implemented with the XML engine of the LIBNAME statement.

## XML IMPORT

Figure 1 shows a sample of XML for the rss XML vocabulary. This XML sample and the accompanying material were downloaded from the SAS web site.

The RSS vocabulary, used to illustrate XML import at the SAS web site, has several features that make it a good choice to illustrate processing of data-centric XML. For instance, it has data in attributes, e.g., version=”0.91”, and elements and it has several levels of hierarchy from the root element, <rss>, to the deepest level, <title>. The right side of Figure 1 shows the rss sample. The left side of Figure 1 shows the XMLMAP file that the SAS XML engine uses to move data from rss to dataset named channel.

Distinguishing features of a map for XMLMAP are at least two. It is itself XML and it relies on the XPATH XML standard. The various XPATH statements in the map use XPATH syntax to define a sequence of XML element type names and attribute names from the <rss> root element to specific data in the rss vocabulary. XPATH syntax is defined in the World Wide Web consortium's XPATH standard. For each path defined in rss, XMLMAP also defines a field in the channel dataset. The XML engine in SAS moves the data point at the end of each path to the designated field in channel. Figure 2 shows how to run XMLMAP in SAS and Figure 3 shows the result of running the rss map with the rss sample in Figure 1. A dataset called channel is created with two fields, title and version.

Figure 1. XMLMAP with a Sample of XML

```
<SXLEMap>
    <TABLE name="channel">
        <TABLE_XPATH> /rss/channel
    </TABLE_XPATH>
        <COLUMN name="title">
        <XPATH> /rss/channel/title </XPATH>
        <TYPE> character </TYPE>
        <DATATYPE> string </DATATYPE>
        <LENGTH> 200 </LENGTH>
        </COLUMN>
        <COLUMN name="version">
        <XPATH> /rss@version </XPATH>
        <TYPE> character </TYPE>
        <DATATYPE> string </DATATYPE>
        <LENGTH> 8 </LENGTH>
        </COLUMN>
    </TABLE>
</SXLEMap>
```

```
<rss version="0.91">
    <channel>
        <title>WriteTheWeb</title>
    </channel>
</rss>
```

Figure 2. Running XMLMAP

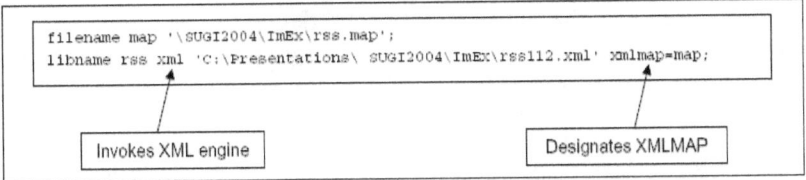

```
filename map '\SUGI2004\ImEx\rss.map';
libname rss xml 'C:\Presentations\ SUGI2004\ImEx\rss112.xml' xmlmap=map;
```

Invokes XML engine          Designates XMLMAP

Figure 3. XMLMAP results

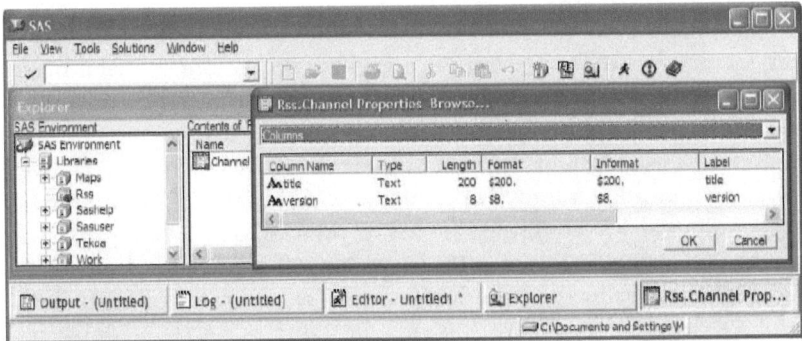

# XML EXPORT

Creating XML via custom tagsets in PROC TEMPLATE and exporting it with the XML engine is a totally different process from importing XML with XMLMAP and the XML engine.

On import, SAS retains none of the hierarchical information in the XML file, and this has a significant implication, particularly when it's time to export XML from SAS. For user-specified XML schemas or DTDs, the export route from SAS to XML goes through customized ODS tagsets and PROC TEMPLATE rather than through the XML mapping file and LIBNAME engine used to import XML. This requires learning what amounts to a new language. That language is described in SAS documentation, particularly the Base SAS Community XML pages at www.sas.com. The URL for SI's XML support is in the "References" section at the end of this chapter. This chapter is concerned with a 100% DATA step solution to XML export and so it will not cover in detail the esoteric subjects of ODS tagsets and PROC TEMPLATE.

Using the SI tools, there is nothing as simple as a "reverse map" that connects a field in a dataset to the user's own XML via a path definition. Instead, the export process, in essence, defines one, and only one, XML schema that it supports and allows users to put a SAS dataset name and SAS field names into that schema along SAS-defined paths. Getting the dataset and field names into the exported XML require programmatically defining a tagset in PROC TEMPLATE.

Figure 4 shows the skeleton of a PROC TEMPLATE for exporting XML and Figure 5 fills in that skeleton for two of the events. Figure 6 shows the SAS code that creates the export XML.

One might think that through carefully defining events, using the special syntax for that in PROC TEMPLATE and the even more special syntax and reserved names supported by the XML engine, it would be possible, although tedious, to have the XML engine export user-defined XML. For example, the author attempted to export the rss XML from SAS after successfully importing it into SAS using the XMLMAP. This is not possible (the impossibility confirmed by a source at SI) for several reasons. First, the XML engine is not case aware. XML element and attribute names are case sensitive but the XML engine is not aware of case. For example, <channel> in Figure 1 is not the same as <CHANNEL> in Figure 7. Second, the XML engine for export puts all data into elements, one field in the source SAS dataset per element, and groups them by source dataset row. For example, "version" in Figure 1, is an attribute on the root element, <rss> and it is mapped to the same dataset as the element content for <title>. It is impossible with the XML engine to export "version" as an attribute on an element that contains other data. Third, the XML engine can export data from just one SAS dataset at a time so it is impossible to put together exported XML that is a composite of data from several source datasets. One can merge data from several source datasets before the export to XML, as long as such a merge makes sense given the key structure of the datasets, and then export the long records to the mirror-image XML that the XML engine can produce. But, XML offers much more flexibility in data structures than this and very often the exact structure is dictated by needs outside the SAS world. It is impossible for the XML engine to match the options that XML offers for data structures.

### Figure 4. Creating the Tagset

```
proc template;
define tagset Tagsets.ZBIioXML;
   define event XMLversion;
   . . .
   end;
   define event table_body;
   . . .
   end;
   define event row;
   . . .
   end;
   define event data;
   . . .
   end;
   define event field;
   . . .
   end;
end;
```

### Figure 5. Defining an Event

```
define event data;
   start:
   break / if !cmp( SECTION , "body" );
   ndent;
   trigger field;
   finish:
   break / if !cmp( SECTION , "body" );
   trigger field;
   end;
```

```
define event field;
   start:
   put "<" NAME ;
   put "> " ;
   put VALUE ;
   put " " ;
   break ;
   finish:
   put "</" NAME ">";
   put nl;
   xdent;
   break;
   end;
```

Figure 6. Running ODS Tagsets

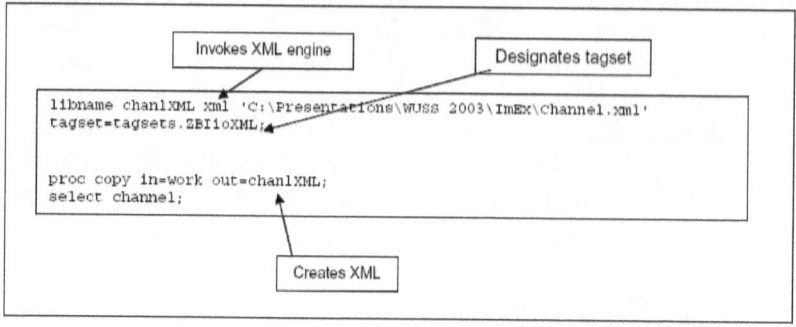

Figure 7. XML Engine-exported XML

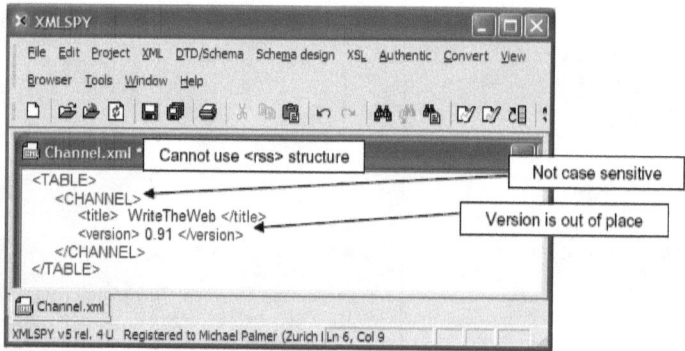

## SAS AND XML : OIL AND WATER?

Given these limitations of the XML engine in SAS, a natural question is whether or not SAS is the right place to work with XML at all. SAS is a truly powerful tool because it combines superb data management capabilities with state-of-the-art statistical capabilities and ties it all together with a fully functional programming environment. In addition, SAS has tremendous cross-platform capabilities. This puts SAS-based systems in the middle of many sophisticated information systems that involve complex human-machine and machine-machine interactions.

XML has become ubiquitous in information technology because it is a vendor-neutral, platform-independent format for self-describing information. XML has become the preferred format for heterogeneous information systems. In other words, SAS and XML really have to work well together. The author's experience, primarily in the pharmaceutical and medical worlds but also with some exposure to financial systems, is that SAS and XML can do better than just work well together. XML can integrate SAS into heterogeneous systems for truly remarkable results with the use of a functional toolkit that feels comfortable to SAS users. The rest of this chapter will describe that toolkit.

## A DATA-STEP XML METHODOLOGY

A straightforward tool for working with XML in the DATA-step can be based on the indexing of levels of hierarchy in an XML instance.

An algorithm for numbering levels of depth in an XML hierarchy and for numbering siblings at a given level satisfies the three conditions given above for an XML solution in SAS:

1.  retain information on the XML parent-child-sib relationships
2.  in numerical indexes
3.  stored in flat SAS records.

But the straightforward solution has a problem. The problem is that, unlike flat files, XML instances for a given XML vocabulary do not necessarily have identical or even similar structures. They can, and often have, very heterogeneous structures. It's even possible to have the identical content, which should end up in identical data structures in SAS, in very different XML structures from the same XML vocabulary. This situation makes the straightforward algorithm unreliable because the indexes that it produces will not be invariant to the way an XML instance happens to be put together. To make the indexing invariant, it has to be tied to the structure of the XML vocabulary for the instance, not to the instance itself. The construction of such an invariant index is a central part of the methodology and software tools discussed below.

The methodology supports highly generic programming, and it has been implemented to take advantage of that capability. In the author's implementation, there are two macros: %importXML and %exportXML. These are available for free from the author.

With these two macros, XML-formatted data from a very broad class of user-defined XML vocabularies can be imported, exported, and processed in SAS without having to leave the base SAS environment. A significant advantage of %importXML and %exportXML over SI's XML tools is that they can always import and export user defined XML without unfamiliar programming techniques. They work very much like XML analogs to INPUT and OUTPUT statements in a DATA-step. This is a significant simplification of XML processing in SAS.

## XML IN THE DATA-STEP

The XML fragment below will be used to illustrate the indexing algorithm. XML statements begin with a start tag of the form <TagName> and end with a tag of the form </TagName>. The scope of a tag may completely include other tags and content:

```
<Tag00><Tag01>Information</Tag01></Tag00>.
```

In addition, a tag may have one or more attributes in its scope: <Tag00 Attribute00="Stuff">. Tags that do not contain other tags or content may be written as empty tags: <Tag02 Attribute01="More stuff"/>.

The XML fragment below has three tag names. <SubjectData> is in the scope of <ODM> and <ItemData> is in the scope of <SubjectData>. <ItemData> has two attributes with data: ItemOID and Value.

```
<ODM>
    <SubjectData>
            <ItemData ItemOID="PT" Value="P002"/>
    </SubjectData>
</ODM>
```

## SAS INSTITUTE'S XML METHODOLOGY

This XML fragment could be readily imported into SAS with the XML engine of the LIBNAME statement using the map file below. The XML engine uses the map file to read the XML, create SAS datasets with map-specified attributes, and import data into the datasets, all as described above.

```
<SXLEMap>
    <TABLE name="ItemData">
      <TABLE_XPATH>/ ODM/SubjectData/ItemData /TABLE_XPATH>
      <COLUMN name="ItemOID">
     <XPATH>/ODM/SubjectData/ItemData@ItemOID </XPATH>
     <TYPE> character </TYPE>
     <DATATYPE> string </DATATYPE>
     <LENGTH> 20 </LENGTH>
      </COLUMN>
      <COLUMN name="Value">
```

```
        <XPATH> /ODM/SubjectData/ItemData@Value </XPATH>
        <TYPE> character </TYPE>
        <DATATYPE> string </DATATYPE>
        <LENGTH> 200 </LENGTH>
          </COLUMN>
    </TABLE>
</SXLEMap>
```

This map file (written in XML itself from an SXLEMap schema) specifies the creation of a table, that is, a SAS dataset named ItemData with two fields, or columns. One field is ItemOID and the other is Value and each has the attributes given in the map file.

The non-SAS thing in the map is the specification of paths. This specification comes from the XML world. The Xpath specification of the World Wide Web Consortium (W3C) is the source. Xpath is the W3C recommendation on how to identify a specific place in an XML instance. Paths are used because, as pointed out above, XML files are hierarchies with parents, sibs, and descendants, and one locates a specific point in a hierarchy by specifying the path to it. As implemented in the XML map, the paths are text strings that can get very long and complicated.

For non-XML data, such as a coma-delimited file or some other text file being imported into SAS, data import would typically take place in the DATA-step and might be done with an INPUT statement, data transformations, validation operations, and merging with other data, instead of with a mapping file. The XML engine skips that initial DATA-step and its familiar syntax and powerful programming capabilities and moves data immediately into a destination SAS dataset. These SAS datasets can, of course, go into the traditional DATA-step processing.

The XMLMAP processing with the XML engine is only for importing XML formatted data into SAS. It has no role in exporting XML and, as mentioned above, the information needed to export XML from the DATA-step is lost by the XML engine with the XML map.

## A DATA-STEP XML METHODOLOGY

As discussed above, XML can be brought into and written from a DATA-step with the aid of an indexing algorithm for the XML hierarchy. For the XML fragment being used to illustrate XML processing, that indexing is straightforward, either manually or in a machine implementation.

To index this fragment, ODM is at the root, or ultimate, level so it has a value of 1 for the root level indexing variable. SubjectData is in the scope of ODM so it inherits a root level indexing variable of 1, and, in addition, since SubjectData is the first tag one level inside the root level, it has a second index variable with a value of 1.

ItemData, inside the scope of SubjectData, inherits its index variables and gets one new one for itself. ItemOID and Value are attributes but, for purposes of indexing, they are treated just like tags inside the scope of ItemData. The XML fragment below shows the complete indexing.

```
1              <ODM >
1 1                <SubjectData >
1 1 1                <ItemData
1 1 1 1                  ItemOID="PT"
1 1 1 2                  Value="P002"/>
                  </SubjectData >
             </ODM>
```

Looking at the indexed XML, it's straightforward to see how it could be stored in a SAS dataset. Figure 8 shows this XML instance, including the indexing, in a SAS dataset.

Figure 8. XML-image SAS dataset with index variables.

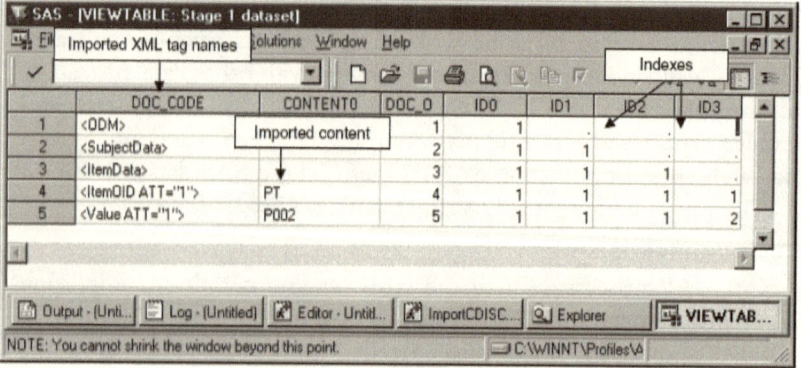

## SIMPLE PROGRAMMING TECHNIQUES WORK

The SAS DATA-step code below shows how this XML imported into a SAS dataset can be processed using familiar DATA-step techniques and put directly into two fields, NAME and VALUE, in a SAS dataset. The SAS variable *content0* holds the imported data. For the ODM example, *content0* equals PT in the first line and *content0* equals P002 in the second line.

```
/*<ItemData ItemOID=""/>*/
if ID01=1 and ID02=1 and ID03=1 and ID04=1 then
    NAME=trim(left(content0));

/*<ItemData Value=""/>*/
if ID01=1 and ID02=1 and ID03=1 and ID04=2 then
    VALUE=trim(left(content0));
    output;
run;
```

In the next XML fragment below, a second <ItemData> element is added and indexed.

```
1      <ODM >
1  1      <SubjectData >
1  1  1        <ItemData
1  1  1  1          ItemOID="PT"
1  1  1  2          Value="P002"/>
1  1  2        <ItemData
1  1  2  1          ItemOID="SEX"
1  1  2  2          Value="m"/>
            </SubjectData >
        </ODM>
```

In order to process this new ItemData, the SAS code would also have to
be modified to pick up the new 1 1 2 element. Obviously, a method of
handling XML in SAS that required custom code to match the XML instance would not be useful.

The indexing algorithm has to recognize repeating XML structures and
give them identical indexes, as below.

```
1      <ODM >
1  1      <SubjectData >
1  1  1        <ItemData
1  1  1  1          ItemOID="PT"
1  1  1  2          Value="P002"/>
1  1  1        <ItemData
1  1  1  1          ItemOID="SEX"
1  1  1  2          Value="m"/>
            </SubjectData >
        </ODM>
```

With both ItemData elements indexed identically, the programs become
generic and more powerful. Figure 9 shows this XML imported into a
SAS dataset.

Figure 9. Invariant indexing in the XML-image SAS dataset

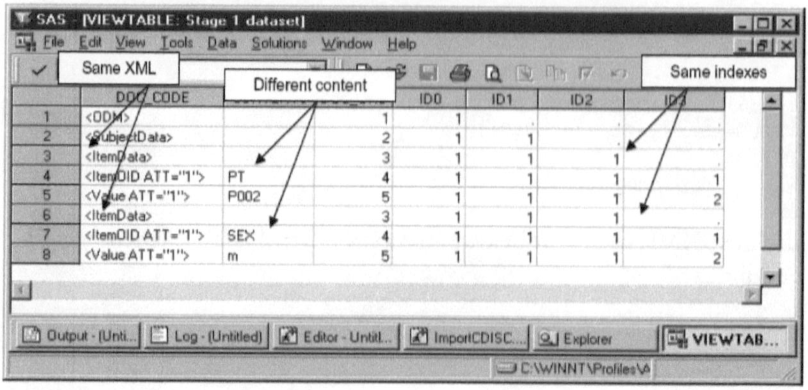

## A GENERAL SOLUTION

A general solution to the need for an indexing algorithm that is invariant to the XML instance, but depends on the underlying structure of the XML vocabulary, is called a canonical document (a candoc). The term candoc, the candoc approach, candoc technology, and implementation tools are called, in Zurich Biostatistics' terminology, Tekoa Technology.

The candoc for the XML fragment under discussion is, in indexed form.

```
1       <ODM >
1 1         <SubjectData >
1 1 1           <ItemData
1 1 1 1             ItemOID=""
1 1 1 2             Value=""/>
            </SubjectData >
    </ODM>
```

The candoc contains no content but defines the permitted tag names, attribute names, and relationships between all tags and attributes. It's a template to guide the import and export of an XML vocabulary. Using the candoc, every ItemOID with a path through the XML of <ODM><SubjectData><ItemData> will have exactly the same ID: 1 1 1 1, and will be processed correctly in the SAS code sample above. In other words, the code sample will work very much like a traditional INPUT statement in a DATA-step.

The indexed candoc enumerates all of the paths through the XML schema or DTD that it supports. The DOC_ORD numbers in Figure 10 show the path enumeration. To streamline the DATA-step programming illustrated above, DOC_ORD numbers can be used instead of the individual indexes.

```
/*<ItemData ItemOID=""/>*/
if DOC_ORD=4 then NAME=trim(left(content0));

/*<ItemData Value=""/>*/
if DOC_ORD=5 then VALUE=trim(left(content0));
   output;
run;
```

This brings the SAS programmer control of XML processing in the DATA-step but does not require knowledge of XPath. Since the %importXML tool automatically indexes any canonical document and automatically indexes any XML instance, the SAS programmer can use familiar DATA-step programming techniques, as shown above, to work with XML.

Figure 10. Canonical Document that guides invariant indexing for import and export.

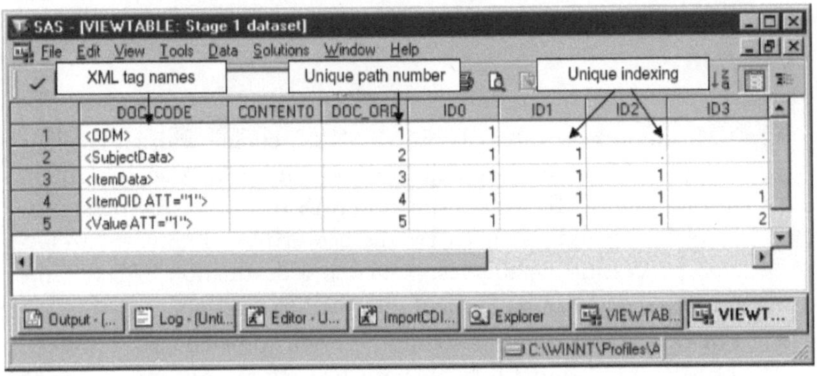

## A 100% BASE SAS SOLUTION FOR ALL XML

Candocs guide the import of XML into SAS and they guide the export of XML from SAS. ZBI's %exportXML tool uses a candoc to write XML from the kind of XML SAS dataset discussed in this chapter. The XML export does not require ODS or Java or perl. Export, like import, is done completely in the base SAS DATA-step using familiar techniques.

Candocs, since they are completely under the control of the user, allow anyone who is comfortable with DATA-step programming to import and export any data-centric XML vocabulary.

The method has been in use successfully for several years and does support real life, complex, consortium developed XML vocabularies such as the pharmaceutical industry's CDISC XML standard for clinical study data. The method has scaled successfully to XML files of over one million records.

## XSLT-TYPE TRANSFORMATIONS

XSLT-type transformations can be done in the DATA-step using this candoc indexing approach. To transform, the index ID values are changed with DATA-step programming statements. Since the index ID values identify paths in XML, one instance can be transformed to another by changing the ID values and exporting the resulting XML with the appropriate candoc.

## SUMMARY

XML's hierarchical, text-based, named content nature makes it cumbersome to import, export, and transform in the DATA-step. SAS Institute's solution handles XML import and export as two separate cases.

- XML import uses the LIBNAME XML engine with an auxiliary mapping file. The mapping file, itself in XML, associates paths through the XML with destination SAS files. This by-passes the DATA-step and also bypasses the powerful and familiar DATA-step processing capabilities. Once in a destination SAS file, the imported data can be brought into the DATA-step.
- For export to XML, SI's solution uses customized tagsets, PROC TEMPLATE, and ODS. These procedures are unfamiliar to many SAS programmers. Also, they can export only XML that itself has the row-column structure of SAS datasets. This is not really a general-purpose solution for XML export. Generic DATA-step writing of XML is not part of the PROC TEMPLATE solution, either.

The various versions of SAS do support direct LIBNAME import and export of a SAS-specific XML schema and some standard non-SAS schemas. This support has varied from version to version of SAS.

An alternative to the LIBNAME XML engine for XML import and PROC TEMPLATE for export is to flatten the hierarchical XML into a numerically indexed representation that presents nothing new to the SAS programmer, unlike native XML. This method is the basis for the import and export of XML that takes place 100% in the familiar DATA step. This DATA-step method has been implemented in a highly generic way, used with real life XML, and scaled up to production-size XML files of more than one million records.

## CONCLUSION

XML and SAS can coexist nicely, for import of XML into SAS, export of XML from SAS, and transformation of one XML instance into another. This is true for any data-centric XML that a user may encounter. SAS is a truly powerful tool because it combines superb data management capabilities with state-of-the-art statistical capabilities and ties it all together with a fully functional programming environment. In addition, SAS has tremendous cross-platform capabilities. This puts SAS-based systems in the middle of many heterogeneous information systems that involve complex human-machine and machine-machine interactions. XML has become ubiquitous in information technology because it is a vendor-neutral, platform-independent format for self-describing information. XML has become the preferred format for heterogeneous information systems. In other words, SAS and XML really have to work well together.

The author's experience, primarily in the pharmaceutical and medical worlds but also with some exposure to financial systems, is that SAS and XML can do better than just work well together. XML can integrate SAS into heterogeneous systems for truly remarkable results with the use of a functional toolkit that feels comfortable to SAS users.

## REFERENCES

SAS Institute "Base SAS Community XML"
http://support.sas.com/rnd/base/index-xml-resources.html (January 30, 2004)

James Clark and Steve DeRose "XML Path Language (XPath) Version 1.0" World Wide Web Consortium (W3C)
http://www.w3.org/TR/xpath (January 30, 2004)

Zurich Biostatistics, Inc. "Presentations"
http://www.zbi.net/NewFiles/leadership.html (January 30, 2004)

seven

# Using ExcelXP to Display SDTM Metadata and More

## Christine Teng
## Shaoan Yu

The Clinical Data Interchange Standards Consortium (CDISC) has established worldwide industrial standards that support platform-independent data standards that enable information system interoperability to improve medical research and related areas of healthcare. Many pharmaceutical companies have started implementation of CDISC data models such as Study Data Tabulation Model (SDTM) and Analysis Data Model (ADaM). As variable names and attributes are standardized, it is very easy to write programs to collect information about the data. The purpose of this chapter is to demonstrate how standardization simplifies work processes. SAS9 provides several approaches to create Excel output. There is an experimental tagset called ExcelXP that is available for download from the ODS Markup Resources site at:

http://support.sas.com/rnd/base/topics/odsmarkup/

The SAS9 ExcelXP tagset generates XML output that conforms to the Microsoft XML Spreadsheet Specification ("XML Spreadsheet Reference", Microsoft Corp.). One can create XML output on a UNIX or Windows platform and the XML output can be read by EXCEL 2002 and later releases. ExcelXP provides simple options to create multiple worksheets. In this chapter, the ExcelXP tagset is used in conjunction with the SAS Dictionary to create metadata documentation for a group of SDTM domains from a mock clinical trial project for demonstration.

## INTRODUCTION

The SAS9 ExcelXP tagset generates XML output that conforms to the Microsoft XML Spreadsheet Specification ("XML Spreadsheet Reference", Microsoft Corp.). It provides the functionality to create multiple worksheets in a workbook as well as multiple tables within a single worksheet. These features are very useful for creating metadata documentation where each domain has its own worksheet with label. It enables quicker accessibility to locate the information for a group of domains. With SAS DICTIONARY and PROC SQL, the metadata documentation can be created without hard coding. The details of using PROC SQL and SAS DICTIONARY will not be covered in this chapter. For more information regarding the SAS DICTIONARY and PROC SQL, please refer to the SAS manuals.

This chapter is not a tutorial about the ExcelXP tagset. Rather, it demonstrates another application using the ExcelXP tagset. The detailed tutorials and references for the ExcelXP tagset can be found at the references section of this chapter. In order to control the appearance of the output within Excel, PROC TEMPLATE can be used to create a style template. A template defines how to format output produced by a procedure or data step. For information about PROC TEMPLATE, please consult SAS9 online documentation site at:

http://support.sas.com/onlinedoc/913.

SAS provides many standard templates that allow for customization. To see a list of templates provided by SAS:

(1) go to the Results windows
(2) right click on Results and select Template
(3) expand sashelp.Tmplmst (See Table-1 in Appendix).

In the macro that builds the metadata documentation, we created a customized style template that uses certain fonts, colors and spacing inside my Excel workbook. This step is not required to use ExcelXP. However, style template makes the output more presentable.

## DESIGN REQUIREMENTS

The following are the requirements for the metadata documentation:
Create a macro program with one parameter DATADIR is used to assign the input library name.

```
%ls_datastruc(datadir = datadir)
```

Create a metadata table inside a worksheet for each domain within the datadir library. The label of each domain should be listed first, followed by the attributes of the variables. (See Table-2 in Appendix) If any variable in the domain has length of label > 40, length of variable name > 8 or length of a character variable > 200, a note will be shown. (See Table-3 in Appendix) If a domain contains a variable name ending with testcd, create a second table after the metadata table in the same worksheet. (See Table-4 in Appendix) After all worksheets of domains are created, create a global dictionary for all test codes defined in the project. (See Table-5 in Appendix)

## IMPLEMENTATION

Since the ExcelXP tagset is still evolving, there are some limitations and hence its functionality may be changed in the future. It is recommended that the user always download the latest update to verify the changes and enhancements. To use the ExcelXP tagset, first download the latest ExcelXP tagset from the SAS ODS MARKUP page. This page also provides links to documentation for using and customizing tagsets. For this exercise, we use the ExcelXP Tagset version dated June 2007. Before using the ExcelXP tagset, check the codes or execute the following to see a list of options available in the ExcelXP tagset:

```
ODS tagsets.excelxp file = "test.xml" options(doc="help");
```

Quick Reference for the TAGSETS.EXCELXP Tagset can also be found in
http://support.sas.com/rnd/base/ods/odsmarkup/excelxp_help.html.

Under the pre-configuration part of the requirement A below, only specifications are described since coding for this part is not the focus of this chapter. The sections, where the worksheets are built, provide more detailed coding information.

## REQUIREMENT A

Create a macro program with one parameter.

```
%MACRO ls_datastruc(datadir= );
```

- Pre-configuration before building the worksheets;
- NULLTBL – A table used to build a header in the global work-

sheets for the requirement E.

- TESTTBL – A table that contains all of the TESTCD and the associated TEST description. The TESTCD values are collected from each domain that has a variable ending with TESTCD. This is used in the requirement E.
- Set up the style template;

```
proc template;
     define style styles.XLStatistical;
     parent = styles.Statistical;
          :
          :
ods listing close;
```

*Set up the workbook; include the ExcelXP tagset code

```
%let _ODSDEST=tagsets.ExcelXP;
ods &_ODSDEST path = "c:\temp\excelXP"
        file = "test.xml"
        style = XLStatistical;
```

1. Build the worksheets (see requirements below);

```
ods &_ODSDEST close;
%MEND;
```

## REQUIREMENT B

Create a metadata table inside a worksheet for each domain defined in the macro parameter datadir.

```
proc sql noprint;
     %*dsetname contains all domains in the libname data-dir;
     select memname into :dsetname separated by '+'
     from dictionary.tables
     where libname="&datadir" and memtype="DATA" ;

     %*examlst contains all domains that have a variable name
          ending with TESTCD;
     select memname into :examlst separated by ' '
     from dictionary.columns
     where libname="&datadir" and memtype="DATA" and name
        like '%TESTCD' ;
quit;

%let num=1;
%let list = %upcase(%scan(&dsetname, &num, +));

%*Use Do-While loop to create individual worksheet;
%do %while (&list. ne );
     %*Create worksheet with defined options;
```

```
ods &_ODSDEST options(absolute_column_width =
    "6, 16, 10, 45, 25"
                                    sheet_interval = "none"
                                    sheet_name = "&list");
%*Print domain name and label at the beginning of the
    sheet;
proc sql;
    select ' ', substr(memname,1) as Data_Set, ' ',
            substr(memlabel,1) as
        Data_Set_Label, ' '
        from dictionary.tables
        where libname = "&datadir" and memtype = "DATA"
            and memname = "&list";
quit;

%*Print domain columns and attributes information;
proc sql;
    select int(varnum) as Pos, upcase(name) as
            VarName, propcase(catx('',type,
            put(length, best5.))) as Type-Len,
        substr(label,1) as Label, ' ' as
            Deriviation_Comments
        from dictionary.columns
        where libname = "&datadir" and memtype = "DATA"
            and memname = "&list"
        order by varnum;
quit;
```

## REQUIREMENT C

If any variable in the domain has length of label > 40, length of variable name > 8 or length of character > 200, a note will be shown.

```
proc sql;
    select int(varnum) as Pos, upcase(name) as VarName,
        propcase(catx('',type,put(length, best4.)))
            as TypeLen,
        substr(label,1) as Label,
        case
        when length(label) > 40 then
            'length of label > 40'
        when length(name) > 8 then
            'length of variable name > 8'
        when length > 200 then
            'length of character value > 200'
        else ' '
        end as Check_Length
    from dictionary.columns
    where libname="&datadir" and memtype="DATA" and
        memname="&list"
    order by varnum;
quit;
```

## REQUIREMENT D

If a domain contains a variable ending with testcd, create a second table after the metadata table in the same worksheet.

```
%if %index(&examlst., &list.) %then %do;
    proc sql;
        select distinct "&list" label='Domain',
                &list.testcd label='Test Code',
            ' ', &list.test Label='Test Description'
            from &datadir..&list.;
    quit;
%end;

%*Ready to build the next worksheet;
%let num = %eval(&num + 1);
%let list = %upcase(%scan(&dsetname, &num, '+'));
%end;
```

## REQUIREMENT E

Create a global dictionary for all test codes defined in the project.

```
ods &_ODSDEST options(absolute_column_width="10, 15, 55, 20"
    sheet_interval="none"
    sheet_name="TestCode");

    proc sql;
        select ' ' label='Purpose: ',' ' label='List of Tests'
            from NULLTBL;
    select distinct domain label='Source',
                paramcd Label='Parameter Name',
            param label='Parameter Description',
            case
            when paramcd eq '' then 'TESTCD value is missing'
            when param eq '' then 'TEST value is missing'
            else ' '
            end as Check_Missing
        from testtbl
        order by domain;
quit;
```

As shown above, with the use of PROC SQL, SAS DICTIONARY tables, standardized SDTM structure, and simple ExcelXP options, we are able to quickly build up the workbook with multiple worksheets that contain the metadata information for a list of domains. This information is very useful to help learn and verify a project database design.

## SUMMARY

ExcelXP is one of the many tools in SAS to create Excel output. It allows simple configurations to generate Excel output. With SAS Dictionary tables, we found it very useful and easy to create documentation for quality assurance purposes. Please visit the SAS support website at:

http://support.sas.com/rnd/base/ods/odsmarkup/index.html

for additional ExcelXP tagset information and examples.

## REFFERENCES

DelGobbo, V. 2006. "Creating AND Importing Multi-Sheet Excel Workbooks the Easy Way with SAS". Proceedings of the Thirty-First Annual SAS Users Group International Conference, 31. CD-ROM. Paper 115.

Gebhart, E. 2005. " ODS Markup: The SAS Reports You have Always Dreamed Of ". Proceedings of the Thirtieth Annual SAS Users Group International Conference, 30. CD-ROM. Paper 85.

Zender, C. 2005. "The Power of Table Templates and DATA _NULL_". Proceedings of the Thirtieth Annual SAS Users Group International Conference, 30. CD-ROM. Paper 88.

PharmaSUG 2006 Paper: "Simple Ways to Use PROC SQL and DICTIONARY TABLES to Verify Data Structure of the Electronic Submission Data Sets" By Christine S. Teng and Wenjie Wang.

SAS Macro Language: Reference
SAS SQL Procedure User's Guide

## ACKNOWLEGEMENTS

The author would like to thank the management team for their encouragement and review of this chapter.

## APPENDIX

Table – 1 (Available Tagsets in SAS®9)

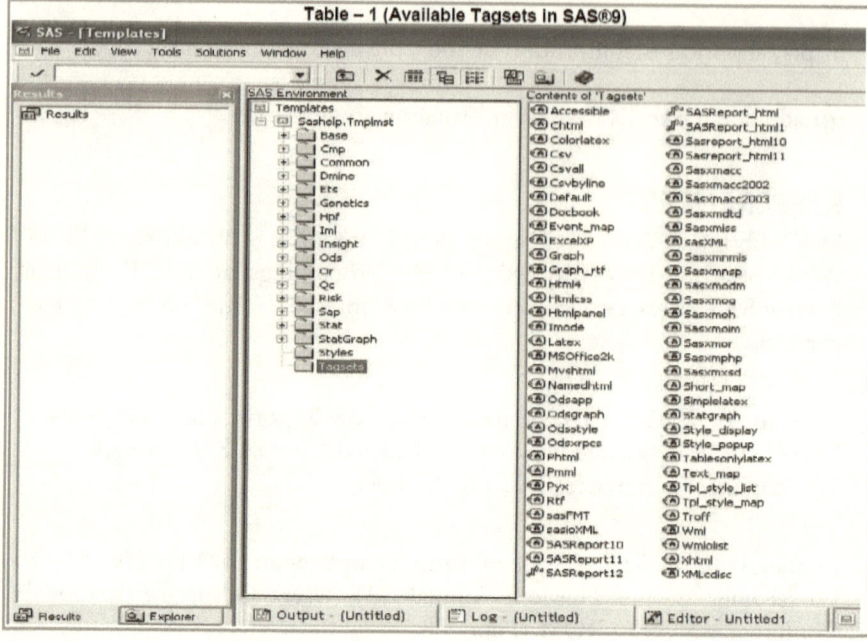

Table – 2 (Requirement B)

| | A | B | C | D | E |
|---|---|---|---|---|---|
| 1 | | Data_Set | | Data_Set_Label | |
| 2 | | AE | | Adverse Events Data Set | |
| 3 | | | | | |
| 4 | Pos | VarName | TypeLen | Label | Check_Length |
| 5 | 1 | STUDYID | Char200 | Study Identifier | |
| 6 | 2 | DOMAIN | Char2 | Domain Abbreviation | |
| 7 | 3 | USUBJID | Char200 | Unique Subject Identifier | |
| 8 | 4 | AESEQ | Num8 | Sequence Number | |
| 9 | 5 | AEGRPID | Char200 | Group ID | |
| 10 | 6 | AEREFID | Char200 | Reference ID | |
| 11 | 7 | AESPID | Char200 | Sponsor-Defined Identifier | |
| 12 | 8 | AETERM | Char200 | Reported Term for the Adverse Event | |
| 13 | 9 | AEMODIFY | Char200 | Modified Reported Term | |
| 14 | 10 | AEDECOD | Char200 | Dictionary-Derived Term | |
| 15 | 11 | AECAT | Char200 | Category for Adverse Event | |
| 16 | 12 | AESCAT | Char200 | Subcategory for Adverse Event | |
| 17 | 13 | AEOCCUR | Char2 | Adverse Event Occurrence | |
| 18 | 14 | AEBODSYS | Char80 | Body System or Organ Class | |
| 19 | 15 | AELOC | Char200 | Location of the Reaction | |
| 20 | 16 | AESEV | Char8 | Severity/Intensity | |
| 21 | 17 | AESER | Char2 | Serious Event | |
| 22 | 18 | AEACN | Char17 | Action Taken with Study Treatment | |
| 23 | 19 | AEACNOTH | Char17 | Other Action Taken | |
| 24 | 20 | AEREL | Char200 | Causality | |
| 25 | 21 | AERELNST | Char200 | Relationship to Non-Study Treatment | |
| 26 | 22 | AEPATT | Char200 | Pattern of Adverse Event | |
| 27 | 23 | AEOUT | Char33 | Outcome of Adverse Event | |
| 28 | 24 | AESCAN | Char2 | Involves Cancer | |
| 29 | 25 | AESCONG | Char2 | Congenital Anomaly or Birth Defect | |

AE / CM / CO / DM / DS / EG / EX / IE / LB / MH / ML / PC / PE / PR / QS / SC / SE / SU / SV / TA / TE /

### Table – 3 (Requirement C)

| | A | B | C | D | E |
|---|---|---|---|---|---|
| 1 | | Data_Set | | Data_Set_Label | |
| 2 | | LB | | Laboratory Findings Data Set | |
| 3 | | | | | |
| 4 | | Pos VarName | TypeLen | Label | Check_Length |
| 5 | | 1 STUDYID | Char200 | Study Identifier | |
| 6 | | 2 DOMAIN | Char2 | Domain Abbreviation | |
| 7 | | 3 USUBJID | Char200 | Unique Subject Identifier | |
| 8 | | 4 LBSEQ | Num8 | Sequence Number | |
| 9 | | 5 LBGRPID | Char200 | Group ID | |
| 10 | | 6 LBREFID | Char200 | Specimen ID | |
| 11 | | 7 LBSPID | Char200 | Sponsor-Defined Identifier | |
| 12 | | 8 LBTESTCD | Char200 | LAB Test or Examination Short Name | |
| 13 | | 9 LBTEST | Char200 | LAB Test or Examination Name | |
| 14 | | 10 LBCAT | Char255 | Category for Lab Test | length of character value > 200 |
| 15 | | 11 LBSCAT | Char200 | Subcategory for Lab Test | |
| 16 | | 12 LBORRES | Char200 | Result or Finding in Original Units | |
| 17 | | 13 LBORRESU | Char200 | Original Units | |
| 18 | | 14 LBORNRLO | Char200 | Reference Range Lower Limit in Original Unit | length of label > 40 |
| 19 | | 15 LBORNRHI | Char200 | Reference Range Upper Limit in Original Unit | length of label > 40 |
| 20 | | 16 LBSTRESC | Char200 | Character Result/Finding in Std Format | |
| 21 | | 17 LBSTNRC | Char200 | Reference Range for Char Rslt-Std Units | |
| 22 | | 18 LBSTRESN | Num8 | Numeric Result/Finding in Standard Units | |
| 23 | | 19 LBSTRESU | Char200 | Standard Units | |
| 24 | | 20 LBSTNRLO | Num8 | Reference Range Lower Limit-Std Units | |
| 25 | | 21 LBSTNRHI | Num8 | Reference Range Upper Limit-Std Units | |
| 26 | | 22 LBNRIND | Char200 | Reference Range Indicator | |
| 27 | | 23 LBSTAT | Char8 | Lab Status | |
| 28 | | 24 LBREASND | Char200 | Reason Test Not Done | |
| 29 | | 25 LBNAM | Char200 | Vendor Name | |

H ◀ ▶ H \ AE / CM / CO / DM / DS / EG / EX / IE \ LB / MH / ML / PC / PE / PR / QS / SC / SE / SU / SV / TA / TE / | ◀ |

### Table – 4 (Requirement D)

| | A | B | C | D | E |
|---|---|---|---|---|---|
| 1 | | Data_Set | | Data_Set_Label | |
| 2 | | LB | | Laboratory Findings Data Set | |
| 79 | | | | | |
| 80 | Domain | Test Code | | Test Description | |
| 81 | LB | ALB | | Albumin | |
| 82 | LB | ALB1 | | ALB | |
| 83 | LB | ALP | | Alkaline Phosphatase | |
| 84 | LB | ALT | | Alanine Aminotransferase | |
| 85 | LB | APTT | | Activated Partial Thromboplastin Time | |
| 86 | LB | AST | | Aspartate Aminotransferase | |
| 87 | LB | BASO | | Basophils | |
| 88 | LB | BILDIR | | Direct Bilirubin | |
| 89 | LB | BILI | | Bilirubin | |
| 90 | LB | BLD | | Urine Blood | |
| 91 | LB | BUN | | Blood Urea Nitrogen | |
| 92 | LB | CA | | Calcium | |
| 93 | LB | CAST | | Casts | |
| 94 | LB | CAST1 | | UCAST | |
| 95 | LB | CASTFAT | | Fatty Casts | |
| 96 | LB | CASTGRA | | Granular Casts | |
| 97 | LB | CASTLEUK | | Leukocyte Casts | |
| 98 | LB | CHOL | | Cholesterol | |
| 99 | LB | CHOL1 | | CHOL | |
| 100 | LB | CL | | Chloride | |
| 101 | LB | CRAMMUR | | Ammonium Urate Crystals | |
| 102 | LB | CREAT | | Creatinine | |
| 103 | LB | EOS | | Eosinophils | |
| 104 | LB | EPIC | | Epithelial Cells | |
| 105 | LB | GGT | | Gamma Glutamyl Transferase | |

H ◀ ▶ H \ AE / CM / CO / DM / DS / EG / EX / IE \ LB / MH / ML / PC / PE / PR / QS / SC / SE / SU / SV / TA / TE / | ◀ |

## Table – 5 (Requirement E)

| | A | B | C | D |
|---|---|---|---|---|
| 1 | Purpose: | List of Tests | | |
| 2 | | | | |
| 3 | | | | |
| 4 | Domain | TESTCD | TEST | Check_Missing |
| 5 | EG | ARATE | Atrial Rate | |
| 6 | EG | INTP | Interpretation | |
| 7 | EG | PR | PR Interval | |
| 8 | EG | QRS | QRS Interval | |
| 9 | EG | QRSA | QRS Axis | |
| 10 | EG | QT | QT Interval | |
| 11 | EG | QTC | QTc Interval | |
| 12 | EG | QTCB | QTc Interval Bazett | |
| 13 | EG | QTCF | QTc Interval Fridericia | |
| 14 | EG | RR | RR Interval | |
| 15 | EG | VRATE | Ventricular Rate | |
| 16 | IE | EX1 | | TEST value is missing |
| 17 | IE | EX1 | Smokes 4 packs a week | |
| 18 | IE | IN1 | | TEST value is missing |
| 19 | IE | IN1 | Age Between 18 and 64? | |
| 20 | LB | ALB | Albumin | |
| 21 | LB | ALB1 | ALB | |
| 22 | LB | ALP | Alkaline Phosphatase | |
| 23 | LB | ALT | Alanine Aminotransferase | |
| 24 | LB | APTT | Activated Partial Thromboplastin Time | |
| 25 | LB | AST | Aspartate Aminotransferase | |
| 26 | LB | BASO | Basophils | |
| 27 | LB | BILDIR | Direct Bilirubin | |
| 28 | LB | BILI | Bilirubin | |
| 29 | LB | BLD | Urine Blood | |

H ◀ ▶ H / EG / EX / IE / LB / MH / ML / PC / PE / PR / QS / SC / SE / SU / SV / TA / TE / TV / VS \ TestCode / ◀

# eight

# A SAS Programmer's Guide to Generating Define.xml

## Michael Molter

How would you like to be able to generate a Define.xml with just a few simple PROC PRINT statements? Not possible, right? Believe it or not, with a well thought out metadata environment, we can make this dream come true, but it would not happen overnight.

CDISC's requirement of an XML based metadata document introduces at least three potentially new challenges to the SAS programmer asked to generate it. One is at least a basic understanding of XML. A second is a thorough understanding of the CDISC specific XML structure of Define.xml. A third is the use of SAS to generate it. All three of these tasks most likely lie outside the scope of what a SAS programmer building clinical databases, tables, listings, and graphs ever needed to know. This chapter addresses all three of these challenges. After a brief discussion of XML basics, we will study carefully the structure of Define.xml. With these tools in place, we will see how the ODS Markup destination provides a powerful tool for generating the final document with the familiar PRINT procedure.

## INTRODUCTION

The Clinical Data Interchange Standards Consortium (CDISC) and pharmaceutical regulatory agencies (such as the Food and Drug Administration (FDA)) are introducing several changes in the clinical trials submission process and with them, several challenges to SAS programmers in the industry. Among such challenges is Define.xml, an XML based submission of a study's metadata designed to tell a regulatory reviewer everything they need to know about the data being submitted. Under the umbrella of Define.xml are many sub-challenges, the collection of which can make the generation of Define.xml an intimidating task. For starters, there is the organization of metadata.

Something that may have received minimal attention at most, in the past, we are now not only forced to think about it, but we have to keep track of it and organize it. We have to consider not only simple data set and variable attributes such as lengths and labels, but also those that CDISC has deemed important such as the role of variables and their expected values, documentation of computational algorithms, and many more. We need to plan a database for it and we have to consider all the different ways to collect this information.

At least a database is something that we as programmers can relate to, but other challenges that lie ahead may be completely foreign to someone who has spent a career creating data sets, tables, listings, and graphs. The most obvious of these challenges is XML – a markup language that is deceitfully similar to HTML from a distance, but up close is different – a markup language that requires each of its documents to be accompanied by XML based support documents like schemas and style sheets. Not only is a good general base knowledge of XML helpful, but a thorough knowledge of the XML structure that CDISC has developed for submitting metadata is critical. Finally, even in our familiar, comfortable SAS environment, the challenge of writing a program that takes the metadata as its input and produces CDISC XML as its output is one to be taken seriously.

When I spell it out like that, the task is an intimidating one, and reading this chapter is not going to have you turning out Define.xmls tomorrow. Companies will need to invest resources in reading several other papers written on the subject, attending talks at conferences, networking, visiting websites, and programming development time. What this chapter will do is help you get your Define.xml off the ground by addressing some of these key challenges. This chapter will not present a full lesson in XML, not only because of space considerations, but also because you do not need a full XML lesson. I will briefly discuss the role of the XML schema and the XSLT style sheet, but will not discuss technical aspects of these support documents because you do not need it – at least not initially. We will look in detail at the XML structure required for metadata submission and pay particular attention to how physically separate parts of the document are to be linked. Finally, we will look at ODS's Markup destination and ODS tagsets as tools for generating the required XML structure. Small samples of instructional SAS code will be scattered throughout this last section. In the end, the goal of this chapter is not to provide you with code to copy that will automatically turn your SAS metadata into a CDISC compliant, XML metadata document; but rather, to provide you a foundation which can significantly sharpen your research and development focus as you begin this journey.

## XML

Allow me to begin with some good news; the learning curve for the general XML knowledge needed to generate Define is not nearly as bad as you might think. Prior knowledge of HTML and markup in general will only serve to help. When you think about learning HTML, or for that matter, any other computer language, you think of two aspects. You have to learn what the keywords are, or the words that have special meaning. The second aspect is syntax, or the ways that keywords are legally combined with literal text and special characters. XML syntax is very similar to that of HTML, and so if you know HTML syntax, you are most of the way there. If you do not, there are not very many rules to remember, and so it should not take you long to pick them up. HTML has predefined keywords. By predefined, I mean that keywords such as "td", when correctly combined with HTML syntax, <td>, have meaning to programs that read these files. Web browsers are programs that not only read the files, but display the files according to the keywords. This gives us the image of a web page. Part of learning HTML is, as mentioned earlier, learning these keywords and understanding how they contribute to what we see on a web page. As odd as it sounds, XML has no predefined keywords. In theory, users make up keywords; in our world, CDISC has done it for us. The next natural question is how made up keywords can have any meaning to anybody. This question will be answered later in this section.

So the task of learning general XML has been significantly reduced from something comparable to learning HTML. The syntax rules are few and simple, and to some, familiar. There are no keywords. And if it's all still too abstract for you, CDISC's Case Report Tabulation Data Definitions Specification (DDS) has thorough examples that give you something to aim for – a structure to which to fit your metadata. We will go through the syntax rules you need to know. We will wrap it up by discussing at a high level how keywords are given meaning. That discussion will be low priority while trying to get your Define off the ground, but may become more important as you try and customize later on. This small amount of relevant theory will then lead us naturally into the next section, where we delve into CDISC defined structure and keywords.

## TAGS AND ATTRIBUTES AND CONTENT, OH MY!

Like other markups, XML is driven by elements, and each element is made up of a pair of tags, and optionally, attributes, text, and other elements or nested elements. An element begins with a start tag which consists of an open angle bracket (<) followed by a keyword that represents the name of the tag (often called the name of the element).

Since CDISC has defined keywords for us, I will not go into detail about naming rules, except that they are similar to naming rules for SAS data sets - they start with letters, but can contain numerals and other characters, and cannot contain spaces. Tag names are case sensitive, so pay careful attention to Define tags that use mixed case (e.g. <ItemGroup-Def>, <CodeList>). Tags may or may not be defined with one or more attributes. When they are, the tag name is followed by a name value pair where the "name" is a keyword representing the name of an attribute and "value" is the value of that attribute, enclosed in quotation marks, single or double. Following all attribute specifications is a closed angle bracket (>) that ends the opening of the element or the start tag.

```
/*Example 1:  a start tag without attributes*/
<GlobalVariables>

/*Example 2:  a start tag with attributes*/
<CodeListItem CodedValue = "Severe">
```

All start tags must eventually be accompanied by an end tag. The end tag is also constructed with angle brackets and a keyword that matches the keyword of its corresponding start tag, but two differences exist. First, whereas start tags can contain attributes, end tags cannot. Second, end tags are always preceded by a forward slash (/). What comes between the start and end tags can vary.

```
/*Example 3:  a start and end tag pair in which the start tag con-
tains no attributes*/
<Decode> … </Decode>
```

Occasionally, start tags are followed immediately by their corresponding end tags. Such elements are referred to as empty. While this is legal, it's not always very practical, and if the start tag contains no attributes, it is not at all practical. Either way, in the case where nothing appears between the start and end tags, XML allows us to take a shortcut. Rather than having a pair of distinct tags, we have one tag with a slash at the end. Example 4 illustrates a specific example of this kind of tag found in Define.xml.

```
/*Example 4:  Short cut for an element with nothing between its
start and end tags*/
<ItemRef ItemOID = "SC.SCTESTCD.ALLERGY" OrderNumber = "1"
Mandatory = "No"/>
```

Alternatively, between its start and end tags, an element can contain content. Content can be in the form of more elements (nested elements), text which contains no tags, or both – also referred to as mixed content. More elements are sometimes described in relation to the element in which they are nested, such as subelements, children, grandchildren, etc..., and the element within which they are nested is referred to as a parent element. These subelements follow the same rules that parent elements follow - naming conventions, start tags with or without attributes and end tags, each surrounded by angle brackets. After the end of a start tag, if the next character is not an open angle bracket, then what follows the start tag is text. Text has no special characters to distinguish it and no rules governing its content. We sometimes refer to this text as the value of the element. This value continues until the end tag of the enclosing element. Example 5 illustrates both subelements and content. The TranslatedText element, a subelement of the Decode element, has the value "NO".

## XML STRUCTURE

```
/*Example 5:  Subelements and text*/
<Decode>
    <TranslatedText xml:lang = "en"> NO </TranslatedText>
</Decode>
```

We are now ready to take a step back from the details of the syntax and look at the broader structure. Though general XML does not require it, many XML documents including Define.xml begin with an XML declaration. Define's is illustrated below.

```
<?xml version = "1.0" encoding = "ISO-8859-1" ?>
```

Except for the declaration, XML elements in which a question mark immediately follows "<" and immediately precedes ">" are referred to as XML processing instructions. Rather than showing up in a browser, these pass along instructions to an application that reads the XML. In

Define, CDISC allows us to follow the declaration with a style sheet processing instruction, or an instruction that tells the browser to apply a style sheet before showing it to the user. We will discuss style sheets a little more in the next section, but for now, we illustrate Define's optional style sheet instruction below.

```
<?xml-stylesheet type = "text/xsl" href = "define1-0-0.xsl"?>
```

The value of the HREF attribute is the name of the external style sheet. Technically, the declaration and the style sheet instruction are not considered XML elements. They do use the angle brackets as delimiters like tags, but note that unlike elements, they do not come in start end pairs or have the slash at the end.

Immediately after these, every XML file must have the start tag of what is known as the root element. The end tag of the root element comes at the end of the file. Put another way, the root element has no parent or sibling elements, and every other element is a descendant of it or nested within it. Define's root element is the ODM element. Within the root element are properly nested subelements. We saw earlier that following the start tag of an element can be text or the start tag of a subelement. "Properly nested" means that any element must close (or in other words, its end tag must appear) prior to the closing of its parent element. In other words, child elements must be opened and closed entirely within their parent elements (or between the start and end tags of their parent elements).

```
/*Example 6:  Proper nesting*/
<GlobalVariables>
    <StudyName>1234</StudyName>
    <StudyDescription>1234 Data Defini  tion</StudyDescription>
    <ProtocolName>1234</ProtocolName>
</GlobalVariables>

/*Example 7:  Improper nesting*/
<GlobalVariables>
    <StudyName>1234</StudyName>
    <StudyDescription>1234 Data Defini  tion</StudyDescription>
    <ProtocolName>1234
</GlobalVariables>
</ProtocolName>
```

# XML SCHEMAS AND XSLT - GIVING MEANING TO YOUR XML

So what does it all mean? How can XML have any meaning if I'm allowed to make up element names and attributes? To answer that question, let's go back in time and consider the early days of HTML de-development. At some point, someone made up elements like <table>, <tr>, <td>, and so on. Today we know these as elements that begin the display of a table, the display of a row in a table, and the display of cell content in a table, respectively, but in the beginning, they were as made up as <GlobalVariables> and <StudyName> illustrated above. They took on their roles as table display elements when someone got around to writing an application – a web browser – that parsed the HTML text and associated elements like these and others with display characteristics. In beginning level XML texts where it's common to draw comparisons between XML and HTML, you will see that HTML is markup that's concerned with the display of data.

In the same paragraph in that text, you will also read that XML is not concerned so much about the display of data as it is about the transporting of data. XML can be transported easily across machines because it's simple text that any machine can read. HTML is simple text that applications we call web browsers can read. These applications not only read it, but they do something with it. Specifically, they separate or parse the elements and attributes and execute display instructions as they process them. So if XML and HTML are nothing more than text, then if we can write applications that read HTML text and do something with it, then we should be able to do the same thing with XML text. In particular, in collaboration with CDISC, regulatory agencies such as the FDA have written applications that read XML such as that found in Define and load the data into data warehouses. A second example is SAS's XML engine that acts as an application that reads XML and transforms it into SAS's proprietary data set format. Internet Explorer can also be considered an XML application, although all it does is display the markup in collapsible sections that are defined by the elements.

## VALIDATION

XML applications are written with expectations. For starters, as input, they expect syntactically correct or well formed XML. Additionally, in order to "do something" with XML content, the application has to be able to identify the content, and it does that by referring to element and attribute names. So what does an XML application do when these expectations are not met – when the syntax is wrong, or when elements identified by the application are not present?

We can begin to understand the answer to this by asking ourselves the same question about a simple SAS program. Consider a program that begins with a DATA step. Before it begins executing the statements, it goes through a compile stage, where it checks for syntax; it checks to see that the data set specified by DATA= exists, and it checks for several other things. If everything is ok, it will execute the statements, but if any fail it will issue log statements and not even try to execute. And where do these checks come from? They are built into the SAS system or the software application.

In some respects XML validation is similar. A computer language's syntax is what makes it useful, readable. Without it, it's just meaningless text. When our SAS syntax is incorrect, the SAS system has no way of knowing how to execute. Similarly, we cannot expect XML parsers to read XML that is not well formed. In a sense, we could say that XML that is not well formed is not even XML. For that reason, just like at SAS's compile time, when we ask an application to process XML, the parser first performs a syntax check. Violations are reported and prevent the application from performing its intended function.

While "well formed" refers to validation on a syntax level, the term valid XML or semantic validation usually refers to another level of validation. Just as data sets named in a SAS program are expected to exist, so too are elements, attributes, and content referred to in XML applications. While this kind of validation is built into the SAS system, an XML application's validation at this level is often defined in a separate XML file called an XML schema. An XML schema is a well formed XML document with predefined element names and attributes that lays out the rules for any XML document that chooses to use it. Schemas have the power to specify which elements and attributes are to be used, what kind of data (string, datetime, integer, etc.) an element contains, how many instances of each element is allowed, the order of the elements, and more. Because it's a separate document, enforcing such rules for a particular XML document (the instance document) requires a reference to the schema. It's then up to the application to read this reference, use the schema to validate the instance document and act on its findings. How it acts on these findings is up to the application and how it's written. We know that SAS does the best it can to continue processing subsequent parts of a program even when an earlier part failed. Of course this fact has its own ramifications. If the MEANS procedure fails and a subsequent DATA step attempts to read the data set output from PROC MEANS, then that DATA step will most likely fail too. Some XML applications may be written to quit after one violation of the schema is found. Others may try to move on and report all findings. Finally, others may not depend on a strict structure and may ignore certain kinds of schema violations or not use a schema at all.

CDISC has created an XML schema document, define1-0-0.xsd, that we must reference as an attribute of the ODM element. This reference is found as two attributes of the ODM root element and is illustrated below.

```
<ODM xmlns:xsi = "http://www.w3.org/2001/XMLSchemainstance"
xsi:schemalocation = "http://www.cdisc.org/ns/odm/v1.2 define1-0-
0.xsd"
```

Internet Explorer is one application that can do a syntax validation of our Define. When an XML instance is not well formed a web page appears with the message "The XML page cannot be displayed" and a description of the error. Unfortunately, IE cannot do a semantic validation of Define, but other validation programs may be available on the internet.

## VIEWING DEFINE.XML
Up to this point the meaning we have attached to an XML document's homegrown keywords has been discussed only in terms of our ability to extract and store XML content. Validation is often built into an application to check an XML document's "extractability". What we have not yet touched on is our ability to view an XML document. In fact we stated earlier that XML is not concerned about display, but that does not mean we do not want to see it. CROs and sponsors may wish to use a more readable version as a reference guide for their data. For that reason, we briefly discuss here the XSLT style sheet.

XSLT, an acronym for XML Style sheet Language Transformation, is an XML based transformation language that has the ability to "transform" your markup into something viewable like HTML. We mentioned earlier that opening Define.xml with Internet Explorer simply displays the markup in color coded collapsible sections. While the ability to collapse and expand elements helps to eliminate clutter when looking at markup, markup transformed into tabular format is much easier to process cognitively. XSLT transforms XML to HTML, or put another way, generates HTML in a way similar to the way the macro facility generates SAS code. Both can generate literal text conditionally or unconditionally, with or without the aid of similar kinds of programming logic. Where they differ is to what conditional and programming logic is applied. Macros often use as input user provided parameters, whereas XSLT uses XML content such as data and attribute values as its input. In order to do that, the XSLT language uses XPATH, a language used to find and extract information in an XML document. Consider Example 8 below.

```
/*Example 8:  an excerpt of an XSLT style sheet*/
<table   border='2' cellspacing='0' cellpadding='4' bgcolor =
"#fffdda">
     <tr> <th colspan='7' align='left' valign='top' height='20'
bgcolor = "#ECECEC">
/*Data sets for Study*/
<xsl:value-of select =
"/odm:ODM/odm:Study/odm:GlobalVariables/odm:StudyName"/>
</th> </tr>
```

Note that everything through the text "Data sets for Study" is valid
HTML markup, and is being generated unconditionally, without logic, by
the style sheet. What is to follow the word "Study" is the name of the
study, which is information to be found in Define.xml. This information
is extracted using the xsl:value of element and the select= attribute. The
value of the select attribute is an XPATH expression that tells the style
sheet which branch of the XML tree to navigate through to extract the
text.

Unlike a schema, style sheet references are not required by XML or by
Define.xml, though some sponsors may require it for their own purposes.
Because of that, CDISC does not currently take responsibility for main-
taining such files, though two different versions are available on their
website (one is for members only).

## TO SUMMARIZE...

What does this all mean to you? Up to this point we have covered a mix
of theory and practice - Define.xml practice. Before getting into the de-
tails of Define.xml in the next section, let's summarize among the theory
we have covered what is particularly relevant to you as you get your De-
fine off the ground.

We began by comparing XML education to HTML education and quickly
saw that for our purposes, learning XML is not nearly the chore it might
appear to be. In part this is because the task of learning predefined key-
words that is common to understanding so many other computer
languages does not exist for understanding general XML, although under-
standing that fact does take some getting used to. We also discussed
syntax. As we will see, we can learn a lot from the Define samples that
CDISC makes available for us, but by taking for granted the proper syn-
tax that these samples illustrate, we lose the ability to comprehend

messages that applications deliver to us when we do violate these rules. For this reason the section above regarding the basic syntax rules such as proper nesting, enclosing attribute values in quotation marks, etc is worth studying and becoming comfortable with.

Believe it or not, the thoroughness of examples such as those found in the DDS combined with some basic knowledge of syntax goes a long way toward at least knowing what metadata goes where in Define. In the next section we will use the DDS examples to discuss Define keywords and linking relationships built into Define, and that will take us even further. A second tier of learning, defined as concepts you may not need right away but would be beneficial to study along the way, would include schemas, style sheets, and namespaces. We did not discuss namespaces and CDISC tells you through its examples how to declare and reference them, but knowing something about them will explain the xmlns: attributes in the root element, as well as the special meaning of elements and attributes that are prefixed with colons. Since CDISC has created a schema for you, you do not have to create your own, but understanding the schema language and how to read define1-0-0.xsd can help you understand structural requirements not illustrated in examples. Using style sheets published by CDISC may be enough, but an understanding of XSLT allows you to customize for your customers (e.g. hardcoded text, colors, column/section inclusion/exclusion), and in some cases, troubleshoot issues such as hyperlinks not working, which may lead to resolution of Define violations.

## THE XML OF DEFINE.XML

At this point, we know a few XML specifics. We know of the existence of other things whose details we need not be concerned with, and we know almost nothing about Define.xml. We know that XML syntax, though illustrated well in published examples, is important to learn right away. We know about semantic validation through an XML schema, but nothing about schema language; about viewing an XML file through a web browser with the help of an XSLT style sheet, but nothing about the XSLT language. While not top priority, these should certainly be somewhere in the middle of your to-do list. Finally, we know that while general XML does not come with a predefined set of tags like HTML does, CDISC has developed a tag vocabulary for us. It's now time for us to get to know not only the vocabulary, but also how the elements are to relate to each other.

We will begin this section by identifying some valuable resources you should have nearby as you get started. Using that, we will go through each section of the markup. As we do this we will discuss the general purpose of each section, but we will leave out details that are available in other resources. We will then conclude by discussing how different sections are related to each through common attribute values.

## SOURCES

As you might expect, the source of most, if not all of your resources will come from CDISC's website - www.cdisc.org. Here you will find a Standards link which takes you to a list of the standards, split between those in production and those in development. Among those in production is the Case Report Tabulation Data Definition Specification (define.xml). Details on this standard can be found by clicking on the hyperlinked text, (CRT-DDS V1.0), found alongside of this description. Along with a detailed description of the standard, you will find links to several files available for viewing or download. These include schema and style sheet files, Define examples, and a PDF file called:

CRT_DDSpecification1_0_0.pdf.

It is from this 45 page file (DDS) that we will be working throughout most of the remainder of this section.

After a few introductory pages, most of the remainder of the DDS is divided into the sections of Define. In each section is an introductory paragraph about its purpose. Following that are tables that describe the section's XML elements and attributes including whether or not they are required. Following the tables are snippets of examples and illustrations of how they are related to other parts of the Define document. After this, beginning on page 39 of the DDS and ending on page 43 is a sample Define, and on page 44 is an outline of the elements that illustrates nesting relationships.

One other important source of information is worth mentioning here. From the CDISC.org home page is another link labeled Public Discussion Forums. While the DDS is thorough in its explanations and its examples, there are always questions it does not answer and situations not illustrated in the examples. As of this writing the DDS is also old and due for revisions. The discussion forums are exactly what they sound like - users from around the world of all levels of experience asking questions. Answers come from other users, as well as members of the CDISC team. Together the forums cover several areas of CDISC, one of which is dedicated to Define.xml. The reader is encouraged to click on this link, briefly set up a profile (or just log on as a guest), and simply browse over the history of questions and answers. A profile is required in order to participate in discussions.

## UNDERSTANDING DEFINE.XML

In order to understand the pieces of Define.xml, we begin with its structure. In layman's terms, we can think of Define.xml and its sections as a book about our study. A book often begins with some combination of a forward, a preface, and acknowledgments. Following that is a table of contents, the body of the book (its chapters), and at the end, appendices that might include an index or explanation of endnotes. In a similar way, the DDS describes Define in terms of a table of contents and Data Definition tables, but we can take it a step further. Define contains a header and high level information about the study to correspond to a book's forward. Define's table of contents, illustrated in tabular form on Page 6 of the DDS, consists of "chapter names" that each correspond to a data set in the database, accompanied by data set attributes such as labels, structure, keys, and more. Define contains an element structure to support this in the ItemGroupDef element. The body of the book is then made up of chapters or Data Definition Tables, each of which corresponds to an item in the table of contents, and provides detailed metadata for the corresponding data set  namely, attributes of each variable in the data set. A sample chapter is illustrated on page 10 of the DDS in tabular form. Define contains this structure in the ItemRef element, a subelement of ItemGroupDef, and the ItemDef element. Finally, Define has its own version of endnote appendices. Just as many terms and phrases in a book require further explanation in an appendix because they are too long to include in the body, many variables in a database require explanation beyond what can fit comfortably into the Comments column. Such information includes explanation of computational algorithms, lists of possible values and decodes (controlled terminology), and explanations of the mixed nature of certain variable values (value level metadata).

This analogy is easily illustrated when viewing a Define that includes a style sheet reference to define1-0-0.xsl, CDISC's published style sheet, with Internet Explorer. The table of contents appears at the top of the web page and looks like the example on page 6. All of the data definitions tables appear after the table of contents, and are also accessible with hyperlinks from the data set name column of the table of contents. The appendices or endnotes follow, which are accessible with hyperlinks from associated variables in the data definitions tables.

From our discussion so far, we can see that Define contains a web of connections or links between different parts of the document. At first this web may seem like something that exists only in theory without any manifestation in the markup, but when we consider the fact that the style sheet is able provide access to one end of the web from another through hyperlinks, we are forced to think otherwise. It is these relationships that will be the main focus of the remainder of this section. While some attention will be given to element structure, the thoroughness of the examples provided in the DDS as well as the global element order on page 44 and the tables that explain the meaning of each element and attribute make it unnecessary to repeat them here. Since the DDS makes clear the order in which elements are to appear, we will continue with the book analogy, noting how relationships are manifested in the markup. We will also note places where this order is slightly different from the element order. In the end, beyond element and content meaning and order, or beyond just the words printed on the pages, we will have seen the story that Define is trying to tell.

We begin our story with the forward - an idea of what is to follow in the book. Define's counterpart includes the XML header plus highlevel study information. In our earlier discussion of general XML we illustrated concepts with examples from Define.xml. Putting those examples together, we get example 9 illustrated below, and also found on page 26 of the DDS.

```
/*Example 9: a sample XML heade*/
<?xml version="1.0" encoding="ISO-8859-1"?>
<?xml-stylesheet type="text/xsl" href="define1-0-0.xsl"?>
<ODM xmlns="http://www.cdisc.org/ns/odm/v1.2"
xmlns:xsi="http://www.w3.org/2001/XMLSchema-Instance"
xmlns:xlink="http://www.w3.org/1999/xlink"
xmlns:def="http://www.cdisc.org/ns/def/v1.0"
xsi:schemaLocation="http://www.cdisc.org/ns/odm/v1.2 de-fine1-0-
0.xsd" FileOID="Study1234"
FileType="Snapshot" ODMVersion="1.2"
CreationDateTime="2008-12-02T13:39:06">
```

We know that the first line is the XML declaration and the second is the stylesheet reference. The third line opens the ODM root element, which is then followed by several attributes before the start tag is closed. Those that begin with xmlns are declaring namespaces and those with a colon following xmlns are associating prefixes with the namespaces. The one without the colon is the default namespace. While the name of the stylesheet could change from one Define to the next (or may not even be referenced in all Defines), the root element and the namespace declarations should appear in your Define exactly the way they appear here - they are not expected to change from one Define to another. The ODMVersion attribute will also remain the same until Define is incorporated in version 1.3.

As seen on page 44 of the DDS, the only first generation child of the ODM root element is the Study element. Because Study has no siblings, its end tag immediately precedes the ODM end tag. Study is then partitioned by two child elements - GlobalVariables and MetaDataVersion. While the three children of GlobalVariables provide more high level study metadata, children of MetaDataVersion begin with information about external documentation, and then move into more detailed metadata. It is with the external documentation elements - def:AnnotatedCRF and def:SupplementalDoc that we begin to see linking between separate parts of the markup.

Sponsors are allowed to submit any number of annotated CRFs or any other supplemental files that they think may aid a reviewer. def:AnnotatedCRF and def:SupplementalDoc are elements that each contain one or more def:DocumentRef child elements. def:DocumentRef is an empty element which contains only one attribute – an identifier attribute called leafID. Throughout this chapter the term "identifier attribute" refers to an XML attribute whose text string value has nothing to do with any metadata or even the study itself, but is used to match the value of an attribute in another element of the document, thereby creating a link or a relationship between the two elements. Such attributes appear frequently throughout Define. It's similar to a SAS data set variable that's used in a BY statement to merge with another data set, but that has no purpose beyond this. In the current situation, def:AnnotatedCRF contains one def:DocumentRef for each annotated CRF file, and def:SupplementalDoc contains one def:DocumentRef for every other linked external file. The leafID attribute of each of these DocumentRef elements contains an arbitrary text string value that matches the value of the ID attribute (another identifier attribute) in a def:leaf element - a sibling to def:AnnotatedCRF and def:SupplementalDoc. In addition to ID, def:leaf contains the xlink:href attribute, whose value contains the relative path (relative to the directory in which Define is located) of the external file. The description of this file or the text that contains the hyperlink is contained in the value of the def:title element - a necessary child element of each def:leaf element.

One use of the AnnotatedCRF element comes from Define1-0-0.xsl. The stylesheet scans through the list of leafID attributes found in the def:DocumentRef elements, and for each one it finds, it uses the leafID value to go find its corresponding path and description information. Once found, it then creates a hyperlink to it. Once finished with the AnnotatedCRF list, it does the same with the SupplementalDoc list.

Like the forward in a book, Define's forward may not play much of a role in the story, but it is still necessary. Though the author's family is not part of the story, the author often states in the acknowledgments that they could not have written the book without their support. Similarly, XML header information is not found in the tables seen in the readable Define, but the document cannot be processed without it. The rest of the forward; the high level study information such as study name, description, and protocol - does not lend itself to tabular presentation. References to some of it can be found scattered throughout the readable version. Examples include "Data sets for study" followed by the value of the StudyName element, links to annotated CRFs and supplemental documents, and the creation date found throughout.

We are now ready to move on to the table of contents and the data definition tables. When we think of a book's table of contents, we think of a list of chapter names, and for each, a corresponding page number where the beginning of the chapter can be found. Put another way, the names in the table of contents can be thought of as high level descriptions of chapters or pieces of the story to be found later, and the page numbers are shortcuts to them. Define's chapters are its data sets or its data definition tables. Its table of contents is a table found in the beginning of Define and contains one row per data set. Each chapter is described in terms of data set level attributes such as labels, data set structure, purpose, keys, and the location of the corresponding SAS transport file. The chapters themselves describe each of the variables in the data set, including label, origin, comments, role, etc. Being an electronic file, page numbers in the table of contents that take you from the table of contents to any data definition table are replaced by hyperlinks. Let's now see how all of these aspects - data set descriptions, variable descriptions, and links from one to the other are manifested in the markup.

Each data set's descriptors are housed in an individual instance of an ItemGroupDef element. ItemGroupDef is a child element of MetaDataVersion, and because each data set gets its own ItemGroupDef, it is the first child of MetaDataVersion that has multiple instances (recall that def:DocumentRef could have multiple instances, but is a grandchild of MetaDataVersion). By looking at the DDS, the reader will note here that we have deviated from the element order required by Define to talk about ItemGroupDef. As you might expect, many of a data set's descriptors are kept in attribute values. For example, the Name attribute is the name of the data set, def:label holds the data set label, and so on (see page 7 of the

DDS for the full list). Other important information however is kept in subelements.

The table of contents not only contains the name of SAS transport files, but it also contains hyperlinks to them. By thinking of these links as links to external files, it should then come as no surprise that markup that lies beneath these links is similar to the markup behind links to annotated CRFs and other supplemental files discussed earlier. Note that one of ItemGroupDef's attributes is def:ArchiveLocationID. Like the LeafID attribute discussed earlier, this is also an identifier attribute. Being an identifier attribute, its value is not part of metadata, but must match the value of another identifier attribute. Just as this matching attribute was found in a def:leaf element, each ItemGroupDef must contain a child def:leaf element. Recall that def:leaf has the ID attribute. In this case, the value of ID must match that of def:ArchiveLocationID. def:leaf must also contain the child def:title element whose value is the text that contains the link.

So where in the markup is the information needed to build each of the data definition tables? For any given table we start with information still found in ItemGroupDef. Among the descriptors of a data set is the role that each variable plays in that data set. This is manifested in the ItemRef element - another child of ItemGroupDef. Every variable in the data set has a corresponding ItemRef. ItemRef is an empty element and so has no values or children, but contains attributes such as Role, whose possible values (or controlled terminology) can be found on page 11 of the DDS, OrderNumber whose integer value describes the variable's physical location in the SAS data set, and Mandatory whose value indicates whether or not the absence of values would render the item incomplete. A data set's data definition table is constructed from this list of ItemRefs, and so contains one row for each variable described in an ItemRef. The existence of these ItemRefs within ItemGroupDef makes it easy to create a hyperlink (using the Name attribute of ItemGroupDef) from the table of contents to the data definition table. There does appear to be one problem though - if you look closely at the data definition table, only one of its columns is an attribute of ItemRef. So where in the markup are the other column values such as Origin, Label, and Comments?

Define requires us to describe a variable in many ways. As mentioned, attributes such as OrderNumber and Role found in ItemRef elements speak specifically to a variable's role in that data set. Other variable descriptors, however, may be more universal. In other words, a variable that might be found in multiple data sets may be described in all data sets with the same set of attribute values. Rather than forcing us to repeat the same set of values in every data set a variable is found in, Define allows us to describe these attributes outside of the context of any specific data set. In markup terms, they are described outside of the ItemGroupDef elements - in ItemDef elements.

For example, consider the STUDYID variable. For reference, the Item-Def attributes can be found on page 12 of the DDS. STUDYID is required in all data sets, and so each ItemGroupDef must contain an Ite-mRef for it. In theory different data sets might have different values for any of the ItemRef attributes that describe STUDYID, but if one set of attribute values for the attributes found on page 12 describe STUDYID in all data sets, then we can get away with just one ItemDef instance. On the other hand, perhaps you choose to include a comment with USUBJID in the DM data set, but not with any other data set. In this case, you will need two ItemDefs for USUBJID - one that includes the comment that will be linked to DM, and the other that does not, that will be linked to all other data sets that have USUBJID.

The remainder of the columns in the data definition tables comes from these ItemDefs. Since each table is made up of information from both ItemRef and ItemDef elements, the markup needs to link these elements. Once again this is done with identifier attributes. ItemRef's ItemOID attribute is an identifier attribute whose value must match the OID attribute value of its corresponding ItemDef element. In SAS terms, think of ItemRef as a data set that contains some, but not all of the ne-cessary information about a list of variables. To get the rest of the information, you have to merge with another data set - ItemDef. The BY variable in this merge would be ItemOID from ItemRef and OID from ItemDef (of course one of them would have to be renamed).

Let's return to the USUBJID example. If this variable is to contain a comment in the DM data definition table, and no comment in any other data definition table such as AE, then we would need one ItemDef that would have the comment, and another that did not. Additionally, the value of the OID attribute in the first ItemDef would match the value of the ItemOID attribute in the ItemRef element that describes USUBJID within the ItemGroupDef element for DM. Similarly, the OID from the second ItemDef (without the comment) would match the ItemOID in the ItemRef that describes USUBJID within every other ItemGroupDef that contains USUBJID. The relevant markup of such a situation is illu-strated below.

```
/*Example 10:  ItemDef - ItemRef relationship*/
<ItemGroupDef name="DM" <ItemRef ItemOID="DMUSUBJID"> >
<ItemGroupDef name="AE" <ItemRef ItemOID="USUBJID"> >

<ItemDef OID="DMUSUBJID" Comment="DM comment">
<ItemDef OID="USUBJID">
```

Additional examples are found on pages 15 and 16 of the DDS.

## APPENDICES

While reading through a book we often find words that are immediately followed by superscripts. We know that this indicates that the preceding word(s) require explanation whose length might interrupt the flow of the story if inserted in the current location. For that reason these explanations are usually placed at the bottom of the page or in an appendix at the end of the book, where the reader can read them when ready.

Many of the variables in the data definition tables also require explanation. Of course the data definition table has the Comments column, but there are two circumstances under which an appendix at the end might be better suited than the Comments column to provide the explanation. Similar to the book analogy, length is one of those reasons. Long lists of controlled terminology squeezed into one cell would make the row for that variable very tall. A second reason is one we have seen before, when we discovered the convenience of one ItemDef instance for documenting the same attributes for a variable found in several data sets. While an explanation for a variable may be easily short enough to fit into a column of a data definitions table, the same explanation may explain several variables throughout the database. Rather than repeating that explanation, we document it once in the appendix, and all the variables to which it applies can reference it. Like the table of contents, the electronic counterpart of page turning is hyperlinks, and as we have seen before, this suggests the need for identifier attributes in the markup to establish these links.

Before we get into the markup, let's briefly look at the three different types of explanations for which markup is available in Define. One is a computational algorithm. Some derived variables should be accompanied by an explanation of how they were derived. A second is controlled terminology. Certain variables have discrete lists of possible values and CDISC requires that they be documented. When these values are coded, we must also provide the decode. A third type which is a little more complicated is value level metadata. CDISC requires that SDTM Findings data be submitted in a normal or vertical data set structure, even when multiple tests are involved. This means having a variable whose values indicate the different tests (--TESTCD and --TEST) and a results variable (-- ORRES). Because each of these tests (each of which can, conceptually, be thought of as a variable of its own, and are sometimes delivered that way by the DBMS) can theoretically have its own set of attributes and its own controlled terminology, each needs to have its own metadata documented. This is done in the value level appendix.

Because the existence of further explanation for a variable can be thought of as an extension of its own metadata, the markup link begins in all three cases within ItemDef. In the case of the computational algorithm, def:ComputationMethodOID is an identifier attribute of ItemDef (illustrated on page 24 of the DDS). In the case of the controlled terminology, the empty CodeListRef element appears as a child to the ItemDef, with an identifier attribute called CodeListOID (page 1921). Similarly, def:ValueListRef is an empty child of ItemDef with ValueListOID as its identifier attribute. This is illustrated on page 23, but note that that illustration refers to the identifier attribute as def:ValueListOID, whereas the example on page 42 leaves off the def: prefix. Technically both are correct, but Define1-0-0.xsl expects no prefix. Links will not work if the prefix is included.

We know that the hyperlink starts in the data definitions tables and ends in an appendix table. Naturally, hyperlinks that start in the data definitions table have corresponding markup in ItemDef elements as we have just seen, but we now consider the markup that corresponds to the target of these hyperlinks. For computational algorithms and controlled terminology, it's straightforward. The def:ComputationMethod element is another child element of MetaDataVersion that appears before the first ItemGroupDef element. The structure of this element is simple: an identifier attribute called OID whose value matches that of the def:ComputationMethodOID attribute in the ItemDef. The description of the algorithm is then the value of the element. This is illustrated on page 24 of the DDS. Similarly, the value of CodeListOID matches the value of the identifier OID attribute in the CodeList element - another child of MetaDataVersion that appears toward the end of the markup. CodeList is a more complex element with more attributes, plus one instance of a child CodeListItem element for each discrete value of the controlled terminology. CodedValue is an attribute of CodeListItem, and the decode is buried as a value of the TranslatedText grandchild element. The Decode element is between CodeListItem and TranslatedText. More details can be found in the DDS.

Value level metadata is more complicated because for any variable subject to it (e.g. --TESTCD), each of the possible values of the variable must also be treated like variables. The --TESTCD variable itself is similar to the other explanation types - the value of the ValueListOID attribute must match the value of the identifier OID attribute found in another child of MetaDataVersion - def:ValueListDef - also found before the ItemGroupDef elements. Since each of this variable's values is also being treated as a variable, we also need an ItemDef for each of them. Keep in mind that most ItemDefs are linked to an ItemRef within an Item-GroupDef. Since these are not actually variables in a data set, ItemRef information such as OrderNumber, Role, and Mandatory cannot be found in any ItemGroupDef. Rather, they are linked to ItemRefs that are children of the def:ValueListDef attribute just mentioned. This relationship is well illustrated on page 23 of the DDS.

## CREATING DEFINE.XML WITH SAS

Until now we have discussed what needs to be produced; it's now time to talk about how to produce it with SAS. In particular, in this chapter we will discuss the use of the Output Delivery System (ODS). If you are a frequent user of ODS this might come as some relief to you thinking that it's as simple as a couple of ODS statements that open and close destinations and maybe a few ODS options, but two questions arise that must be addressed whose answers are not simple: which ODS destination will we use, and what data sets hold the metadata to be output to this destination?

To the first question, the short answer is the markup destination - but that's only the beginning. Opened without any options, this destination produces valid XML with a generic set of tags and attributes. Though valid, it is certainly not CDISC xml, and as of the writing of this chapter, SAS has no destination that will produce CDISC xml. For that reason we have to create our own destination with an ODS tagset. Though a full explanation of how to create tagsets and all the tools available to do so is beyond the scope of this chapter, a significant portion of this section will be dedicated to discussing important concepts of output delivery with tagsets, including some of the PROC TEMPLATE syntax, the event model, and tagset variables. We will also spend some time talking about capturing system information and PROC results and writing it all out to the output file. For a more comprehensive discussion, the reader is encouraged to read any of the selections mentioned in the references section at the end of this chapter. In the end, though a complete tagset will not be provided, adequate discussion of the issues to consider should be enough to get the reader started on building their own.

Of course just mentioning the Output Delivery System as a tool for generating output implies that we have something to output - most likely, something that started in one or more SAS data sets. In our case, using ODS means that we have to organize our metadata into one or more data sets, or what we will call a metadata database (MDDB). In reality, your metadata will come from one of many different sources. Some of it, such as variable attributes, may be captured programmatically, while others may be hardcoded from protocol text. In this chapter all discussions of using ODS will be based on the assumption that the reader has decided on a structure for their MDDB and a method for building it that will meet their needs. Some may decide to use Excel spreadsheets for data entry while others may use SAS's PROC FSEDIT; some may create one data set for each domain in their MDDB while others may choose to combine the metadata from all domains into one data set; some may choose to put all controlled terminology into one data set while others may split it into multiple data sets. Although examples will assume specific structures, they are for demonstration only and are not meant to suggest best practices.

After general tagset discussion we will immediately dive into capturing and writing PROC PRINT results. In the end, the object will be to have a tagset to be used with the markup destination that will allow us to simply apply PROC PRINT to all data sets in the MDDB in the proper order once the destination is opened, as in the example below.

```
/*Example 11:  Generating Define.xml with ODS's markup destina-
tion*/
ODS markup tagset = your-tagset-name file = "file-name.xml" ;
proc print noobs data = MDDB-data set-1 ; run;
proc print noobs data = MDDB-data set-2 ; run;
proc print noobs data = MDDB-data set-3 ; run; etc.

ODS markup close ;
```

## THE MARKUP DESTINATION

When we think of ODS, we think of the different file formats we can send our results to, such as PDF, CSV, RTF, and HTML. We do this with a small handful of statements with a handful of options, and POOF - we have our output. With trivial changes, we can easily change formats. We do this without giving hardly any thought to the work that ODS has to do - capture the results of the PROC and surround them with just the right markup in just the right places.

System and PROC options, global statements such as TITLE and FOOTNOTE as well as global ODS statements, and the ability to manipulate style and table templates gave us more freedom to customize output than we ever thought we needed. Then came XML.

Users realized that while the options, statements, and templates that they could manipulate gave them indirect access to certain parts of the markup, other parts of the markup were untouchable. This realization became most apparent when SAS programmers began to have a need for generating XML. RTF and HTML were one thing - they had predefined keywords (tag names, attributes, etc) that SAS could hardcode into the software - but how could SAS be expected to create markup like XML that had no predefined tags, a markup whose tag names we get to make up? How could SAS be expected to generate text such as ItemGroupDef or any other text that CDISC has defined? SAS does have an XML destination but its keywords and output structure are not what is required by CDISC. Users now need more than just statements and options for ODS to translate into markup - they need direct access to the markup. They need the ability to bypass the translation and write the markup themselves. That's where tagsets come in.

Tagsets have been around in one form or another since ODS has been around. After all, it takes more than magic to start with an ODS statement that opens a destination and another to close it, and end with complex markup. Somewhere in SAS's source code has to be instructions on how to create that markup. In addition to these instructions, the source code also has to have the ability to capture dynamic information. This includes not only the results of PROCs, but also text from TITLE and FOOTNOTE statements and any other global or system information that needs to be translated into markup. In a nutshell, when SAS gave users tagsets, they handed over this source code.

On the surface, the idea is a simple and familiar one. After all, since long before ODS has been around we have known how to use a DATA step to capture and manipulate data, and write a combination of hardcoded literal text and manipulated dynamic data to a text file one record at a time. The tagset, written with the TEMPLATE procedure, is the same set of instructions applied to PROC output (and other global parameter values such as titles and system options). We will refer to this as markup data. The tagset has many of the data manipulation tools that the DATA step has including most of the same functions, variable and array functionality, statement blocks, DO/WHILE iterative looping, conditional logic, and more, though much of the syntax is somewhat different. Of course the FILE statement is unnecessary because the output file is named in the ODS statement that opens the Markup destination, but it does have the PUT statement (and some derivatives of PUT) with most of the same functionality (line pointers and trailing @s are among the DATA step PUT features not available in the tagset's PUT). In other words, once data is available, a tagset can manipulate and write it out the same way the DATA step does with minor differences in syntax. What's different is how data is captured.

We know that data is available to the DATA step through variables and each carries different information about each record. Markup data is also available through variables, but it does not come from data records. We also know the DATA step as an active piece of SAS code - every executable statement is sequentially applied to every record read. A tagset is a template, and template code is more passive. It's normally separated into pockets of code, each of which is only executed when it's called upon from somewhere else. In an ODS style definition, these pockets are called elements, each of which is executed when it's loaded into a stylesheet. In a tagset, the pockets are called events, and an event's code is executed when ODS is building a file and calls for that event.

That's how ODS builds a file - in a sequence of discrete steps, at each of which it executes a specific event's code defined in the tagset. This is how ODS has always worked. In the early days, tagsets and their event definitions were simply part of SAS's source code. Today, SAS makes its tagsets available to us, and through PROC TEMPLATE, we can inherit and modify them. Additionally, we can use PROC TEMPLATE to create our own from scratch. The latter is what we need to generate Define.

So how does ODS know which events to call? The answer depends on what part of the file it's building, but for the most part, the pattern of event calling is consistent with the markup pattern found in markup files that contains tables. Most files begin with a high level header section that consists of "onetime" elements. Correspondingly, in the beginning, ODS calls events, each of which should be defined to write markup normally found in the beginning, and each of which should only be called this one time. Some tagsets may be defined to allow for embedded style sheets. In such cases, ODS will call the same event over and over again, in each case, with differences in style variables. These style variables get their values from the ODS style definition being used. Each call corresponds to a different element in the style definition, and results in a different style class in the embedded stylesheet.

These first few events, all called before the PROC is processed, are fairly static, except for the stylesheet events which are only called when a stylesheet is to be included, and whose variable values are derived from the style definition specified on the style= option on the ODS statement that opens the destination. In fact since these are called before the PROC is processed, you can close the destination without executing any PROC and still get output that comes from these preliminary events. When a PROC is included, ODS calls an event that will generate a title if a title exists, a byline if it exists (if the PROC code contained a BY statement), and soon after, an event that generates markup that corresponds to the beginning of a table. If the PROC generates five columns, ODS will call the column header event five times. If you ask for a header to span multiple columns, ODS will call for the appropriate events the appropriate number of times. After column headers, events are called to generate markup containing actual data. At this point ODS is dynamically calling events dictated by PROC results.

More specifically, what's dynamic is the number of times events are called, if at all, but what is not dynamic is the order in which events are called. This is something we count on from ODS - an order of event calls that corresponds to the order in which markup should appear. For example, we count on the SYSTEM_TITLE event which gives us access to the title in the TITLE statement to be called before events that generate PROC results. We expect events with byline information to be called between events with titles and events with table information, and we expect events that carry table header information to be called before those that carry table body information. Not only that, but we also count on ODS to help us generate properly nested markup.

Maybe one of the most compelling reasons to use ODS over other methods is the tagset's ability to write nested markup. As an example, consider the root element which, by definition, contains nested within it all other elements, usually at different levels. We know that while one event will generate "<ODM", the rest of the ODS output is generated through multiple event calls, many of which are called dynamically according to factors such as PROC results. The nature of nested markup is that markup in one part of the document is naturally tied to markup in a later part, so how can we build this relationship between two separate areas of the markup into the event model that generates it? How can we tie the generation of "</ODM>" to the generation of "<ODM" (or in general, any end tag to its corresponding start tag)? The answer is through event states.

When a tagset defines an event in states, then event calling begins to take on a nested pattern. Specifically, when a tagset defines a start state and a finish state, then a call to this event will execute only the code in the start state at first. Events that ODS deems to be nested within this event, or that carry markup to be nested within the tags generated with the start state of the "parent event", will then be called, and after their code finishes executing, the finish state of the parent event will then be executed. Conveniently, like the predetermined order of event calling, the nesting pattern that ODS uses to call events is an intelligent one, meaning that the pattern closely resembles the pattern of nesting found in markup files. For example, the first event that ODS calls (starting in SAS 9.1.3) is called Initialize, and the second is called Doc. The Initialize event, like an empty element, has no event calls nested within it. If defined with start and finish states, the code in the finish state will execute immediately after the code in the start state, and so there is no reason to define this event in your tagset with states. Correspondingly, as we know, XML files (and sometimes HTML files) have declarations at the beginning of the document. Since these also have no nesting, one might use the Initialize event to generate the XML declarations. In terms of nesting, the Doc event is to event calls as the root element is to the markup. Just as the root element opens at the beginning (after the XML declarations) and closes at the end of the document, all event calls are nested within the call to the Doc event. This means that while code such as put "<ODM" found in the start state will generate markup in the beginning of the file, code such as put "</ODM>" found in the finish state will generate markup at the end of the file.

```
/*Example 12:  Initialize and Doc event definitions*/
define event initialize ;
    put "<? xml version="1.0" encoding="windows-1252"?>" ;
    put "<?xml-stylesheet type="text/xsl"   href="define1-0-
0.xsl"?>" ;
end ;

define event doc ;
    start:
    put "<ODM" ;
    finish:
    put "</ODM>" ;
end;
```

Other examples of this event nesting exist too. The Doc event has two child events - a shorter Doc_head and a longer Doc_body - similar to the GlobalVariables and MetaDataVersion children of the Study element in Define. Inside Doc_body is the call of the Proc event corresponding to the beginning of PROC processing. Within the Proc event is a Table event, and within that are Header event calls for each column. After the

Header events end, a Row event is called for each row of the table, and within each is a Data event for each cell.

Up to this point we have seen that ODS creates files by calling events that define markup generation in a pattern that resembles common markup structure, and that the tagset is a template for defining such events. Traditionally such a template has been a part of SAS's source code, but is now available to SAS programmers through PROC TEMPLATE. The problem is that SAS programmers do not know the names of the events that ODS calls, the order in which they are called, or their nesting pattern. Adding to the problem is the fact that the events called sometimes depend on PROC results and global settings. We have mentioned a few here, but for a programmer to be able to associate a piece of markup with a particular event, we need complete documentation. Oddly enough, we can get this kind of information from any one of a class of tagsets called mapping tagsets.

Consider the mapping tagset illustrated in Example 13 below.

```
/*Example 13:  a mapping tagset to document events and their call
order*/
proc template ;
   define tagset eventorder ;
   default_event = "all" ;
   indent=3;

   define event all ;
     start:
     put event_name " (START)" nl ;
     ndent ;

     finish:
     xdent ;
     put event_name " (FINISH)" nl ;
   end;
end;
```

Mapping tagsets like the one in example 13 are not used for creating deliverable output like Define.xml, but instead they help us learn about system and SAS metadata (not clinical metadata) such as event names. In this case we are defining a tagset called Eventorder that defines only one event called "all". As we know, ODS will call for several events, none of which are defined in this tagset, but because "all" is declared to be a default event (with the DEFAULT_EVENT= statement), its code will be executed as a substitute for undefined events. Note that each PUT statement combines literal text with a variable reference. We will discuss event variables in more detail soon, but for now, know that its value is the name of the event being called. As in the DATA step, literal text is

contained in quotation marks. Though it looks like another variable reference, "nl" moves the pointer to the next line. Following the PUT
statement in the start state is an NDENT statement which moves the
pointer to the right three spaces (as dictated by the INDENT= statement, used for readability). Similarly, the XDENT statement in the finish
state moves the pointer to the left three spaces. We now put this tagset
to practice in the following manner.

```
ods markup tagset=eventorder
   file = "proc print event order.txt" ;
   title "tagset testing" ;

proc print noobs data = sashelp.class(obs=2) ;
   var name sex age height weight ;
run;

ods markup close;
```

The resulting file can be found in appendix A. What may first stand out
about this output is the fact that it looks nothing like what you expect
from PROC PRINT. Maybe what's most noteworthy though comes at
the end. We can see from the PROC PRINT code that this will produce
a table with two data rows (plus a header row) and five columns. At the
end of the output file we see an event called Table_head being called.
Nested within that is a call to the Row event, and nested within that are
five calls to the Header event - one for each column header. After that,
the Row event finishes, and because the header will have only one row,
the Table_head event finishes. Then comes the Table_body event. Note
that within this event call are two calls back to the Row event, each with
five calls to the Data event nested within them. The two Row calls correspond to the two data rows of the table, and again, the five Data calls to
the five columns of data. Once Table_body finishes, all other events in
which it was nested finish too.

## EVENT VARIABLES

We mentioned earlier that markup data is available through variables and
since then we have seen examples of them. Style definitions from style
templates make their way into markup by way of style variables.
EVENT_NAME, whose values, as illustrated in example 13 above, reflect the name of the current event being called, is an event variable that
might fall under the metadata umbrella. Other metadata variables include
SASVERSION, ENCODING, DATE, and TIME. Many of these may
not be useful in generating markup, but they are available and remain static across event calls. Other variables such as VALUE and NAME do

carry dynamic data to be inserted into the markup and have the potential to change with every new event call. In all, between style and event variables, ODS has access to more than 500 variables. Though many are documented in the Online Documentation, many questions are still outstanding. How do I capture something global like titles? Do they populate a variable in the first event call and then remain static across all event calls like some metadata variables, or do they become available at just one event call and then disappear? If the latter, which event call? What other metadata is available? How do I know which cell of a table a data value represents? Earlier we saw how a mapping tagset can serve as documentation about events and their call order. We will now create another to document event variables and values.

Consider the mapping tagset illustrated in Example 14 below.

```
proc template ;
    define tagset allvars ;
    default_event="all" ;
    define event all;

    put "EVENT: " event_name NL ;
    put "======================================" NL ;
    putvars event _name_ " = " _value_ nl ;
    put "======================================" NL ;
    put NL ;
    end;
end;
```

Once again we have a tagset with just one event defined, but because it's deemed to be a default, its code will be executed at every event call. Here we use the PUTVARS statement with the EVENT keyword. For any given event call, SAS will cycle through all of the event variables with non-missing values for that call and write to the file what follows the EVENT keyword. Note that once again, this combines literal text - the equal sign and surrounding spaces enclosed in quotes - with variable references _NAME_ and _VALUE_. At any given iteration, _NAME_ is the name of the variable at that iteration and _VALUE_ is its value. An excerpt of the output generated using this tagset and the PROC PRINT code above is illustrated in Appendix B.

Though Appendix B is not the complete output file, we can start to gain an appreciation for the role that the variable VALUE plays. To answer our question regarding the availability of the title, we see that in the SYSTEM_TITLE_SETUP event call, VALUE holds the title. In the Proc_Branch event, VALUE holds the name of the PROC used. With each call to the Header event nested within Row nested within Table_head, VALUE contains the column headers, and in the Data event calls, it contains results of the PROC. For the most part, though more than 500 variables exist, VALUE contains most of the text that would be seen through a browser.

Keep in mind that this example comes with certain initial conditions - PROC PRINT with two observations and five variables, the NOOBS option on the DATA statement, one title, etc. The reader is encouraged to modify these conditions and observe the effect on the output. For example, try labeling the variables, use a BY statement, sum numeric variables, use an ID statement, use different system options, try with different PROCs or multiple PROCs. Also try modifying the mapping tagset. If the PUTVARS statement produces too much unnecessary output, try modifying the first mapping tagset by adding the value of the VALUE variable as illustrated below in example 15.

```
/*Example 15:  adding VALUE to the EVENTORDER tagset*/
define event all ;
    start:
    put event_name " (START) VALUE=" value nl ;
    ndent ;

    finish:
    xdent ;
    put event_name " (FINISH)" nl ;
end;
```

In addition to the variables provided to us by SAS, tagset authors have the ability to create their own variables called memory variables. Unlike data set variables that are created with statements that have no keywords, memory variables are created with the EVAL statement (numeric variables) and the SET statement (character variables). Memory variables are always referenced with dollar signs.

```
/*Example 16:  creating memory*/
set $charvar "character variable" ;
eval $numvar index($charvar, "r") ;
```

List variables and Dictionary variables are two special types of memory variables that work like arrays. Similar to the DATA step array, list variables associate a numeric index with a string while dictionary variables associate a string with another string. For list variables, this is accomplished with the SET statement and a set of square brackets that either encloses a number to which the string is being associated, or nothing, which simply assigns the string to the next available numeric index in the list. For dictionary variables, the index is a quoted string. With both types of arrays the index can be replaced with a variable reference that resolves to an integer or a quoted string. Unlike DATA step arrays, no declaration of the dimension of the array is needed.

```
/*Example 17:  list and dictionary variables*/
set $listvar[1] "first list index" ;
set $listvar[2] "second list index" ;
set $listvar[] "third list index" ;

/* Added to the end of the array */
set $listvar[$numvar] "numvarth index" ;
set $dictionvar ["one"] "first dictionary index" ;
set $charvar "character variable" ;
eval $numvar index($charvar, "r") ;
```

## GETTING STARTED ON YOUR DEFINE TAGSET

We have now been through the theory and are ready to put it all to practical use. We will do that by taking another look at Example 12, but with a few changes.

```
/*Example 18:  Initialize and Doc events revisited*/
define event initialize ;
    put "<? xml version="1.0" encoding=" encoding "?>" ;
    put "<?xml-stylesheet type="text/xsl" href="define1-0-0.xsl"?>"
;
end ;
define event doc ;
    start:
    put "<ODM>" ;
    put "<Study>" ;

    finish:
    put "</Study>" ;
    put "</ODM>" ;
end;
define event doc_head ;
    start:
    put "<GlobalVariables>" ;

    finish:
    put "</GlobalVariables>" ;
end;
define event doc_body ;
    start:
    put "<MetaDataVersion>" ;

    finish:
    put "</MetaDataVersion>" ;
end;
```

Notice that in this example, we are not writing out any of the attribute specifications for the root ODM element, the Study element, or the subelements of the GlobalVariables element. These observations speak to the primary focus of discussion, but before we get into those details, let's make a few other observations.

We first note that in the first declaration, the value of the encoding attribute is now an event variable reference rather than quoted literal text. This suggests that the event variable has a meaningful value at the time that the Initialize event is called. This variable in particular is a system metadata variable whose value remains consistent across all event calls. Values of other event variables such as VALUE and NAME are not so predictable.

We have also added a few more PUT statements to more events that write out opening and closing Define.xml tags. Before we move on, it's important that we closely examine the event structure of example 18 and remind ourselves how this produces the element structure required by Define. In order to do that, we revisit PROC PRINT output in Appendix A generated from the tagset illustrated in Example 13.

In example 18 we added PUT statements to add three more tag pairs, but why did we put them where we did? More specifically, why did we put one of them in the Doc event that also writes out the opening and closing of the root element, and the other two in separate events? Why did we choose the events we did for these tag pairs? We can easily answer these questions by comparing the event call pattern (order of event calls and their nesting structure) in Appendix A to the element structure (order of elements and their nesting structure) required by Define.xml. Define starts with XML declarations that have no nesting. Likewise, when an ODS destination is opened, it begins by calling the Initialize event that has no nested event calls within it, making Initialize a good candidate for generating these declarations. After Define's declarations is the opening of the root element, which of course does not close until the end of the document. The Study element opens after the root element opening tag and then closes immediately before the close of the root element. Likewise, after executing statements in the Initialize event, ODS then calls the Doc event, inside of which all other event calls are nested, making Doc a good event to generate the opening tags of the ODM and Study elements in the Start state and the end tags in the Finish state. GlobalVariables is a child element of Study, but unlike Study's relationship to ODM, Global-Variables is not an only child - MetaDataVersion is GlobalVariable's one and only sibling. Because, according to Appendix A, the Doc event call is the only "child event call" of ODM, generating these tag pairs with the Doc event would not have supported this sibling relationship. On the other hand, the Doc event call does have two nested sibling event calls

Doc_Head and Doc_Body that correspond to the two child elements of Study. For that reason, we used these events in example 18 to generate these tag pairs.

Before we rely too heavily on the structure suggested by Appendix A, it's important that we keep in mind the conditions under which this was generated. An important question is how different Appendix A would look under different conditions. Recall that this was generated with a single PROC PRINT, the NOOBS option, reading only two observations and reporting on specific variables in a specific order indicated in the VAR statement. A title was also provided. For our purposes, this set of conditions is close to what we want to achieve open the destination, PROC PRINT each data set of the MDDB (in the correct order), and close the destination. The most significant departure from Appendix A conditions is the use of multiple PROC PRINTs. We will briefly discuss here how event calls would change from a logical point of view, but the reader is encouraged to experiment and see for themselves.

We mentioned earlier that initial event calls are relatively static, but then get more dynamic when the PROCs get processed. We also mentioned that because these static events are called before PROCs are processed, we can actually open an ODS destination and close it without any PROCs. In other words we can think of these events as being associated with the opening of the ODS destination. We can see from Appendix A that these initial events include precisely the events we defined in example 18 above. Once ODS is finished opening the destination, then it stands to reason that it's ready to start processing PROCs. Correspondingly, as seen in Appendix A, the first and only child of the call to the Doc_Body event is a call to the Proc event. It's at this point that event calling gets more dynamic. Nested within Proc are events called, for example, when a title is used and when a BY statement is used. The number of nested Row event calls depends on the number of rows that result (in this case, specified by the OBS= option in the PROC statement), plus another for the header. Nested within each Row event call are calls to the Data event, the number of which corresponds to the number of columns in the table. In this case, that's a function of the number of variables named in the VAR statement, plus the use of the NOOBS option in the PROC statement. Once enough Row events are called to complete the construction of the table, ODS finishes the processing of the PROC by executing the finish states of events nested within the Proc event. Once this is over, two things can happen. One is the closing of the destination, which corresponds to the call of the finish states of the initial static events. We see this in Appendix A. The other option is that another PROC can be processed, which would correspond to a new call to a new Proc event, and the PROC processing events start over again with the second PROC.

So far, things have worked out pretty well for us. Up to this point, the pattern that ODS uses in calling events, and in particular, the pattern of nesting, corresponds exactly to the pattern of elements and their nesting in Define.xml. We can be confident that the opening tags in the beginning of Define as well as their corresponding end tags will be generated only once  at the beginning and the end of the file because the instructions for writing the text are in events that correspond to the opening and closing of the ODS destination, each of which we know happens only once. It's tempting to want to continue this pattern of event definition and see how much of the rest of Define (e.g. the ItemGroupDefs) we can accurately generate in this manner, but we soon discover that because of the variety in structure across child elements of MetaDataVersion, some adjustments will be necessary.

For starters, with a quick glance at Appendix A, it appears that the pattern breaks down within DOC_BODY, for the simple reason that MetaDataVersion contains several child elements and DOC_BODY contains only one child event call to Proc. However we also just reasoned that Doc_Body will actually contain one child Proc event call per PROC PRINT, and so if the number of PROC PRINTS matches the number of child elements of MetaDataVersion, then maybe we have restored hope of having an event call structure that exactly matches Define's element structure. This also suggests one possible structure for your MDDB  each data set carries metadata for exactly one child element instance of MetaDataVersion. With this MDDB structure, we simply define the Proc event in the tagset to write out the markup for each child element of MetaDataVersion, and then by running PROC PRINT on each data set in the MDDB we get the right number of child elements.

One obvious problem with this solution as it is stated here is that we do not want to write out the same markup for each child of MetaDataVersion because different groups of these child elements have different element and attribute structures. For example, the def:AnnotatedCRF element contains no attributes and one or more def:DocumentRef child elements, while the def:leaf element contains two attributes and exactly one def:title child element. ItemGroupDef contains several attributes and several instances of the ItemRef child element, and each CodeList element contains attributes as well as multiple levels of nesting. This means that if we are going to try and generate these elements from the Proc event, then that event definition will have to contain conditional PUT statements based on which child element (or group of elements) it is generating.

Conditional logic in tagsets is no problem (though the syntax is different from the DATA step's conditional logic), but we run into another bump in the road. Suppose we have a data set in our MDDB that contains all of the metadata that belongs in the ItemGroupDef element associated with the AE data set. This includes attributes of the ItemGroupDef element as well as attributes of each ItemRef child element. In the Proc event we can easily generate the literal text "<ItemGroupDef" and we can even generate the name of the first attribute plus the equal sign, but if the value of this attribute is contained in a data set of the MDDB that we are PROC PRINTing, then according to Appendix B, we do not yet have access to this value. In fact, as we pointed out earlier, we do not have access to it until the Data event is called, which is several levels of event call nesting deep within the call of Proc. This means that if we choose to generate markup from the Proc event, we are limited to generating literal text up until the occurrence of the first PROC result, and that to generate the PROC results, we will have to do so with the Data event.

We started this discussion and developed this approach as a way to generate the child elements of MetaDataVersion, but it could also be one way to generate some of the markup that we skipped in example 18 in particular, the ODM and Study attributes and the values of the child elements of GlobalVariables. Recall in that example that we had an event call structure that perfectly matched the element structure in the header of Define. Suppose now that we decide to store the ODM attributes in a data set of the MDDB for PROC PRINTing. Because we cannot get PROC results until the Data events start getting called, we cannot generate any of the header markup that follows these attributes until the Data events. That means we would have to remove the "<Study>" text as well as the entire Doc_head and Doc_body events. At most, you could use the start and finish states of the DOC event to generate the opening and closing of the root element (ODM). Optionally, you might also choose to use the finish state of Doc to generate the closing tags of the Study and MetaDataVersion events to make sure they close at the end of the file.

This is certainly one viable option, but because you are removing that assurance you had that the opening and closing tags were going in the right places, you will need to take caution in how and when you generate these with this approach. The positive side is the use of the SAS data set for keeping such metadata. On the other hand, as a developer you might look at the ODM attributes and decide that across studies, they stay static enough to hardcode them into your tagset and not store them in a data set. This is another viable option that runs the same risk that hard coding runs in any application  a decline in flexibility and an increased likelihood of having to change application code. The positive side is that you can continue to use the event definitions of example 18.

Finally, one other option that offers more flexibility than hard coding, allows the event structure of example 18, and involves no storage in a data set is macro variables. Like other templates, the tagset language has the MVAR statement which allows you to declare macro variables that are to be resolved when the tagset is used rather than when it is compiled. Of course this would require the initialization of such macro variables before opening the ODS destination (e.g. %LET). References to such macro variables in the tagset definition do not include ampersands.

We noted earlier that different children of MetaDataVersion have different element and attribute structures. Because of that, generating these children requires conditional logic. We now conclude this section by looking at some examples that demonstrate this. In example 19, suppose we have a data set in our MDDB called "ACRF" that will be used to generate our def:AnnotatedCRF element. Because this element contains only one piece of data - the leafID attribute, which is actually an attribute of the def:DocumentRef subelement - our data set contains only one variable to hold all such attribute values. Running PROC PRINT on this data set, we know that the event variable VALUE will contain the value of that one data set variable when the Data event is called. Example 19 below demonstrates how we might define the Table and Data events to generate this part of the markup.

```
/*Example 19:  generating the def:AnnotatedCRF element*/
define event proc ;
start:
put "<def:AnnotatedCRF>" nl / if $tablename eq "ACRF" ;;

finish:
put "</def:AnnotatedCRF>" nl / if $tablename eq "ACRF" ;;
end;

define event data ;
putq "<def:DocumentRef leafID=" VALUE "/>" nl / if $tablename eq
"ACRF" ;
end;
```

Several parts of this example are worthy of note here. Note the syntax of conditional statements. Note also the new PUTQ statement which wraps double quotes around the resolution of the variable references (in this case, around the value of VALUE in the Data event definition). Finally, note the condition based on $tablename. Remember that dollar signs precede memory variables, or variables created by the developer in the tagset definition. In this case, the memory variable was created in an earlier event that captured the name of the data set being processed.

Example 19 illustrates the generation of a relatively simple element. The simplicity comes from the fact that though AnnotatedCRF has a child element, only one piece of metadata is present, and so the data set in the MDDB only needed one variable. This meant only one call to the Data event for each Row call, and so we knew that when Data was called, the value of the event variable VALUE always represented the one leafID attribute. In example 20 below we illustrate the more complex def:leaf element which contains three pieces of metadata two attribute values for def:leaf plus an element value for the def:title child element. We will assume that a data set in the MDDB called "LEAFID" has three variables that hold this metadata. Furthermore, for reasons we will see soon, we will name these three data set variables for the attributes and elements they represent, replacing colons (illegal in variable naming) with underscores. That gives us the variables ID, xlink_href, and def_title. Note also that the letter casing of the variables is important.

The difficulty of having multiple variables corresponding multiple calls of the Data event within each Row event call, is that as the developer we have no control over the order in which these variables become available, which reflects their order in the data set. In this case, because def:title is a child of def:leaf, we need to be able to write out the def:leaf element and its attributes before we write out the def:title value. If this def:title value is not the third of the three variables in the data set, then rather than writing it to the output file right away, we need to hold on to it until we are ready to write it. This brings us to another approach to writing PROC PRINT results to the file  rather than writing them out as we receive them in the Data event, use the Data event to store them in a dictionary variable. Since we know that we have processed an entire row when we hit Row's finish state, we can write them out from here.

Furthermore, we can use the fact that we named the data set variables for the attribute and element names to create a dictionary variable whose string indices are easy to remember. After all, if we assign the PROC results to simple memory variables like $a1, $a2, and $a3, we still would not know which of these holds, for example, the ID attribute. However, with PROC PRINT, the value of the NAME event variable in the Data event is the name of the data set variable being processed. We therefore use each call of the Data event to associate a data set variable's name with its value. At Row's finish state when these are all collected, we write them out the way we need to.

```
/*Example 20:  Creating the leafID element using a dictionary
variable*/
define event data ;
set $data_values[name] VALUE ;
end ;

define event row ;
start:
unset $data_values ;

finish:
break / if section ne "body" ;
do / if $tablename eq "LEAFID" ;
put "<def:leaf ID=" $data_values["ID"] "xlink:href=" $da-
ta_values["xlink_href"] ">" ;
put "<def:title>" $data_values["def_title"] "</def:title>" ;
put "</def:leaf>" ;
done ;
end;
```

Let's analyze example 20 first by noting some new statements. UNSET followed by a variable name simply clears that variable of any values. BREAK means to exit the event. Statement blocks begin with DO and with DONE instead of the DATA step's END. We also notice a reference to the SECTION event variable. The Row event is called not only for data rows but also header rows. The code following the conditional BREAK in Row's finish state should only be executed for data rows, not header rows, which is why this conditional BREAK is there. We also note that in the Data event, the index is not an integer (list variables) or a quoted string, but rather a reference to an event variable. The index becomes whatever this variable resolves to during that call of Data. For example, if the first variable in the data set LEAFID is def_title, then def_title is the value of NAME during the first call to the Data event.

If in the data set, the value of def_title is "Annotated CRFs #1", then as we know, this becomes the value of VALUE during the same Data call, and so $data_values[ "def_title"] = "Annotated CRF". The beauty of this approach is that even if def_title is the first variable in the data set, the fact that it is written last does not matter because before anything is written, all three data values are stored in the dictionary variable, each associated with a string that matches the name of the data set variable that held its value. At the end of the row everything is written out and the slate (dictionary variable) is wiped clean and the process starts again for the next row.

Finally, unlike example 19, the element name in this example is generated along with its attributes and child elements, rather than in the PROC event. That's because the MDDB structure was such that each observation in LEAFID represented a new def:leaf element, whereas the observations in ACRF each represented a def:DocumentRef child element.

The techniques described in example 20 as well as any others used throughout this chapter are among many that you as a developer can use to generate your markup. The purpose of this section of the chapter is to demonstrate how the event model works and how to use event definitions in your tagset not only to write markup to the file but also to capture event variable values when they are available. The techniques illustrated above are not claimed to be better than any others, but rather were used as a means to fulfill this purpose. In the meantime, they also illustrated tagset tools that are available to you, as well as some of the difficulties involved in directing ODS to deliver output.

In fact even the use of ODS is not necessarily the unanimous choice for SAS tools. Other developers have made creative use of the macro facility and the DATA step to accomplish the same purpose. For me there were three reasons for choosing ODS. One reason is that SAS is working closely with CDISC to provide support for Define.xml, and that support will come in the form of ODS tagsets. Different companies will make different decisions when that time comes; those that convert to using SAS's new tools from using their own tagset will have spent valuable time considering things like MDDB structure, the inner workings of ODS, and the ability to modify SAS's new tagset if necessary; those that continue to use their own can still learn from what SAS has produced. A second and more technical reason is ODS's ability to incorporate complex levels of nesting with the event model and in particular, start and finish states. And finally, in some ways to me it feels more natural. With the level of responsibility for our metadata that CDISC requires, organized storage in a database is necessary. Define.xml can be thought of as a copy of your MDDB in a different file format. SAS programmers sometimes make copies of data sets with PROC PRINT. With time spent up front for development, users can do what's natural to them manipulate data and PROC PRINT it.

Although it is not completely natural. We have provided no functionality for titles and footnotes or PROC PRINT features like BY and ID statements. This tagset was written in a box for one purpose only. Also, we noticed at times the dependency of the tagset code on external factors. We assumed data set variable names that matched attribute and element names. We also assumed that the order of the PROC PRINTs will correspond to the order of Define's elements. Such restrictions on the use of an ODS destination is something we are not used to, but then again, most ODS destinations create markup for tabular output  markup that is relatively uniform, unlike the varied nature of MetaDataVersion's children. This tagset can only generate valid Define.xml if the environment is set up right. This suggests that the tagset development is tied in with the structure of the MDDB and each of the data sets it contains. For that reason, some may feel that to ensure the right environmental conditions, use of the tagset must be part of a bigger application, perhaps wrapped in a macro. These are decisions to be made by the development team and the expected users.

## CONCLUSION

The challenges a SAS programmer faces in the pharmaceutical industry can be daunting, depending on one's experience. They present opportunities for learning technologies that cannot be expected to be learned over night. This chapter makes no claim that you will be generating perfectly valid and compliant Define.xmls immediately after reading it. Instead, in addition to other resources including the references mentioned at the end, it is intended to be one of several resources, and hopefully one that is condensed enough to be one of the first ones you reach for. The specific techniques and assumptions used may or may not be suitable for your environment, but hopefully they at least provided you the tools to develop your own.

## REFERENCES

Gebhart, Eric "ODS Markup, Tagsets, and Styles! Taming ODS Styles and Tagsets." Proceedings of the SAS Global Forum Users Group International Conference, April 2007.

Molter, Mike "A Tiptoe Through the Tagset Field." Proceedings of the SAS Global Forum Users Group International Conference, April 2008

Clinical Data Interchange Standards Consortium. "Case Report Tabulation Data Definition Specification (define.xml)", February 2005 http://www.cdisc.org/models/def/v1.0/CRT_DDSpecification1_0_0.pdf

Harold, Elliotte Rusty and Means, W. Scott. (2004) "XML in a Nutshell".

Sebastopol, CA: O'Reilly Media, Inc.

## APPENDIX A

The following PROC PRINT output using the tagset from example 13 illustrates the order of event calling and the event nesting pattern.

```
initialize (START)
initialize (FINISH)
doc (START)
  doc_head (START)
    doc_meta (START)
    doc_meta (FINISH)
    auth_oper (START)
    auth_oper (FINISH)
    doc_title (START)
    doc_title (FINISH)
    stylesheet_link (START)
    stylesheet_link (FINISH)
    javascript (START)
      startup_function (START)
      startup_function (FINISH)
      shutdown_function (START)
      shutdown_function (FINISH)
    javascript (FINISH)
  doc_head (FINISH)
  doc_body (START)
    proc (START)
      anchor (START)
      anchor (FINISH)
      page_setup (START)
        system_title_setup_group (START)
          title_setup_container (START)
            title_setup_container_specs (START)
              title_setup_container_spec (START)
              title_setup_container_spec (FINISH)
            title_setup_container_specs (FINISH)
            title_setup_container_row (START)
              system_title_setup (START)
              system_title_setup (FINISH)
            title_setup_container_row (FINISH)
          title_setup_container (FINISH)
        system_title_setup_group (FINISH)
      page_setup (FINISH)
      system_title_group (START)
        title_container (START)
          title_container_specs(START)
            title_container_spec (START)
            title_container_spec (FINISH)
          title_container_specs (FINISH)
          title_container_row (START)
            system_title (START)
            system_title (FINISH)
          title_container_row (FINISH)
        title_container (FINISH)
      system_title_group (FINISH)
      proc_branch (START)
```

```
leaf (START)
  page_anchor (START)
  page_anchor (FINISH)
  output (START)
    table (START)
      rowspec (START)
        cellspec (START)
        cellspec (FINISH)
        cellspecsep (START)
        cellspecsep (FINISH)
        cellspec (START)
        cellspec (FINISH)
        cellspecsep (START)
        cellspecsep (FINISH)
        cellspec (START)
        cellspec (FINISH)
        cellspecsep (START)
        cellspecsep (FINISH)
        cellspec (START)
        cellspec (FINISH)
        cellspecsep (START)
        cellspecsep (FINISH)
        cellspec (START)
        cellspec (FINISH)
      rowspec (FINISH)
      colspecs (START)
        colgroup (START)
          colspec_entry (START)
          colspec_entry (FINISH)
          colspecsep (START)
          colspecsep (FINISH)
          colspec_entry (START)
          colspec_entry (FINISH)
          colspecsep (START)
          colspecsep (FINISH)
          colspec_entry (START)
          colspec_entry (FINISH)
          colspecsep (START)
          colspecsep (FINISH)
          colspec_entry (START)
          colspec_entry (FINISH)
          colspecsep (START)
          colspecsep (FINISH)
          colspec_entry (START)
          colspec_entry (FINISH)
        colgroup (FINISH)
      colspecs (FINISH)
      table_headers (START)
        header_spec (START)
          sub_header_colspec (START)
            col_header_label (START)
            col_header_label (FINISH)
          sub_header_colspec (FINISH)
          sub_header_colspec (START)
            col_header_label (START)
            col_header_label (FINISH)
          sub_header_colspec (FINISH)
          sub_header_colspec (START)
            col_header_label (START)
```

```
                        col_header_label (FINISH)
                    sub_header_colspec (FINISH)
                    sub_header_colspec (START)
                        col_header_label (START)
                        col_header_label (FINISH)
                    sub_header_colspec (FINISH)
                    sub_header_colspec (START)
                        col_header_label (START)
                        col_header_label (FINISH)
                    sub_header_colspec (FINISH)
                header_spec (FINISH)
            table_headers (FINISH)
            table_head (START)
              row (START) header (START)
                header (FINISH)
                header (START)
                header (FINISH)
                header (START)
                header (FINISH)
                header (START)
                header (FINISH)
                header (START)
                header (FINISH)
              row (FINISH)
            table_head (FINISH)
            table_body (START)
              row (START)
                data (START)
                data (FINISH)
                data (START)
                data (FINISH)
                data (START)
                data (FINISH)
                data (START)
                data (FINISH)
                data (START)
                data (FINISH)
              row (FINISH)
              row (START)
                data (START)
                data (FINISH)
                data (START)
                data (FINISH)
                data (START)
                data (FINISH)
                data (START)
                data (FINISH)
                data (START)
                data (FINISH)
              row (FINISH)
            table_body (FINISH)
          table (FINISH)
        output (FINISH)
      leaf (FINISH)
    proc_branch (FINISH)
  proc (FINISH)
  doc_body (FINISH)
doc (FINISH)
```

## APPENDIX B

The following PROC PRINT output using the tagset from example 14 illustrates event variables and their values by event call.

```
EVENT: system_title_setup
===========================================================
anchor = IDX
toclevel = 1
colcount = 1
event_name = system_title_setup
encoding = windows-1252
operator = mmolter
date = 2009-01-13
sasversion = 9.1
saslongversion = 9.01.01M3P02022006
time = 11:02:47
state = start
value = tagset testing
page_count = 1
total_page_count = 1
firstpage = 1
proc_name = Print
dest_file = body
bodyname = C:\Documents and Settings\mmolter\My Documents\SGF
2009\variable values.txt
tagset = putvars1
style = Default
javadate = 2009-01-13
javatime = 11:02:47-05:00
data_viewer = Report style_element = SystemTitle

EVENT: proc_branch
===========================================================
name = Print
label = The Print Procedure
anchor = IDX
toclevel = 1
colcount = 1
event_name = proc_branch
encoding = windows-1252
operator = mmolter
date = 2009-01-13
sasversion = 9.1
saslongversion = 9.01.01M3P02022006
time = 11:02:47
state = start
value = Print
proc_count = 1
total_proc_count = 1
page_count = 1
total_page_count = 1
proc_name = Print
dest_file = body
bodyname = C:\Documents and Settings\mmolter\My Documents\SGF
2009\variable values.txt
```

```
tagset = putvars1
style = Default
javadate = 2009-01-13
javatime = 11:02:47-05:00
data_viewer = Report
style_element = Con-tentProcName
=========================================================

EVENT: data
=========================================================
type = string
name = Sex
dname = Sex
label = Sex
anchor = IDX
colstart = 2
row = 2
colwidth = 1
scale = 0
precision = 0
colcount = 1
event_name = data
encoding = windows-1252
operator = mmolter
date = 2009-01-13
sasversion = 9.1
saslongversion = 9.01.01M3P02022006
time = 11:02:47
section = body
state = start
col_id = 2
value = M
output_name = Print
output_label = Data Set SASHELP.CLASS
proc_count = 1
total_proc_
count = 1
page_count = 1
total_page_count = 1
proc_name = Print
data_row = 1
dest_file = body
bodyname = C:\Documents and Settings\mmolter\My Documents\SGF
2009\variable values.txt
tagset = putvars1
style = Default
sasformat = $F
unformattedtype = string
unformattedwidth = 1
javadate = 2009-01-13
javatime = 11:02:47-05:00
data_viewer = Report
style_element = Data
last_stacked_value = 0
first_stacked_value = 0
==========================================
===
```

# SDTM Attribute Checking Tool

### Ellen Xiao

Converting clinical data into CDISC SDTM format is a high priority of many pharmaceutical/biotech companies. Most of these companies are ready to invest in obtaining a SDTM conversion tool that can do the job specifically designed for their company or to hire a CRO to convert the data for them. CDISC STDM conversion may sound like an easy job given the various available tools. What is important is not to overlook is the validation of the resulting CDISC SDTM data. It can be quite challenging and time consuming to validate SDTM submissions manually. Three targets or perspectives of validation can be categorized as structure, content and attributes. Here, I would like to focus specifically on a SDTM Attribute Checking Tool used to check between SDTM data and the define.xml.

## INTRODUCTION

The 1999 FDA "Electronic Submission (eSub) Guidance" and the "Electronic Common Technical Document (eCTD) Specification" specify that a document describing the content and structure of the included data should be provided as part of the submission. This document is known as the data definition document (e.g., "define.pdf" in the 1999 guidance). The Data Definition Document provides a list of the datasets included in the submission along with a detailed description of the contents of each dataset. To increase the level of automation and improve the efficiency of the regulatory review process, the define.xml as published by the CDISC define.xml team is the preferred type of data definition file which is more suitable for providing the different types of metadata required to adequately describe data in the SDTM format. An additional benefit of define.xml is its machine-readability. Inconsistency between the document and real datasets is unavoidable. Common inconsistencies can be a difference in labels (truncation, typo in the label, extra blanks, special non-displayable characters etc.), different lengths of variables, extra/fewer variables etc.Any discrepancies may lead the regulatory agency reviewer question the overall quality of the deliverables which may cause unexpected delays of drug approval. Thus, capturing and correcting these discrepancies is as important as creating the documents and CDISC data themselves. To capture all these inconsistencies manually is time consuming and error-prone. Developing a tool to do the consistency check is a more practical way of solving this kind of issue. And this kind of tool can actually be used across platforms and companies.

## SDTM ATTRIBUTE CHECKING

A series of SAS macros have been developed that can be used to check each SDTM domain against the define.xml to maintain consistency between the datasets and the define.xml. The SAS macro is called INF1-3 CheckInFormWithDefine which includes a calling program to %compare0define and macros (%parse, %exdde, %exdde, %parse2, %charnum, %defaut, %read etc.

### %PARSE2 MACRO:

This macro reads in a token list separated by a delimiter defined in the macro parameter and assigned each token to different global macro variables from &macronam.1 to &macronam&j (&j is the total number of tokens listed ) and assign total number of tokens to &macronam.0.

```
%LET sub_lst=%scan(&lst,&i,&dlm);
    %do %while("&sub_lst" ne "");
        %do;
            %let j=%eval(&j+1);
            %global &macronam&j;
            %let &macronam&j=&sub_lst;
        %end;
        %let i=%eval(&i+1);
        %LET sub_lst=%scan(&lst,&i,&dlm);
    %end;
%let &macronam.0=&j;
```

### %EXDDE MACRO:

This macro is mainly used for importing data from Excel (define.xml) into SAS which provides many flexible features in the data importing process. Such as, reading multiple sub-sheets nested within one Excel file with a single macro call which reduces the CPU time for data transfer.

1. Set up default values for some macro parameters. This feature allows the user to minimize the effort and allows use of the default values for the parameters and to define others.

   - Convert parameters STARTC and ENDC to numbers if they are letters by calling macro %charnum. Since the head of the Excel file column was displayed as character(s), the user may define macro variables &StartC (start column to read) or &EndC (end column to read) as character(s). This macro convert &StartC and/or &EndC from character(s) to number(s).

           *%charnum*(StartC); *%charnum*(EndC);

   - Set up default values for macro parameters not specified such as, start row, start column, end row and end column of the excel spread sheets to read in etc..

```
%if %length(&&&dvar) eq 0 %then %do;
   %let &dvar = &dvarv;
   %if &dvar eq fmt %then %do;
      %if &var ^= %str(col&StartC.-col&EndC.) %then %do;
         %parse2(lst=&var,macronam=varlst,dlm=%str( ));
         %let &dvar = sysfunc(translate(%sysfunc(
         repeat($30.c,%eval(&varlst0- 1))),"  ","c"));
      %end;
   %end;
%end;
```

2. If logic checks fail, error messages will be printed in the log file/window and the macro will end execution. The logic checking was established at the beginning of the macro. Instead of running the whole program, the logic checking makes it possible to stop the program execution when logic checking failed; which provide great efficiency for the user to identify the error(s) in the very early stage.

   The following logic checks are included in the program:
   - Check if the Excel file exist.
   - Check if the required macro parameters exist.
   - Check if "start row number", "start column number", "end row number" and "end column number" values defined from macro parameters larger than 0.
   - Check if "start row", "end row" have specified with numeric number instead of character.
   - Check if "end row" is larger than or equal to "start row" and "end column" is larger than or equal to "start col-

umn".

Below is an example of failed logic checking and the related error message that is generated at the SAS log file/window.

```
@@@@@@@@@@@@@@@@@ Message from Macro EXDDE @@@@@@@@@@@@
@ Logic_Err = 2.                                        @
@ Parameters RAWDIR, FILE, and OUTDATA are required,      @
@ and MUST BE SPECIFIED.                                  @
@ Please try again.                              @
@@@@@@@@@@@@@@@@@@@@@@@@@@@@@@@@@@@@@@@@@@@@@@@@@@@@@@@@@@@;
```

The error message clearly indicates which part of the program needs to be modified.

- Read in data from each worksheet, and combine them into one dataset.
- Get the domain list from metadata and create a macro variable &domainlist which can be used to define a macro parameter to read the define.xml sheet by sheet.

```
select distinct scan(memname,1,"$") into: domainlist SEPARATED by
'|' from sashelp.vtable where libname='DEFINE' and
length(scan(memname,1,"$"))=2 or upcase(memname)='RELREC$';
```

- Call %parse2 to separate the Excel file (define.xml) sheet by sheet into different macro variables and save the total number of sheets read in into a macro variable &sh0.
- Macro %read: use dynamic data exchange to read the Excel file (define.xml) which provides the feature to handle format inconsistency within a column. It drops columns not needed and flag the sub-sheet origin of the data. It checks if the Excel file is open, and the related sheet name may need to be verified.

```
filename one dde
"Excel|&rawdir\[&file..xls]&&sh&i!
r&startR.c&startC:r&endR.c&endC"
```

- Open Excel file. The DDE approach requires the Excel file (define.xml) to be opened during the data Processing. This macro integrates the function of opening the Excel file with an X command. If the macro parameter &Excel has been defined as "ON", the user need to manually open the Excel file before submit the SAS program, otherwise the program will open the Excel file. By defining the macro parameter &sleep, the user can specify the number of seconds that a SAS data step is suspended from execution while opening up the Excel file.

- Close Excel window if not comparing the data between Excel and SAS. By defining the macro parameter &debug, the user can control if the Excel file need to leave as open for validation purpose.
- Combine data sets from different sub-sheets. In this step multiple sheets from one Excel file are combined into one SAS data set with the variable FLAG identifying the sheet origin of each record.
- Delete blank records

## CONCLUSION

SDTM Attribute Checking Tool is a handy tool to perform user acceptance checking by end users. For both internal and external CRO SDTM conversion, we can always use the same tool to verify the consistency of the SDTM data. It is a cost effective way to provide greater flexibility to users by providing options to generate customized checks and reports specific to user requirements, both for SDTM domains and for user-defined datasets. Detail implementation of this solution is also available in the macro user menu. Together with SDTM Checker, the whole SDTM validation process can be more complete and thorough. It also keeps users away from tedious work and keeps users focus on other important tasks.

## APPENDIX

CDISC SUBMISSION DATASET DEFINITION METADATA EXAMPLE (STUDY DATA TABULATION MODEL IMPLEMENTATION GUIDE: HUMAN CLINICAL TRAILS. WWW.CDISC.ORG)

| Dataset | Description | Location | Structure | Class | Purpose | Keys |
|---|---|---|---|---|---|---|
| DM | Demographics | dm.xpt | One record per subject | Special Purpose Domains | Tabulation | STUDYID, USUBJID |
| CO | Comments | co.xpt | One record per comment per subject | Special Purpose Domains | Tabulation | STUDYID, USUBJID, COSEQ |
| SE | Subject Elements | se.xpt | One record per actual Element per subject | Special Purpose Domains | Tabulation | STUDYID, USUBJID, ETCD, SESTDTC |
| SV | Subject Visits | sv.xpt | One record per actual visit per subject | Special Purpose Domains | Tabulation | STUDYID, USUBJID, VISITNUM |
| CM | Concomitant Medications | cm.xpt | One record per recorded medication occurrence per subject | Interventions | Tabulation | STUDYID, USUBJID, CMTRT, CMSTDTC |
| EX | Exposure | ex.xpt | One record per constant dosing interval per subject | Interventions | Tabulation | STUDYID, USUBJID, EXTRT, EXSTDTC |
| SU | Substance Use | su.xpt | One record per substance type per reported occurrence per subject | Interventions | Tabulation | STUDYID, USUBJID, SUTRT, SUSTDTC |
| AE | Adverse Events | ae.xpt | One record per adverse event per subject | Events | Tabulation | STUDYID, USUBJID, AEDECOD, AESTDTC |
| DS | Disposition | ds.xpt | One record per disposition status or protocol milestone per subject | Events | Tabulation | STUDYID, USUBJID, DSSTDTC, DSDECOD |
| MH | Medical History | mh.xpt | One record per medical history event per subject | Events | Tabulation | STUDYID, USUBJID, MHDECOD |
| DV | Protocol Deviations | dv.xpt | One record per protocol deviation per subject | Events | Tabulation | STUDYID, USUBJID, DVTERM, DVSTDTC |

# EXAMPLE OF DEMOGRAPHICS

## DM (COPY FROM CDISC.ORG)

dm.xpt, Demographics — Version 3.1.2, February 21 2007. One record per subject, Tabulation

| Variable Name | Variable Label | Type | Controlled Terms, Codelist or Format | Role | CDISC Notes | Core | References |
|---|---|---|---|---|---|---|---|
| STUDYID | Study Identifier | Char | | Identifier | Unique identifier for a study | Req | SDTMIG 2.4.4 |
| DOMAIN | Domain Abbreviation | Char | DM | Identifier | Two-character abbreviation for the domain. | Req | SDTMIG 2.4.4, SDTMIG 4.1.2.2 SDTMIG Appendix C2 |
| USUBJID | Unique Subject Identifier | Char | | Identifier | Identifier used to uniquely identify a subject across all studies for all applications or submissions involving the product. This must be a unique number, and could be a compound identifier formed by concatenating STUDYID-SITEID-SUBJID. | Req | SDTMIG 2.4.4, SDTMIG 4.1.2.3 |
| SUBJID | Subject Identifier for the Study | Char | | Topic | Subject identifier, which must be unique within the study. Often the ID of the subject as recorded on a CRF. | Req | SDTMIG 2.4.4 |
| RFSTDTC | Subject Reference Start Date/Time | Char | ISO 8601 | Record Qualifier | Reference Start Date/time for the subject in ISO 8601 character format. Usually equivalent to date/time when subject was first exposed to study treatment. Required for all randomized subjects; will be null for all subjects who did not meet the milestone the date requires, such as screen failures or unassigned subjects. | Exp | SDTMIG 4.1.4.1 |
| RFENDTC | Subject Reference End Date/Time | Char | ISO 8601 | Record Qualifier | Reference End Date/time for the subject in ISO 8601 character format. Usually equivalent to the date/time when subject was determined to have ended the trial, and often equivalent to date/time of last exposure to study treatment. Required for all randomized subjects; null for screen failures or unassigned subjects. | Exp | SDTMIG 4.1.4.1 |
| SITEID | Study Site Identifier | Char | | Record Qualifier | Unique identifier for a study site. | Req | |
| INVID | Investigator Identifier | Char | | Record Qualifier | An identifier to describe the Investigator for the study. May be used in addition to SITEID. Not needed if SITEID is equivalent to INVID. | Perm | |
| INVNAM | Investigator Name | Char | | Synonym Qualifier | Name of the investigator for a site. | Perm | |

| Variable Name | Variable Label | Type | Controlled Terms, Codelist or Format | Role | CDISC Notes | Core | References |
|---|---|---|---|---|---|---|---|
| BRTHDTC | Date/Time of Birth | Char | ISO 8601 | Record Qualifier | Date/time of birth of the subject. | Perm | SDTMIG 4.1.4.1 |
| AGE | Age | Num | | Record Qualifier | Age expressed in AGEU. Usually derived from RFSTDTC and BRTHDTC, but BRTHDTC may not be available in all cases (due to subject privacy concerns). | Exp | |
| AGEU | Age Units | Char | (AGEU) | Variable Qualifier | Units associated with AGE. | Exp | SDTMIG Appendix C? |
| SEX | Sex | Char | (SEX) | Record Qualifier | Sex of the subject. | Req | |
| RACE | Race | Char | * | Record Qualifier | Race of the subject. Sponsors should refer to "Collection of Race and Ethnicity Data in Clinical Trials" (FDA, September 2005) for guidance regarding the collection of race (http://www.fda.gov/cder/guidance/5656fnl.htm). If multiple race responses are collected and one is designated as the primary race, RACE should hold the primary race. If the primary race was collected via an "Other, Specify" field and the sponsor chooses not to map the value to one of the 5 designated values, then the value of RACE should be 'OTHER'. If multiple races are collected and none is designated as primary, then the value of RACE should be 'MULTIPLE', and the additional information will be included in the Supplemental Qualifiers dataset. If a subject does not provide race information, the value of RACE should be 'UNKNOWN'. | Exp | |
| ETHNIC | Ethnicity | Char | (ETHNIC) | Record Qualifier | The ethnicity of the subject. Sponsors should refer to "Collection of Race and Ethnicity Data in Clinical Trials" (FDA, September 2005) for guidance regarding the collection of ethnicity (http://www.fda.gov/cder/guidance/5656fnl.htm). | Perm | |
| ARMCD | Planned Arm Code | Char | * | Record Qualifier | Short name for ARM (may be up to eight characters). | Req | SDTMIG 4.1.2.1 |
| ARM | Description of Planned Arm | Char | * | Synonym Qualifier | Name of the Arm to which the subject was assigned. | Req | SDTMIG 4.1.2.1, SDTMIG 4.1.2.4 |
| COUNTRY | Country | Char | (COUNTRY) | Record Qualifier | Country of the investigational site in which the subject participated in the trial. | Req | |
| DMDTC | Date/Time of Collection | Char | ISO 8601 | Timing | Date/time of demographic data collection. | Perm | SDTMIG 2.4.5, SDTMIG 4.1.4.1 |
| DMDY | Study Day of Collection | Num | | Timing | Study day of collection measured as integer days. | Perm | SDTMIG 2.4.5, SDTMIG 4.1.4.1 |

* Indicates variable may be subject to controlled terminology. (Parenthesis indicates CDISC/NCI code-list code value)

# EXAMPLE OF COMPARISION RESULT

Discrepancy of extra variable definition

```
Study:  XXXXXX-XXX      11:51 Sunday, May 17, 2009
SDTM Data Vs. Mapping Specification:
List of Variables in SDTMPLUS, but not in Define.xml

Obs  Memname  Name     Label      Vartype
53   SUPPQUAL IDVAR    IDVAR      Char
54   SUPPQUAL IDVARVAL IDVARVAL   Char
55   SUPPQUAL QEVAL    OEVAL      Char
56   SUPPQUAL QLABEL   OLABEL     Char
```

Discrepancy of label

```
Study:  XXXXXX-XXX      19:51 Sunday, May 24, 2009
SDTMPLUS Data Vs. Mapping Specification: List of Variables with
Non-matched Labels

Obs Memname Name     Exllabel           Label
203 CF      CFTEST   Test               CFTEST
204 CF      CFTESTCD Test Short Name    Test Short Name
205 CF      CFTPT    Planned Time       CFTPT
                     Point Name
206 CF      CFTPTNUM Planned Time       CFTPTNUM
                     Point Number
```

Discrepancy of variable length

Study: XXXXXX-XXX 19:51 Sunday, May 24, 2009
SDTMPLUS Data Vs. Mapping Specification: List of Variables with
Non-matched Variable Length

| Obs | Memname | Name | Exltype | Vartype | Exlength | Length |
|-----|---------|--------|---------|---------|----------|--------|
| 749 | QS | QSBLFL | Char | Char | 20 | 1 |
| 750 | QS | QSDRVFL | Char | Char | 20 | 1 |
| 751 | QS | QSDTC | Char | Char | 19 | 16 |
| 753 | QS | QSDTI | Char | Char | 19 | 4000 |

# REFERENCES

[1] Define.xml http://www.cdisc.org/content1057

# Managing Clinical Data Standards: An Introduction to SAS Clinical Data Integration

### Michael Kilhullen

As the adoption of industry data standards grows, organizations must consider how to effectively implement and manage data standards across a large—often global—user base. SAS Clinical Data Integration is built upon a centralized metadata repository that is ideal for centrally deploying and managing data standards. Built on SAS data integration technology, it provides a visual and metadata-driven environment that facilitates the conversion of data to standard formats while collecting more detailed information about the decisions you make during this process. SAS Clinical Data Integration provides specialized interfaces that further leverage the metadata to help you more effectively work with and manage clinical standards. This chapter will present SAS Clinical Data Integration features, including how to import, customize, and manage standards metadata, how to monitor and analyze how users consume metadata during the clinical development process, and how metadata is leveraged to provide consistency and reusability across your organization.

## INTRODUCTION

SAS Clinical Data Integration 2.1 is a new product offering from SAS that focuses on pharmaceutical industry needs for transforming, managing, and verifying the creation of industry mandated data standards such as the Clinical Data Interchange Standards Consortium (CDISC). The product relies on SAS Data Integration to provide centralized metadata management using the SAS Metadata Server and the tools to visually transform data. SAS Clinical Data Integration enhances usability by adding new metadata types, plug-ins, and wizards that assist with clinically oriented tasks such as importing data standards, creating studies and submissions, and adding specialized transformations for transforming clinical data to a standard data model. It also leverages the SAS Clinical Standards Toolkit to provide validation and conformance checking.

## UNDERSTANDING THE CLINICAL METADATA ENVIRONMENT

SAS Clinical Data Integration facilitates the collection and management of metadata across your organization (Figure 1). Most metadata is generated by clinical programmers while they define how the operational data is converted to a data standard. This is a very repeatable process but often needs to be adjusted based on variations in the way that data is collected and analyzed between studies. As multiple studies are processed, the study administrators must ensure that the clinical programmers are creating domain tables that comply with a data standard. As new custom domains are defined, or existing domains are modified, the data standards administrator must be able to understand, evaluate, and potentially apply the changes to the centralized data standards. Finally, a study administrator is likely overseeing several studies that might have different clinical programmers assigned. It is important to maintain a consistent work environment, especially if clinical programmers need to work on studies simultaneously, or transition to a new study more quickly. Moreover, because metadata is being collected at all stages of the process, managers can use metadata to monitor the transformation process and generate reports.

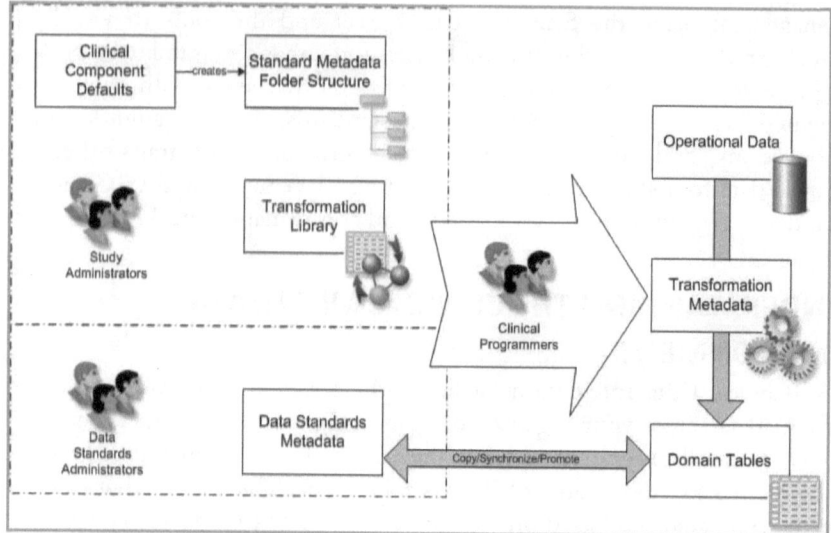

Figure 1: Typical Metadata Collected during a Clinical Trial

In SAS Clinical Data Integration, clinical metadata is stored in the meta-data server as properties of metadata objects. Most metadata is related to creating standardized data and is stored as part of the table and column metadata objects. In some cases, new metadata objects are created to specifically address the business needs of managing standards. For example, studies and submissions have their own metadata representation in the SAS Metadata Server that is based on a common metadata object called a clinical component (Figure 2). In addition to having specialized metadata about the study or submission, clinical metadata objects they also catalog the metadata contents (such as jobs, reports, tables, and so on) created by users, define the versions of standards that are allowed for a study or submission, and enable additional processes such as importing, exporting, and archiving. SAS Clinical Data Integration ensures that data standard domains are implemented only as part of a data standard, study, or submission. When data standard domains are implemented in a data standard, we refer to these as templates because they are used as the basis for the actual data and metadata collected by a study or submission.

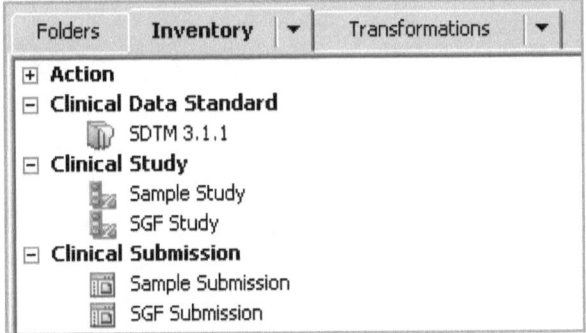

Figure 2: Clinical Metadata Types

# MAINTAINING CONSISTENT METADATA CONTENT

SAS Clinical Data Integration can be configured by an administrator to create default metadata content when clinical components are created (Figure 3). This allows you to maintain consistent content between studies or submissions. For example, the administrator can define a standard metadata folder structure for studies. When the new study wizard finishes, it creates the metadata folders (Figure 4). The administrator can also define standard libraries to ensure that the correct SAS library statements are generated. This scenario is useful when your organization implements standard reporting macros that depend on specific library references to gain access to data and store results. Notice in Figure 4 that the library reference names are updated to include the study name to promote better usability when you need to select a library from a list of all library objects.

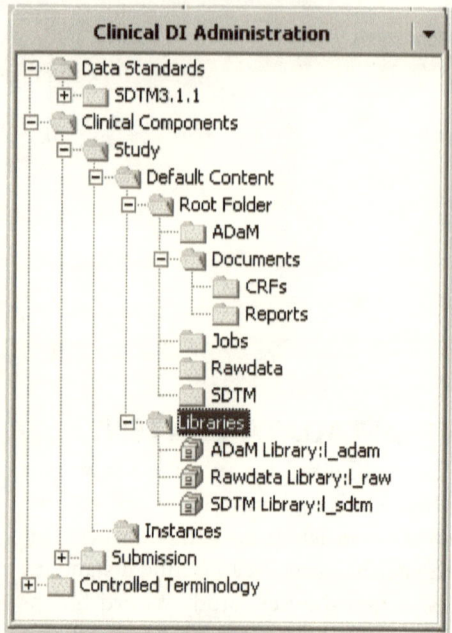

Figure 3: Default Content Defined for Studies

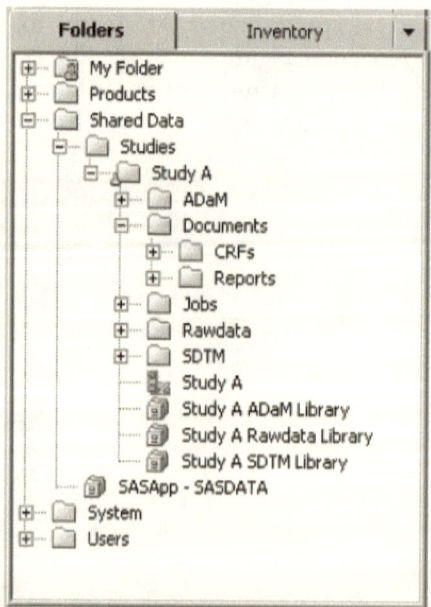

Figure 4: Content Created for a New Study Based on Defaults

In addition to default content, SAS Clinical Data Integration also helps manage the clinical content within a folder. As a best practice, a folder should contain tables with the same type of data, and typically should use the same SAS library for physical storage. This means that you should not find CDISC Study Data Tabulation Model (SDTM) tables mixed with CDISC Analysis Data Model (ADaM) tables in the same folder. (Figure 4 reflects this best practice). SAS Clinical Data Integration plug-ins enforce this rule by defaulting selection windows based on existing content within the selected folder. For example, once a domain is created using the SDTM 3.1.1 data standard, only new domains based on the same standard version can be added to the folder.

## WORKING WITH DATA STANDARD METADATA

Data standards are managed exclusively in the SAS Metadata Server. Therefore, every user of SAS Clinical Data Integration has access to the same domain templates, validation checks, and terminology. All data standard related plug-ins are designed to use the centralized metadata and help simplify creating domains during study transformations (Figure 5). Clinical programmers do not need to figure out where the standards are stored or which standards to use for a particular study. Instead, the study manager defines these settings as part of the study definition and the plug-ins ensure that only applicable standards are displayed to programmers. For example, if a Study Manager defines the study to use SDTM version 3.1.2, the SAS Clinical Data Integration plug-ins will not display any other SDTM versions.

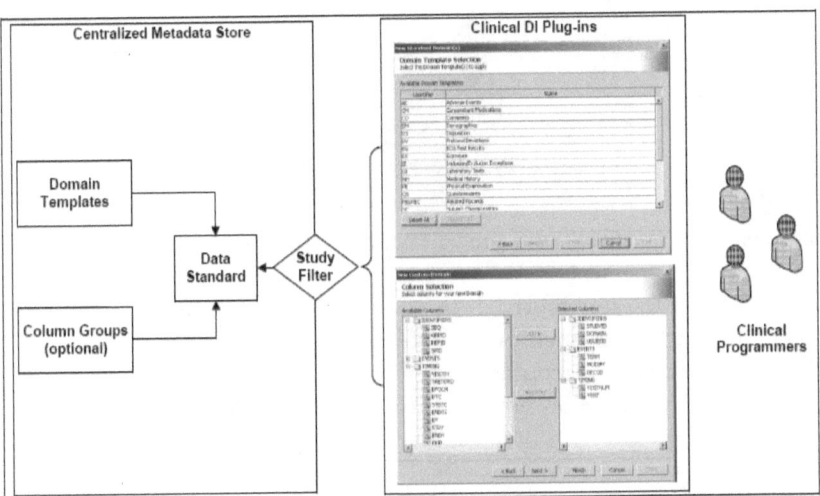

Figure 5: Example of Leveraging Centralized Data Standards with Plug-ins

Accessing the domain or domain template metadata is the same for administrators and programmers. Clinical metadata is accessible through standard SAS Data Integration Studio dialog boxes that are enhanced by SAS Clinical Data Integration plug-ins. Additional tabs are added where the clinical metadata is displayed (Figure 6). If you have edit permissions, then you can change the values of the clinical metadata. Changes are considered study or submission specific. That is, changes do not propagate back to the data standard template. The same is true of changes to data standard templates; they do not propagate to registered domains. Other tools are available in SAS Clinical Data Integration to compare domains to templates and selectively apply changes if needed.

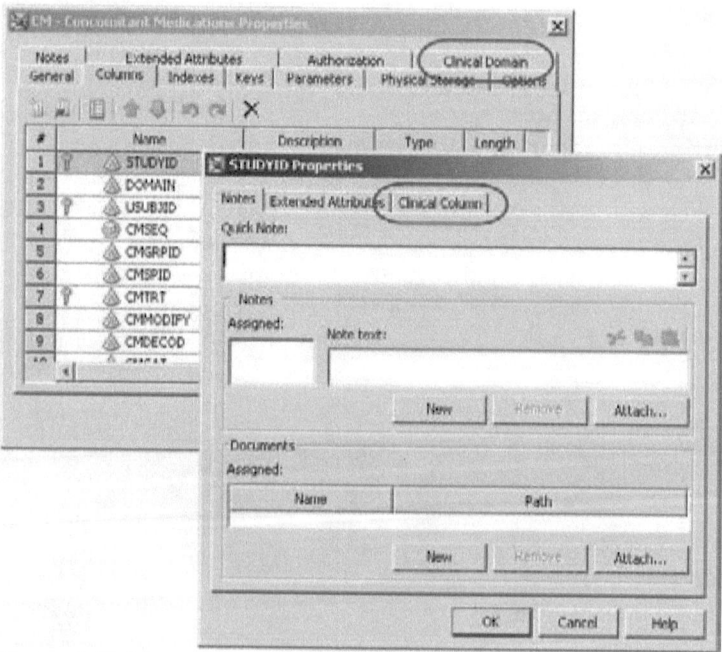

Figure 6: Table and Column Clinical Properties

Clinical properties are displayed on property tabs as a table (Figure 7). Depending on how properties are defined, they might be displayed as a text or a selection list. Properties will have default settings, but you can adjust them depending on how you use the standards in your organization.

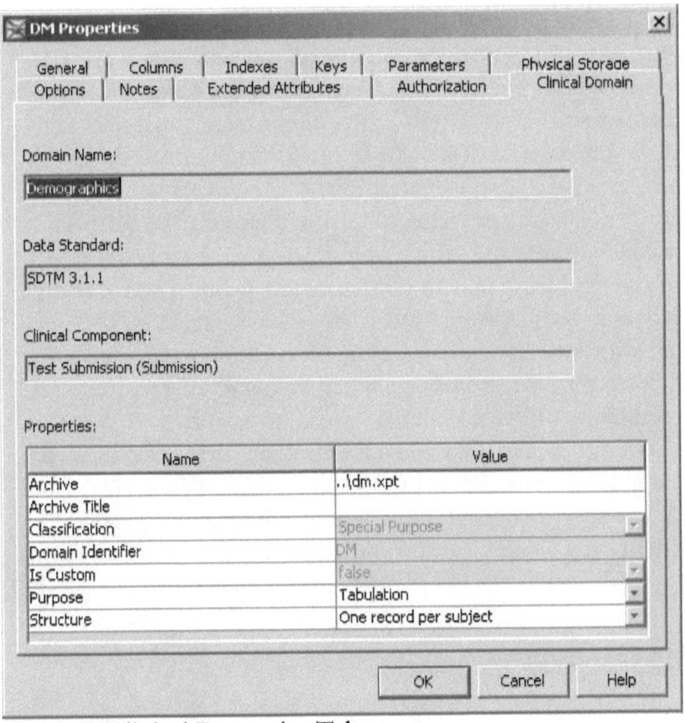

Figure 7: Clinical Properties Tab

SAS Clinical Data Integration supports a common property model for data standards, studies, submissions, and domains. The property model is largely based on the SDTM. However, it has been generalized so that you can add your own modified SDTM implementations or internal data standards. The properties collected for clinical objects are summarized in Table 1. In addition, you can add custom properties and notes to any metadata object.

| Clinical Metadata Type | Additional Properties Managed by SAS Clinical Data Integration |
|---|---|
| Data Standard | Formal name, version, type, base standard type, vendor, supports toolkit validation |
| Study | Study title, short study title, phase |
| Submission | Submission title, short submission title |
| Domain | Identifier, purpose, classification, structure, archive location, archive title |
| Domain column | Term, origin, role, core, display format, qualifiers, XML type, XML codelist, algorithm, whether the column contributes to the key |

Table 1: Additional Properties Available for Clinical Objects

## CONTROLLING HOW PROPERTIES ARE USED

While the CDISC data standards dictate what you need to collect, and in some cases what a property should contain, how your company uses a data standard will vary depending on how well the data standard integrates into your established business processes. In some cases, the values are strictly implemented. That is, clinical programmers can select only from a list of allowable values. If a value is not found, you need to contact the data standards administrator to add the content. When the data standards administrator adds the value, you can then edit the properties and select the value. Other companies prefer a less strict approach. If a value is not available in a list, you can type in a new value. The value you provide is considered study specific and does not propagate to the data standard. Rather, the data standards administrator periodically evaluates the values used for a property across many studies and adjusts the standard values accordingly. Other companies prefer to simply have the user type in values without a list. Whichever approach fits your business needs, SAS Clinical Data Integration provides the flexibility to allow you to define how a property is collected, including whether the property is required, dependent on a lookup list, customizable by the user, and so on (Figure 8).

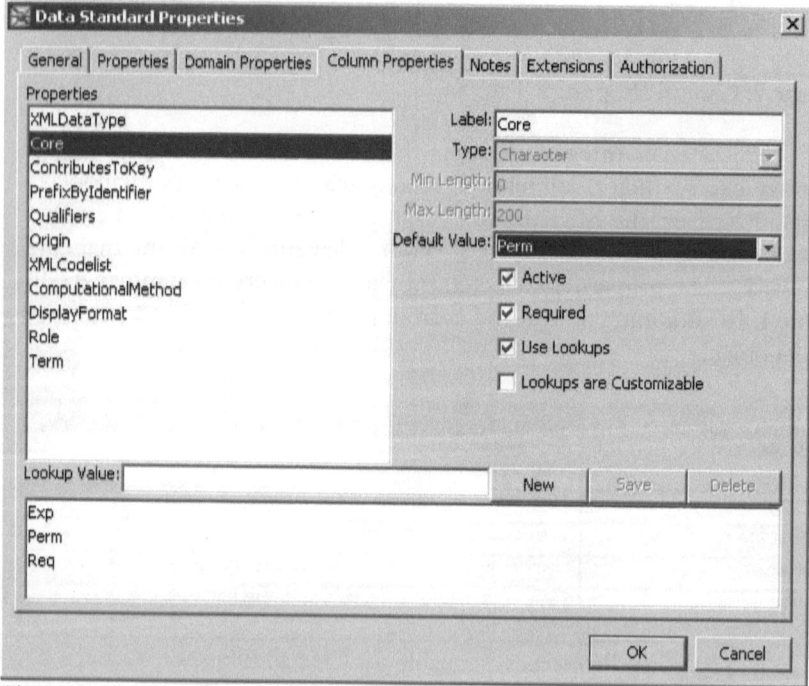

Figure 8: Column Property Model Editor

## CREATING CUSTOM DOMAINS

Certain CDISC standards, such as SDTM, support user-defined domains, which are domains needed for clinical data that is not defined as a standard domain in the SDTM implementation guide. In this case, the underlying data model is used to assemble the new domain (Figure 9). Data models are generalized into column groups that can support both industry standards and vendor-specific data standards. Column groups are simply a logical grouping of columns that are combined and organized into a domain. The columns within a column group will also contain default metadata values, which will be copied to the new domain when created.

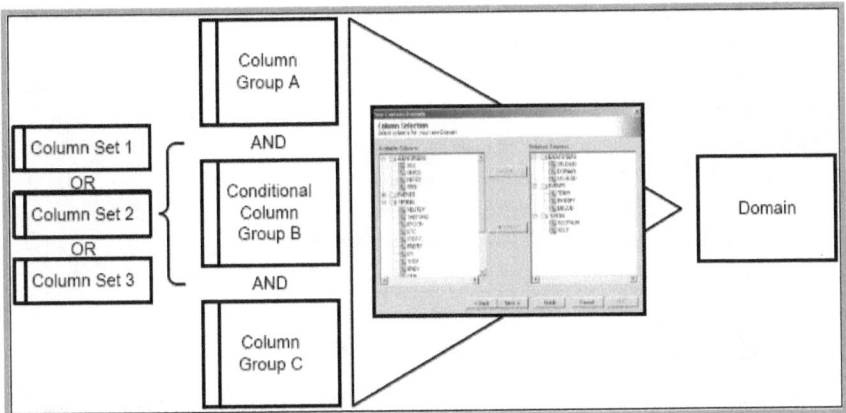

Figure 9: Assembling Column Groups into a Domain

Column groups can also be considered conditional. That is, columns can be selected from one column set within the conditional column group but not another column group. This would be the case for SDTM where a domain can contain only intervention, event, or finding columns, in addition to identifier and timing columns.

If a data standard uses an underlying model, SAS Clinical Data Integration provides a wizard to guide you in defining the custom domain. Data standard administrators can use the same wizard to design new domain templates. Alternatively, they can identify and promote custom domains defined by users in studies and submissions to the data standard. Finally, you might know of a custom domain created for another study that has not been promoted to a data standard. Rather than recreate it, SAS Clinical Data Integration can copy it as long as it is based on the same data standard version used by your study. In doing this, metadata settings are preserved and the necessary metadata relationships to the new study are automatically adjusted.

## SYNCHRONIZING DOMAIN METADATA

When domains are created in a study or submission, the metadata stored in the data standard templates are copied. This allows users to modify the metadata according to the study requirements without impacting the metadata that others might be using for other studies. This, of course, means that clinical programmers can change any attribute of the domain, including labels, lengths, formats, types, and column order. Furthermore, after the domain is copied, the data standards administrator might change the template metadata based on trends in how it was used in other studies. For example, it is common to adjust character column lengths to avoid truncation in a study that collected more text. If the standard administrators find that programmers are frequently changing the length, they can change the length in the domain template so that manual adjustments are no longer necessary. SAS Clinical Data Integration provides a refresh domain plug-in that compares a domain with the data standard template used to create it (Figure 10). It will identify differences found and allow the clinical programmer to choose which changes to apply to the domain.

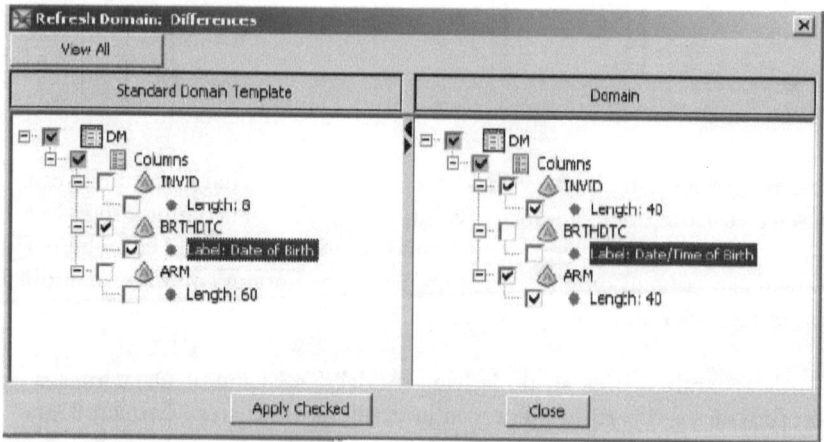

Figure 10: Refresh Domain Metadata

## ANALYZING THE USE OF CLINICAL DATA STANDARDS

As data standards are consumed by your organization, a data standards administrator can monitor how the data standards are being used. SAS Clinical Data Integration makes this easy because of the wealth of metadata collected about standards and how they are used. The data standards administrator can select from a list of clinical components that are based on the data standard selected. The metadata about the domains created are compared and displayed in a table that shows you what columns were used in the domains across the clinical components. This will be useful when clinical programmers are consistently adding new columns and you need to make a decision about adding one to the domain template. Finally, custom domains are also displayed in the comparison so that you can see which custom domains are being added frequently to clinical components. In this case, the data standards administrator can choose to promote the custom domain. This will add the metadata for the selected custom domain to the data standard, making it easier for other programmers to create it.

## LEVERAGING THE SAS CLINICAL STANDARDS TOOLKIT

The SAS Clinical Standards Toolkit is a SAS macro approach to supporting clinical data standards in Base SAS. It supports defining data standard domains, conversion of domains between CDISC models, and validation and conformance checks. It provides periodic updates when new standards and new versions of standards are released. Once the updates are applied to the toolkit, they are automatically detected by SAS Clinical Data Integration during the import and validation processes.

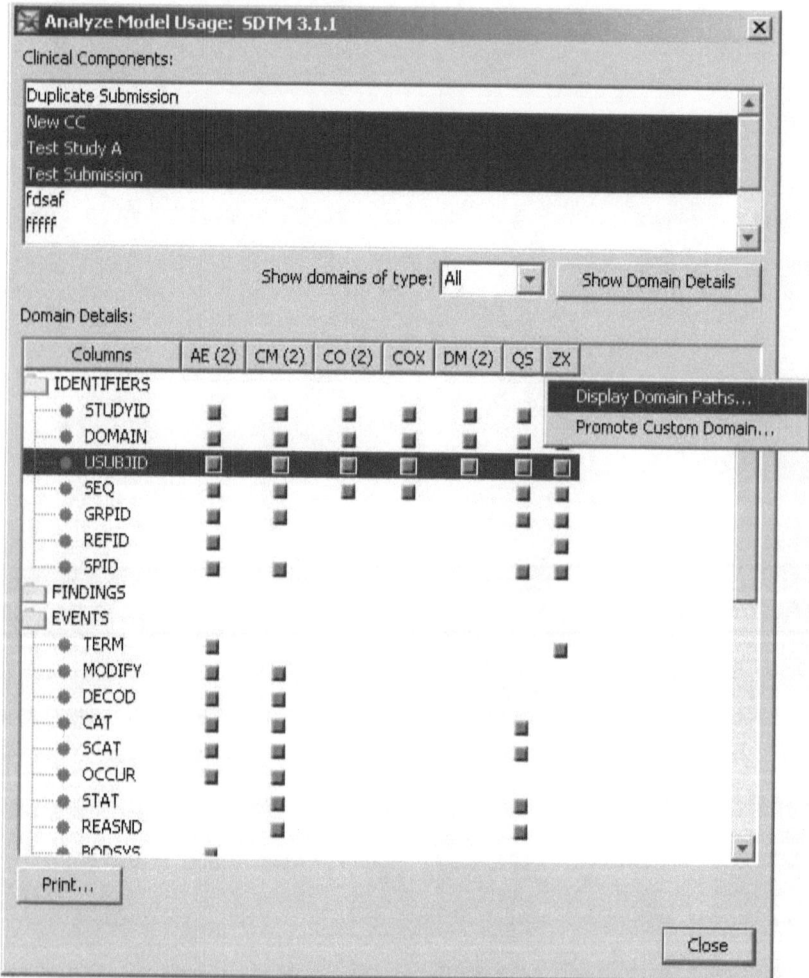

Figure 11: Analyzing How Standards Are Being Used

SAS Clinical Data Integration greatly simplifies the use of the SAS Clinical Standards Toolkit. First, it assumes control of all clinical metadata.

This means that once metadata is imported from the SAS Clinical Standards Toolkit, the powerful features found in SAS Clinical Data Integration are used to manage the data standard definitions. When the SAS Clinical Standards Toolkit macros are used in the transformation process, the metadata needed by the SAS Clinical Standards Toolkit is automatically exported and restructured for execution. Secondly, SAS Clinical Data Integration adds graphical user interfaces to SAS Clinical Standards Toolkit macros. This adds a metadata-driven approach to defining SAS Clinical Standards Toolkit tasks. Finally, validation checks and terminology are also imported into the metadata server and are displayed as manageable objects in the clinical administration interfaces.

## IMPORTING DATA STANDARDS METADATA

SAS Clinical Data Integration provides a Data Standards Metadata Import Wizard to help data standards administrators select and load metadata. This is a one-time process per model version; once metadata loaded, the SAS Metadata Server manages changes and additions to the data standards. The wizard prompts you to select the standard and version from the toolkit, displays the metadata content in detail for verification, and then imports the metadata (Figure 12). Once imported, the standard and domain templates are surfaced through SAS Clinical Data Integration Server plug-ins. Custom versions of standards can also be imported from the SAS Clinical Standards Toolkit. Assuming that the custom data standard is registered to SAS Clinical Standards Toolkit, when the metadata import wizard is run, the custom data standard will automatically appear in the data standard selection lists.

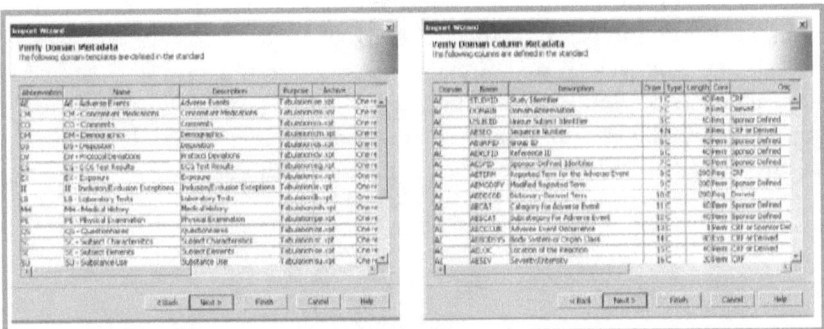

Figure 12: Sample Displays from the Metadata Importer

## VALIDATING DOMAIN CONTENT AND STRUCTURE

As data standard domains are implemented in studies and submissions, the structure and content can vary from the data standard. You must periodically verify that the domains maintain conformance to the data standard. SAS Clinical Data Integration provides a transformation to run validation checks and generate reports through the SAS Clinical Standards Toolkit. The SAS Clinical Standards Toolkit provides 143 unique SDTM 3.1.1 validation checks. These checks are derived from three sources: the CDISC-SDTM WebSDM™ documented checks, checks supporting loads into the Janus study data repository, and checks added by SAS which are based on data management and cleansing experiences building CDISC-SDTM domains using SAS products and solutions. The validation checks are designed to enable an assessment of the consistency of data values within a specific column, between columns, across records within a specific data set, and across data sets. In addition to the provided validation checks, the data standards administrators can create their own customized compliance checks using the Manage Compliance Checks dialog box (Figure 13).

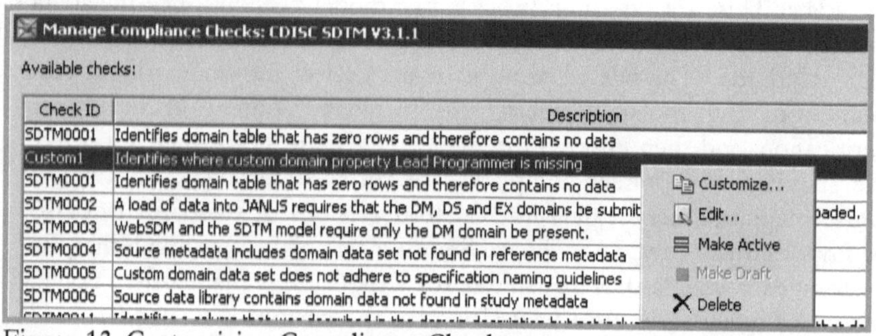

Figure 13: Customizing Compliance Checks

The CDISC-SDTM Compliance transformation is provided for use in building validation jobs. You specify the data standard you wish to validate against, and select the domains to be assessed and the set of compliance checks you wish to run (Figure 14). The model compliance transformation allows you to add as many checks as desired. It also offers filtering capabilities to help find the necessary checks.

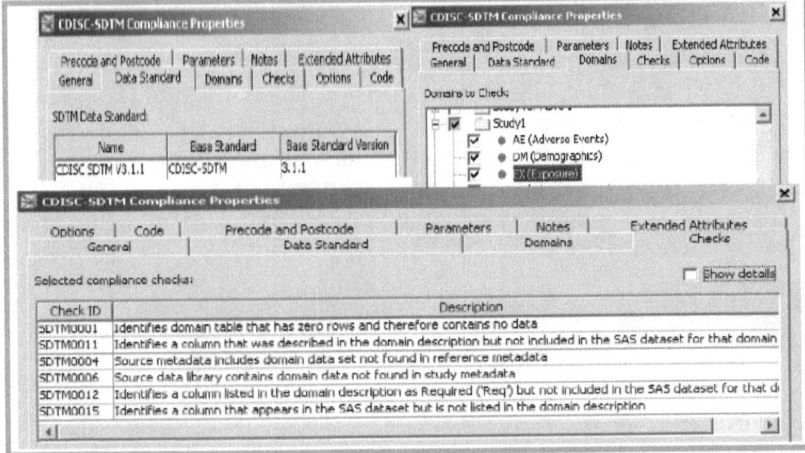

Figure 14: Examples of the CDISC-SDTM Compliance Transformation

After the job runs, two data sets are produced. The results data set contains the findings of the compliance assessment and the metrics data set contains summary statistics on the validation process (Figure 15).

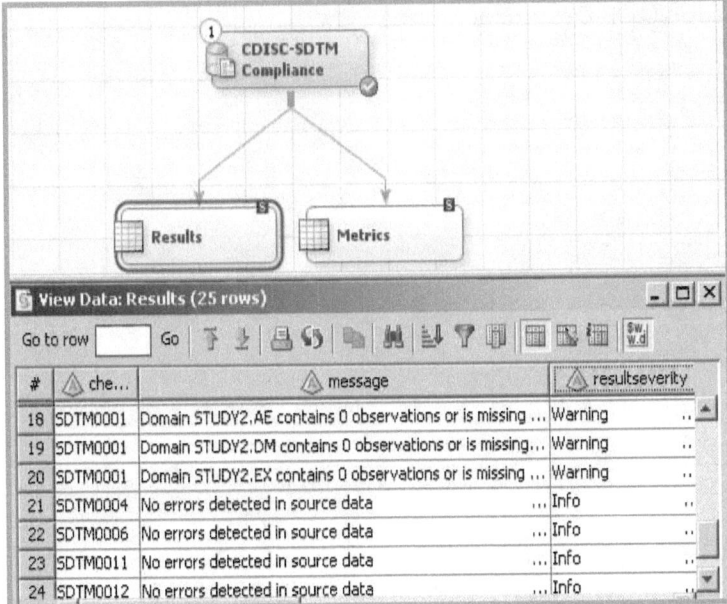

Figure 15: CDISC–SDTM Compliance Transformation and Results Data Set

## GENERATING CRT-DDS

The metadata managed by SAS Clinical Data Integration can be published to CRT-DDS using the CRT-DDS Transformation (Figure 16). This transformation extracts metadata and passes it on to the SAS Clinical Data Standards Toolkit for define.xml creation. The transformation allows you to specify properties to control encoding, log level processing, and an output style sheet (Figure 17).

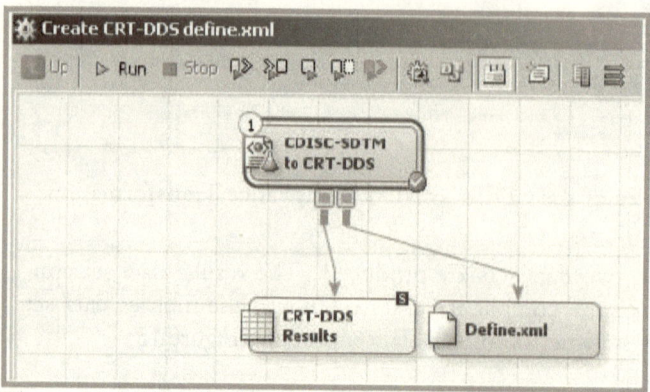

Figure 16: CRT-DDS Define.xml Process Flow

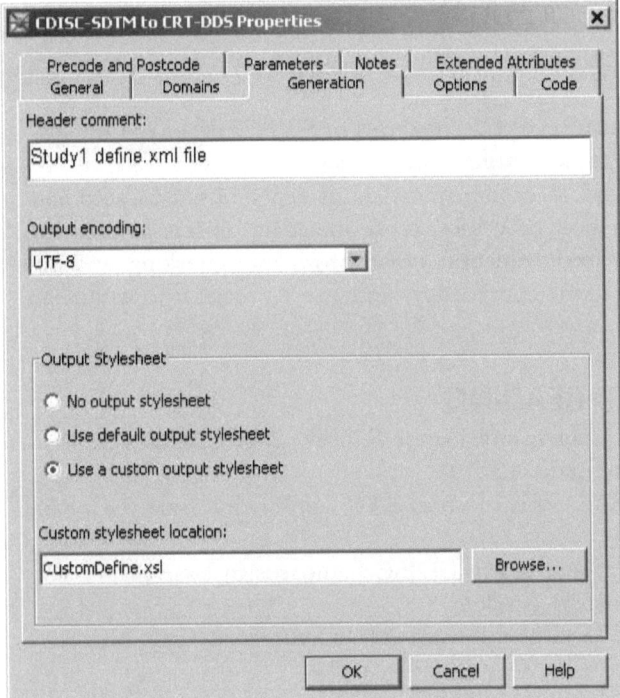

Figure 17: CDISC-SDTM to CRT-DDS Transformation Properties

After the job runs, a define.xml file and a results data set are produced. The Results data set documents the results of the generation of the CRT-DDS file. The define.xml file contains summary information about each of the domain data sets, detailed information about each column in each domain, and code list information (Figure 18).

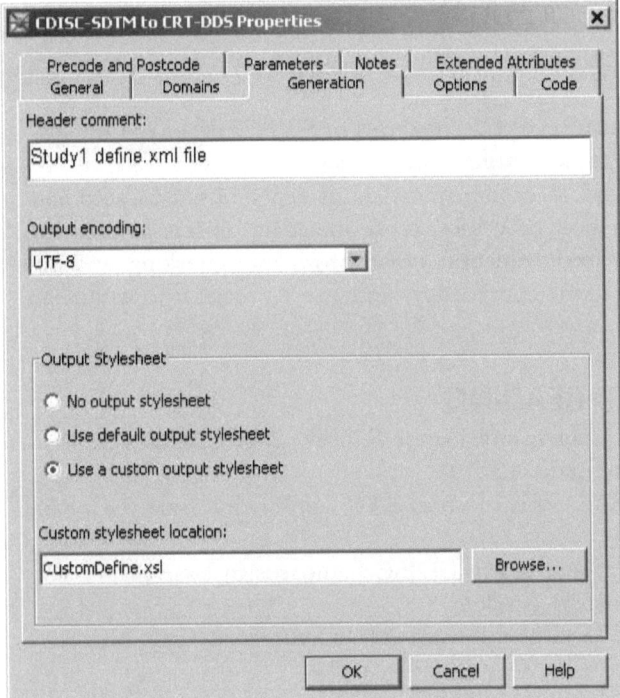

Figure 18: Examples of CRT-DDS

## CONCLUSION

This chapter has shown several key features of SAS Clinical Data Integration 2.1 related to implementing and managing CDISC standards. By centrally collecting and managing metadata, it can be used to automate setup and transformation processes, reuse metadata objects to expedite data standardization, feed validation and conformance checking, and improve the administration, consistency, and use of standards within an organization.

## RECOMMENDED READING

Hunley, Eric, Gary Mehler, and Nancy Rausch. 2009. "What's New in SAS Data Integration Studio 4.2"
Proceedings of the SAS Global Forum 2009 Conference. Cary, NC: SAS Institute Inc.
Villiers, Peter. 2009. "Supporting CDISC Standards in Base SAS Using the SAS Clinical Standards Toolkit."
Proceedings of the SAS Global Forum 2009 Conference. Cary, NC: SAS Institute Inc.

# eleven

# A Tiptoe through the Tagset Field

### Michael Molter

The flexibility that the markup destination has added to ODS is comparable to the benefits ODS originally brought to SAS output, but it comes at a price known as the tagset. With ODS, we could display results in web pages without HTML knowledge; in Word without RTF knowledge. Developers soon realized though that having ODS do all the work was not always ideal; that on occasion, users could benefit from having some control over how markup was generated. Just as templates instruct ODS on display customization, tagsets instruct ODS on markup customization. The advantages are clear – even more flexibility in the generation of output. The price is similar to that paid for display flexibility – more TEMPLATE procedure syntax, and an understanding of how ODS constructs files from these instructions.

Great accomplishments often come from modest beginnings. This chapter is your modest beginning. From the edge of the field we will get "the lay of the land" with discussions on background, purpose, and use with the markup destination. With one foot in the field we will look at examples of markup that require slight tweaking and available documentation to guide us. Further into the field, we will produce simple informational tagsets, and inch out further with tagsets that inherit and manipulate those that SAS provides. By the end of the chapter, the reader will see in the distance many undiscovered areas, but hopefully the curiosity generated by the path taken thus far will lead to further exploration and bridges to greater accomplishments.

## INTRODUCTION

Let's face it, the Output Delivery System (ODS) has spoiled us, and in many ways. For starters, there was flexibility in file formats. For years, the use of long DATA steps with lots of PUT statements was how output was delivered to word processing or spreadsheet programs. When the output came from PROCs, this took place only after the output was collected from the PROC, manipulated, and organized in a data set in a way that optimized the delivery of the output. Significant trial and error in order to place the output in the exact right spot was also common. An alternative was to use the ASCII-based output file that SAS produced. With ODS and these "things" called "destinations", we could, with some simple syntax, have the best of both worlds — we could use the PROC output produced by SAS, but deliver it, instead of to an ASCII file, to other formats such as Word, PDF, HTML, and others. In addition, ODS gave us something we never had before — control over certain aspects of the output — particularly, how a table was laid out, and the appearance or style attributes of the file. With some knowledge of the TEMPLATE procedure and how a file or a table was broken into "pieces" (elements), we could create global templates that, when specified as part of the simple ODS syntax, would define how the file looked. Additionally, some PROCs allowed for "inline" styling that would remove the need for a global template. With the ability to deliver SAS output to different file formats without tedious DATA steps, and the additional freedom to customize its appearance, the world of SAS output was a better place to be.

## CONTROL VS. CONVENIENCE

The beauty of it all was in what I call the "magic of ODS." All we had to do was to learn more SAS syntax. We could create and customize an HTML file without knowing anything about HTML; a Word file without knowing about RTF. By creating one global template with syntax defined by SAS, ODS knew how to translate it into the language of our choice. It's the same convenience we enjoy when we go to a restaurant and pay someone to cook our dinner and bring it to us, or when we pay someone to fix our car when it needs repairs. Not only does it save us work, but sometimes we may be letting someone more knowledgeable than ourselves complete the necessary task.

One person's convenience, though, is another person's loss of control. While one is comforted by the fact that an expert mechanic is fixing their car, another feels helpless handing the reins over to someone else - not knowing exactly how each decision is made, what the quality and the cost of each part is, how much caution is being exercised. By creating and then using style and table templates or inline styling, we are asking ODS to translate PROC TEMPLATE (or other procedures) syntax into the destination language in the area of the file where styles or tables are created. Other areas unrelated to styles and tables are untouchable. To many, allowing ODS to be the "mechanic" is all they need, but another group of programmers has evolved since the original days of ODS. These programmers prefer to bypass the "interpreter", "speak" in the native language themselves, and have access to any part of the file. They sacrifice the convenience of a tool that works for all destinations in favor of infinite control of a destination of their choice. The tagset is their means for gaining this control.

## SCOPE

This chapter is intended to get your feet wet by introducing the tagset to you as a means of fixing the flaws in your ODS output. The object of this chapter is a soft, gentle introduction to tagsets. Most SAS users have a need for procedure output, and yet tagsets and the Markup destination are still in relatively early stages of development. Many users have heard nothing about tagsets. Many who have, know of a reputation of being difficult to program. Putting these facts together, it's reasonable to wonder how many programmers are producing less-than-ideal output that they do not realize can be customized or do not know how to. In this chapter we will discuss the basic concept and structure of a tagset. Moving past the abstract and into the concrete, we will then look at examples of output from tagsets supplied to us from SAS, identify candidates for customization within each, and develop resources (including other tagsets) to help us identify what part of the tagset was responsible for those areas. With some background on terminology and syntax, we will inherit the original tagset and modify it to produce the desired text.

Tagsets offer us something we have never had before – control over any or all of the text (markup) that makes up the file being produced. As you can imagine, this has broad implications, well beyond this chapter's scope of customizing ODS output. For the most part, we will stick to discussions about statements, options, syntax, variables, and other tools that are relevant to our examples. We will also be focusing mostly on making small modifications to pre-existing tagsets through inheritance. Tagsets that are built "from scratch" or almost from scratch, such as those supplied by SAS, require a thorough knowledge of the steps that ODS takes to create a file and the relationship between ODS and the PROC. Though this will be briefly discussed in this chapter, a detailed discussion is beyond our scope. Hopefully, such knowledge can be accumulated with experience. Finally, even further beyond our scope, as we move into

SAS version 9.1 and later 9.2, tagsets begin to form the basis of the new graphic templates. Beyond ODS, they are used with the XML Libname engine as well as the creation of files from the CDISC procedure.

You will also notice that most of the examples use HTML. This is not to suggest that HTML is the only markup tagsets can generate. On the contrary, text that constitutes valid RTF that Word can read, or valid XML that Excel can read, or any other markup, can be generated just as easily in the same way that HTML is generated. Version 9.1 however does not have usable RTF tagsets from which we can inherit. While a discussion of HTML or any other markup is beyond our scope, the reader that is unfamiliar with HTML will be glad to know that the examples in this chapter require very little if any HTML knowledge. What is necessary to know will be explained. The examples in this chapter assume version 9.1.3.

## CONCEPTS

What do you think of when you think of the PRINT procedure? What kind of display do you associate with code such as the following?

```
proc print noobs data=sashelp.class(obs=10) ;
var name sex age height weight ;
run;
```

Most likely, you picture something that resembles Figure 1.

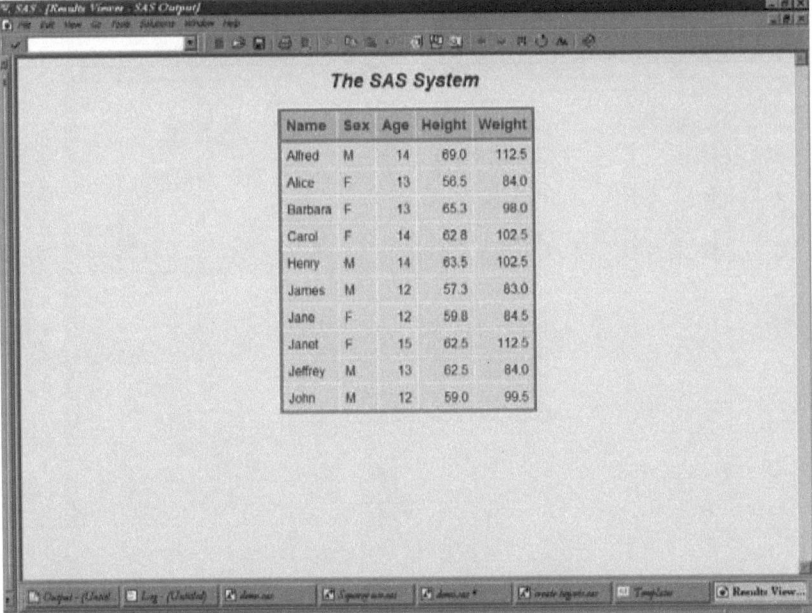

Figure 1

And why wouldn't you? Everything you can do in PROC PRINT is designed with this type of output in mind. The VAR statement allows you, the user, to decide what the columns are, or, put another way, how data is laid out horizontally across a page. Style attribute syntax (not seen in this example) controls aspects of the report such as colors, fonts, column width, and cell alignment.

Counter to every pre-conceived notion about what PROC PRINT output should look like, Figures 2 through 4 also illustrate snippets of output from the code above. How can this be? Let's first look at Figures 2 and 3.

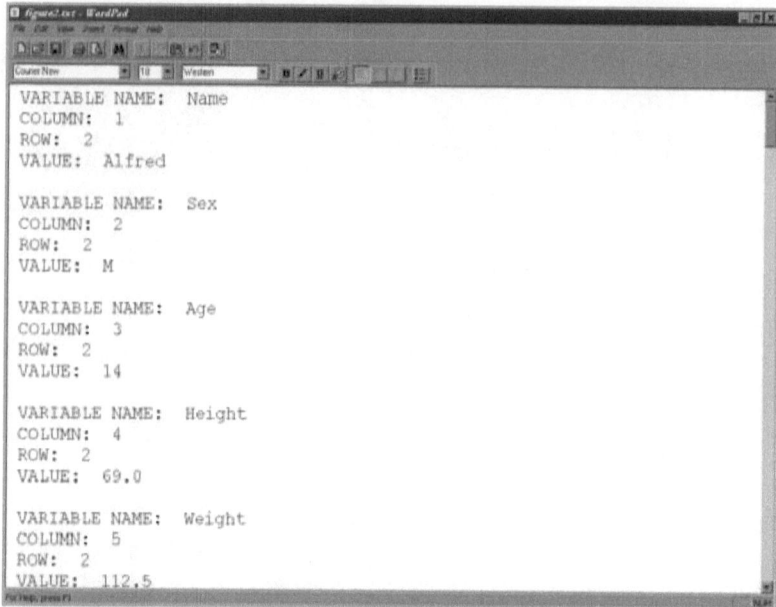

Figure 2

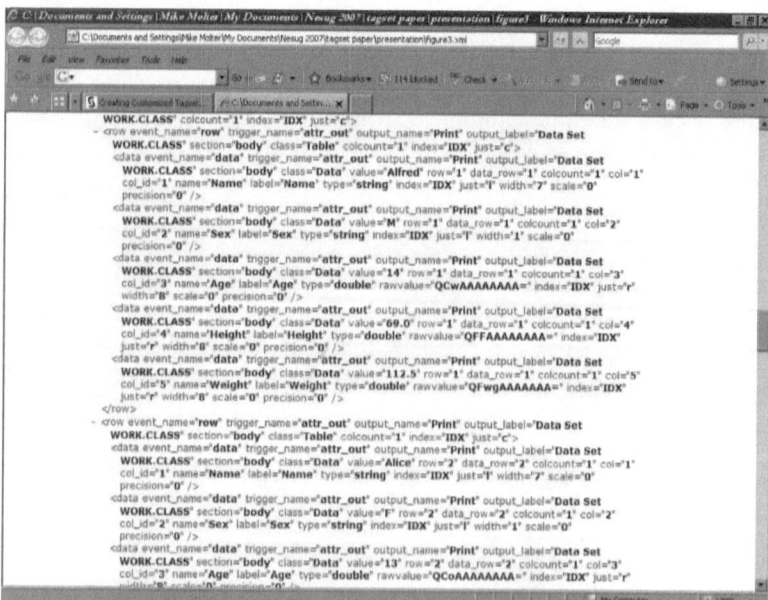

Figure 3

By comparing each of these to Figure 1 above, you will notice (if you look carefully) that the data is there. The problem is that despite telling PROC PRINT exactly how we want columns laid out with the VAR statement, neither of these outputs has columns, or at least, columns that are in one-to-one correspondence with the variables listed in the VAR statement. Figure 4 is even more counter-intuitive.

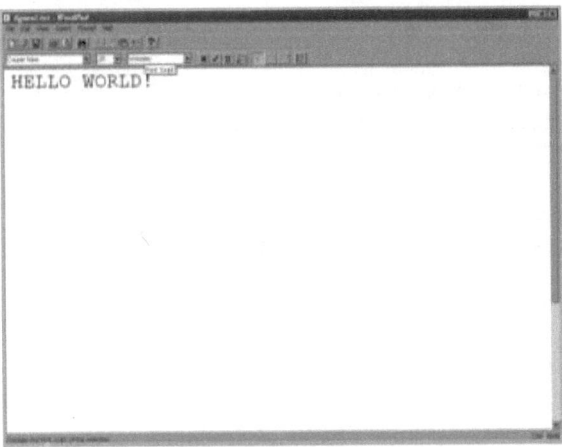

Figure 4

Not only are there no columns, there is not even any data! The statements whose purpose is to lay out the display of the table appear to be having no effect.

Our surprise at the results illustrated by Figures 2 thru 4 speaks to our natural tendency to confuse the roles of ODS with the PROC. These figures help point us in the right direction. The job of the PROC is to analyze the data, and in the case of PROC PRINT, to lay out the table. Like an advisor to the president, the PROC then delivers this information to ODS. Of course the president has several advisors. Continuing with this analogy, ODS has input coming from other sources such as global statements (e.g. TITLE statements, OPTIONS statements, ODS statements, etc.). In the end, just like the president, the decision rests with ODS as to how to use this information, and ultimately, as its name implies, to deliver the output. In the early days of ODS, this was done with the magic of ODS – a gap in our knowledge about the spectrum that starts with raw data and ends with deliverable output. Now, and more so in the future, the tagset is available for users to provide instructions to ODS on how to use and deliver the output.

Incidentally, let's make sure we understand exactly what this "output" is. Let's return to Figure 1. We are tempted to say that this is produced by ODS, but the truth is that this is produced by a program such as Internet Explorer, Microsoft Word, or Adobe Acrobat that reads the "real" file and displays it in its own way. To see this "real" file, open the same file with Notepad. The text you see in this view of the file is called markup. Figure 5 illustrates a snippet of the HTML markup that Internet Explorer interprets as Figure 1. Markup is a text file that contains not only the text you see through the viewing program (e.g. Internet Explorer), but also special instructions called tags that do not show up in the viewing program's view, but that the viewing program uses to display the file. HTML uses angle brackets to surround its tags. A tagset is a SAS file that provides instructions to ODS on how to generate text. To customize something like HTML, we simply customize the markup being generated.

```
figure1.html - Notepad
File  Edit  Format  View  Help
<col>
<col>
<col>
</colgroup>
<thead>
<tr>
<th class="l Header"  scope="col">Name</th>
<th class="c Header"  scope="col">Sex</th>
<th class="c Header"  scope="col">Age</th>
<th class="c Header"  scope="col">Height</th>
<th class="c Header"  scope="col">weight</th>
</tr>
</thead>
<tbody>
<tr>
<td class="l Data">Alfred</td>
<td class="l Data">M</td>
<td class="r Data">14</td>
<td class="r Data">69.0</td>
<td class="r Data">112.5</td>
```

Figure 5

## THE EVENT MODEL

So delivering output really means generating text, but what do we mean by "instructions to ODS on how to use and deliver output"? If all we are dealing with is a text file, then all we need is FILE and PUT statements, right? With this approach, however, we end up building the file manually by ourselves – we provide all the markup to create a table, its column headers, the correct number of rows and columns, even the cell content itself. All of this is information generated by the PROC, but with this approach, we can only capture it by running the PROC, dumping the information to a data set, and then reading it with a DATA step. Tagsets, on the other hand, allow us to define general rules for generating separate pieces of the text. For example, if we are creating a table that has five columns, we define in the tagset a general rule for creating the markup that defines a column, and ODS knows (from the PROC) to apply that rule five times, and when to apply it. Each of these rules is called an event. ODS creates a file in a sequence of discrete steps, each of which calls an event. When the ODS statement is issued, a certain boiler plate of events is called, starting with INITIALIZE, then DOC, and a few more. After that, the PROC is processed and more events are called. These events transfer information such as data values, column and row numbers, style attributes, etc, from the PROC to the markup by way of event variables. Just as PUT statements in a DATA step write text as a combination of literal text and the values of data set variables, the tagset event uses PUT to write markup as a combination of literal text (e.g. tags) and information passed to the event by the PROC through event variables.

The tagset is a mechanism for the modular definition of output generation that allows us to take full advantage of information gathered by the PROC while it is processing. "Modular definition" here refers to the event model – defining each piece of output independent of each other. A tagset is simply a collection of events that together define the entire file. Its modular nature allows us to modify one piece without affecting the others. This is done through inheritance and redefining an event in the same way we inherit style templates to modify individual style elements. "Taking full advantage of information gathered by the PROC while it is processing" means that through the event, we simply tell ODS "here's how to generate this text." When to generate it and how often is left up to ODS and the PROC. Additionally, the text itself does not all have to be literal. By supplying event variable names in the PUT statements in the same way we supply data set variable names in PUT statements in a DATA step, we can generate dynamic text that only the PROC knows. Maybe most importantly, this can be done while the PROC processes, rather than with a DATA step after the PROC has finished processing.

## CHALLENGES AHEAD

We have discussed the event in theoretical terms, but to use the event to tell ODS what to do at certain steps in the process requires something more concrete. What are the names of the events, and in what order are they used? Armed with this knowledge and central to our efforts in this chapter, how do we associate a part of the output with an event? Once we have that, what tools are at our disposal? What are the names of the event variables? For which events does any given variable carry useful information, and for how long is this information available? In the following sections we will use the answers to these questions to begin building our own tagsets.

## BUILDING THE TOOLBOX

As is the case with table and style templates, tagsets are stored in template stores. A template store is a unit of storage specifically for templates and tagsets that, like Windows directories, allows for directory structures within itself. SAS ships two template stores for our use: TMPLMST, a read-only store in the SASHELP library that contains all the SAS-supplied tagsets in a directory called TAGSETS; and TEMPLAT, a read-write store in the SASUSER library. We use the ODS PATH statement to tell ODS which store to either look for a tagset we are trying to use or save a tagset we are trying to create (unless overridden by the STORE= option on the DEFINE TAGSET statement). Each store is specified as a two-level name beginning with the libref associated with the directory in which the store is located, followed by a period and then the name of the store. If multiple stores are listed, ODS will search for tagsets in stores in the order in which they are listed. When creating a tagset, if the first write-access store listed on the ODS PATH statement does not exist, the store will be created. When no ODS PATH statement is used, the implied order is SASHELP.TMPLMST followed by SASUSER.TEMPLAT. One can view a tagset definition (SAS-supplied or user- created) by clicking in the Results window in PC SAS, clicking the View menu, and choosing Templates. The template stores will be listed in the left frame. By expanding the SASHELP.TMPLMST store, one will see folders, most of which contain table templates, but one, Tagsets, that contains tagset definitions. By expanding this folder and double-clicking any of the tagsets on the right side, the definition can be browsed.

## USING TAGSETS

Three different methods exist for using a tagset for ODS output, one of which you may have used before without knowing it. Certain ODS destinations call a tagset behind the scenes. Examples of such destinations include PHTML, HTML4, and CSV.

A second method is available when your tagsets are stored in subdirectories within the template store. When this is the case, you can specify the path within the store as if it were another destination. Consider the following statements.

```
libname mypath "c:\my documents" ;
ods path sashelp.tmplmst(read) mypath.tagstore(update) ;
ods mytags.tag1 file="using_tag1.html" ;
```

In the third statement, SAS is looking for a tagset called TAG1 in a folder called MYTAGS. It first looks for it in the TMPLMST template store located in the SASHELP directory. Not finding it there, it then looks in the template store TAGSTORE located in the MYPATH directory in My Documents.

The third method uses MARKUP as the name of the destination, specifying the tagset in the TAGSET= option, as in the following.

```
ods markup tagset=mytags.tag1 file="using_tag1.html" ;
```

Slight differences exist between the second and third methods. The second method requires the tagset to be stored inside a folder (or any level of subfolders) within the template store. ODS MARKUP does not have this requirement. If TAG1 was not contained within any folder of the TAGSTORE template store, we could specify TAGSET=TAG1 on the ODS MARKUP statement. On the other hand, without the ID= option set, ODS only allows us to have one instance of any particular destination open at a time. Suppose we want to send output to multiple files with different tagsets. Consider the following.

```
ods phtml file="file1.html" ;
ods mytags.tag1 file="file2.html" ;
ods mytags.tag2 file="file3.html" ;
proc print data = sashelp.class ; run ;
ods _all_ close ;
```

The above code is valid because we have three "destinations" open. Suppose, however, that TAG1 and TAG2 are not contained in directories within the template store, forcing us to use the MARKUP destination to produce FILE2 and FILE3. The MARKUP destination can only be open for multiple instances if the ID= option is specified as below.

```
ods phtml file="file1.html" ;
ods markup (id=f2) tagset=tag1 file="file2.html" ;
ods markup (id=f3) tagset=tag2 file="file3.html" ;
proc print data = sashelp.class ;
run ;
ods _all_ close ;
```

## WRITING TAGSETS

As mentioned earlier in the scope, the tools we discuss will, for the most part consist only of those needed to modify markup in the examples. At this point we will discuss those tools in general terms. Each tool will then be discussed in more detail when the time comes to use it. We begin by looking at the structure of a tagset.

As with other aspects of the tagset, its structure is similar to that of a style template definition within PROC TEMPLATE, as seen below.

```
PROC TEMPLATE ;
   DEFINE TAGSET tagset-name ;
   tagset statements
   DEFINE EVENT 1; event statements END ;
   DEFINE EVENT 2; event statements END ;
   etc...

   END;
RUN;
```

The first statement after the PROC statement is the DEFINE TAGSET statement. Tagset-name can be a one-level name or a multi-level name in which levels are separated by periods and represent directories in the store. For example, in the statement define tagset level1.level2.tag1, level1 represents a top-level directory in the template store, level2 represents a sub-directory of level1, and tag1 is the name of the tagset stored in the level2 subdirectory. If the directories do not exist in the store, they will be created. As mentioned earlier, the store to which the tagset is saved is the first one on the ODS PATH statement that has write-access. This can be overridden by specifying / store= followed by the name of a store (an existing one or one to be created) immediately after the tagset name.

Following the DEFINE TAGSET statement and before the event definitions are the tagset statements or tagset attribute statements. Three of the more common statements are the INDENT=, PARENT= and the DEFAULT_EVENT= statements. INDENT= specifies how many spaces to the right text is to be moved when the NDENT statement is found within an event definition, and spaces to the left when an XDENT statement is found. PARENT= specifies the name of a tagset (found by searching the stores in the ODS PATH statement) to inherit.

Events in the "child" tagset override events of the same name in the parent tagset. When an event is called that is not defined in the child tagset, the parent tagset is checked. When an event is requested that does not exist anywhere, nothing happens. On the other hand, we can use DEFAULT_EVENT= to specify an event that will be used in the absence of the event that was called. We will see soon that this can be a useful tool in learning about which events are used by which PROCs and in which order they are used.

We now move into the event definition and begin with an event's state.

Because of the hierarchical nature of markup, events that produce markup are often defined with a start state and a finish state. Most tags in markup are accompanied by a closing tag. It's often the case, especially with markup that produces tables, that before a tag is closed, that another "opening" tag will appear. Another way of saying this is that markup languages allow tags to be nested within other tags. In order to create such markup, ODS needs to call the event that corresponds to the inner tag before it completes the instructions in the event that corresponds to the outer tag. For that reason, the outer event will be defined with a start state which contains instructions for text generation before nested events are called. The finish state then contains instructions for generating text after text has been generated for nested events. The syntax is as follows.

```
DEFINE EVENT ;
start:
   event statements
finish:
   event statements
END ;
```

Just as the data set variable describes a particular aspect of data, the event variable describes a particular aspect of the output delivery process. More specifically, the data set variable provides a unique piece of information about each observation of a data set, but the output delivery process has no counterpart to the observation. The aspect of the output delivery process that a given variable describes occurs at a particular moment in time (when a particular event occurs) in the process. When that moment or event has passed, the value of the variable is gone (though in some cases it may resurface in another event). For example, suppose you issue a TITLE statement in order to put a title at the beginning of your output. At least one of the events among those that ODS and the PROC use will now have access, through a variable, to the text that makes up this title. To get it into the markup in a place where the viewing program will interpret it as a title, the tagset must include in the definition of this event a PUT statement that writes this title to the file while the value of the variable contains it.

The data set variable, in a well-structured data set, typically provides the same information for each observation, but because the event variable is time-sensitive, describing only a piece of the process, several events may use the same variable for their own purposes. Never is this more true than with the event variable VALUE, one of the most common variables used. Let's go back to the TITLE example. In an event that is used early in the process, the value of VALUE is the text that makes up the title. Later in the process, the PROC event might use VALUE to hold the name of the PROC. Even later in the HEADER event, VALUE will hold the column header for the first column. At this point, the value of COLSTART, another event variable that, not being as flexible as VALUE, usually only serves one purpose, holds the value of 1. Still in HEADER, when COLSTART changes to 2, VALUE then holds the column header of the second column. We will soon develop ways to know which events use which variables to hold information that is important for us.

ODS and the PROCs make use of over 500 variables to share information and generate text. Some can be classified as metadata while others are more directly related to the output. Many of the latter are populated by the PROC while others are populated by system options, ODS options, and other global statements. We have discussed VALUE and COLSTART – other common ones include COLCOUNT which, when captured at the right time, holds the number of columns in a table; EVENT_NAME, the name of the SAS event which, though not useful in output, will help us in our quest for information about events; COLSPAN and ROWSPAN which hold the number of columns/rows a cell is spanning. A full list of variables can be found in the Online Documentation.

Inside the event the user can create variables using the SET or EVAL statements. As a general rule, EVAL is used for numeric variables while SET is used for characters. EVAL can be used for mathematical and logical operations, while SET can be used to create character variables and arrays. Most user-created variables are classified as memory variables and are preceded by a $ both in the SET or EVAL statement that defines them as well as when referring to them. Stream variables, preceded by $$ when created and referenced, are also available, and are used to hold large amounts of data. The beauty of a user-created variable is that it retains its value until it is either explicitly re-initialized or it is deleted with the UNSET statement. This means that if necessary, we can capture the value of a variable when it has meaning to us, and hold onto it until we need it. Many of the DATA step functions and operators are available.

Other familiar DATA step concepts such as conditional statement execution, iterative execution, and statement blocks have a place in event definitions, albeit with a slightly different look. The syntax of a conditional statement has the condition placed at the end of the statement following a slash. While it can use familiar DATA step functions, more efficiency is realized from the use of tagset functions such as CMP whose two arguments are tested for equality; ANY and EXIST which return a value of TRUE when any of the variables listed in the argument are populated and all are populated, respectively; NOT which negates a condition and CONTAINS which looks for the second argument in the first argument. ELSE is allowed, but only within a statement block that begins with DO and ends with DONE. Iterative looping is achieved with the WHILE condition on the DO statement and works just like the DO-WHILE statement in the DATA step.

A variety of different PUT-type statements are also available. PUT works exactly as it does in the DATA step, with one exception that holds true for all flavors of PUT – when a variable name follows literal text (enclosed in quotes), if the variable has no value, the literal text preceding it will not be output. Other useful flavors of PUT are PUTQ which wraps quotation marks around the value of a variable being output, PUTLOG which directs output to the log file, and PUTVARS, which loops through all the variables in a variable group (e.g. memory variables, event variables, etc.) and with each iteration, populates the variable _NAME_ and _VALUE_ with the name and value of the current variable, respectively. PUTVARS is most useful when followed by a combination of literal text and _NAME_ and/or _VALUE_, which will generate output for each variable in the variable group.

Though many other event statements exist, other common ones include NDENT, XDENT, TRIGGER, and BREAK. NDENT has the effect of indenting any text that is output after the NDENT statement by an amount specified in the INDENT= statement outside of any event definition. XDENT has the opposite effect. BREAK stops and exits the event, ignoring subsequent statements, and is commonly executed conditionally. The argument of the TRIGGER statement is the name of another event, and has the effect of interrupting the current event to execute statements in the triggered event. It's important to know that while a triggered event is executing, the value of the event variable EVENT_NAME is still the name of the SAS event and not the triggered event. The variable TRIGGER_NAME holds the name of the triggered event. Also, if TRIGGER is executed during a particular state (e.g. the Start state), then only that state will be triggered from the triggered event, unless explicitly stated otherwise (e.g. trigger other event to finish).

## GETTING STARTED

Our toolbox is now off to a good start. We will get into more details on those that we have discussed and any new ones as they become necessary, but we are now ready to begin building some tagsets of our own. The first tagset we will start with can be thought of as another addition to our

222 | ANALYZING CLINICAL DATA

toolbox. After that we will develop the tagsets that produced figures 2 through 4 above. Finally, we will use these additional tools for modifying pieces of ODS output.

We will begin by answering a question we posed earlier: what are the names of the events that ODS calls, and in what order are they called? To answer this, we will make use of the event variable EVENT_NAME. For starters, as each event is called, all we want it to do is tell us what its name is. We can do this by writing a tagset with one event that writes out the name of the event, and set this as the default event.

```
proc template ;
   define tagset info1 ;
      default_event="basic" ;
      embedded_stylesheet=yes;
      define event basic ;
         put "The name of this event is " event_name nl ;
      end ;
   end ;
run ;
```

Recall that the default event is always used when ODS calls for an event that is not defined with the tagset. In this case, without a parent tagset, the BASIC event is always used sine no others are defined. Also note the use of the EMBEDDED_STYLESHEET statement. By setting this to Yes, we are assured that stylesheet markup is contained in the same file as the rest of the markup, as opposed to being directed to an external file or nowhere at all. In this case, we include it in order to see what style events are called. Finally, note the "nl" at the end of the PUT statement. This moves the pointer to the next line. We will now use the tagset to create two different files.

```
(1) ods markup tagset=info1 file="info1.txt" ;
    ods markup close ;

(2) ods markup tagset=info1 file="info1a.txt" ;
    proc print noobs data=sashelp.class(obs=10) ;
       var name age sex height weight ;
    run ;
    ods markup close ;
```

Example (1) has the unusual feature that an ODS destination is being opened and closed with nothing happening in between. This allows us to know what events ODS calls, and in what order, before a PROC is ever processed. They are INITIALIZE, DOC, DOC_HEAD, DOC_META, AUTH_OPER, DOC_TITLE, and STYLESHEET_LINK. When no stylesheet is included, the next events are JAVASCRIPT,

STARTUP_FUNCTION, SHUTDOWN_FUNCTION, and DOC_BODY. When a stylesheet is included as in our example here, between STYLESHEET_LINK and JAVASCRIPT is EMBEDDED_STYLESHEET, STYLES, many calls to STYLE_CLASS, and SHORTSTYLES.

When a PROC is included, you will see the same events as listed above at the beginning of your output, followed by the events the PROC uses. For the most part, all the PROCs use the same skeleton of events, but in some cases, slight differences do exist. For example, the REPORT procedure keeps column number information in the DATA event, but the cell content in the PUT_VALUE event immediately following DATA, whereas PROC PRINT, like many other PROCs, makes no use of PUT_VALUE, keeping column number information and cell content both in DATA. Typically, the first event after DOC_BODY (the last event before the PROC takes over) is the PROC event which, among other things, holds the name of the PROC. You will see that the next set of events are "setup" events, setting up things like the title, the table, cell specs, row specs, table headers and others. We know the data is coming when we next get to events like HEADER, ROW, and DATA.

I have mentioned only a few of the events here – the list from top to bottom is fairly long. Often times the task of finding the event you are looking for and where it fits in with the others is just as challenging as identifying the event of interest in the first place. The best rule of thumb when trying to get a general idea of when events occur is to think of the tasks involved in building a table and the order in which they should be performed. First, the file needs to be built, then the PROC begins, titles are put in place, the table as a whole is set up, then the headers are filled in, rows are defined, and finally, column by column, data cells are filled in. For the most part, when trying to customize pieces of output, it is the later events that we have to work with. When changing the table itself, the events that follow the table setup are what we are interested in.

With some idea of what events are used and the general order in which they are used, let's now try and get an idea of when different types of information show up at what point in the process. We will do this simply by adding a few variables to the above tagset.

```
proc template ;
   define tagset info2 ;
      default_event="basic" ;
      embedded_stylesheet=yes;
```

```
define event basic ;
    start:
    put "EVENT_NAME:   " event_name nl ;
    put "HTMLCLASS:    " htmlclass nl ;
    put "COLCOUNT:     " colcount nl ;
    put "COLSTART:        " colstart nl ;
    put "COLSPAN: " colspan nl ;
    put "ROW:      " row nl ;
    put "VALUE:   " value nl ;
    put "STATE:   " state nl ;
    put nl ;

    finish:
    put "EVENT_NAME:   " event_name nl ;
    put "HTMLCLASS:    " htmlclass nl ;
    put "COLCOUNT:     " colcount nl ;
    put "COLSTART:        " colstart nl ;
    put "COLSPAN: " colspan nl ;
    put "ROW:      " row nl ;
    put "VALUE:   " value nl ;
    put "STATE:   " state nl ;
    put nl ;

    end ;
  end ;
run ;
```

With this tagset we have added a couple of new features. Maybe the one that stands out the most is the use of the Start state and Finish state. This will give us a good idea of when events are nested inside of each other. Also notice the "put nl ;" at the end of each state. This has the effect of inserting a blank line between events in the output. Figure 5 illustrates a snippet of PROC PRINT output, using the data set SASHELP.CLASS and the tagset above.

```
VARIABLE NAME:  Age
COLUMN:  3
ROW:  9
VALUE:  15

VARIABLE NAME:  Height
COLUMN:  4
ROW:  9
VALUE:  62.5

VARIABLE NAME:  Weight
COLUMN:  5
ROW:  9
VALUE:  112.5

VARIABLE NAME:  Name
COLUMN:  1
ROW:  10
VALUE:  Jeffrey
```

Figure 5

Let's see what kind of information some of these variables provide. Keep in mind that PUT statements in tagsets that combine literal text with variable names will only produce output for a text-variable combination when the variable has a value. If it does not, the text that precedes it will not be generated. For our purposes here this is a useful feature of the PUT statement. It means that for any given event, if, for example, we are missing the output COLCOUNT:, we know that this variable has no value in this event. EVENT_NAME always has a value, and because the BASIC event in this tagset was defined with states, STATE will always have a value too. Beware though, sometimes variables are populated with meaningless, or even worse, misleading information. COLCOUNT is an example of the latter. COLCOUNT claims to hold the number of columns in the table, but before the table is set up, this variable has a value of 1. The VAR statement in our PROC PRINT listed five variables, so the table should contain five columns, and later when the table begins to set up, COLCOUNT will have a value of 5. COLSPAN in this example never has a value. This variable does become useful in PROCs such as PROC REPORT that allow us to have spanning headers. As mentioned earlier, VALUE is a multi-purpose variable that holds the name of the PROC early, later the title from the TITLE statement, and even later, cell data values. ROW and COLSTART, as expected, hold row and column numbers respectively as the table is constructed. Finally, we have HTMLCLASS, which holds the name of the stylesheet class to be used. A detailed discussion on HTML style classes is beyond the scope of this chapter (though it will be discussed more in an upcoming example), but by adding PUTVARS STYLE followed by a combination of _NAME_, _VALUE_, and possibly some literal text will provide the name (_NAME_) of each style variable and its value (_VALUE_) for each event. Adding this to a tagset similar to those above will generate output that resembles the style element definitions in a style template.

Let's now return to Figures 2 through 4. These last couple of examples have illustrated how the output from Figure 2 can be generated. Though it has a much different appearance than that of Figure 2, Figure 3, upon close inspection, is not much different. It contains a few more variables, is laid out in a more horizontal, XML format, and is viewed through Internet Explorer, but like the others, provides variable and value information about each event. Tagsets like this are often referred to as mapping tagsets. SASHELP.TMPLMST contains several mapping tagsets, such as EVENT_MAP and SHORT_MAP. EVENT_MAP was used to generate Figure 3.

Unlike Figures 2 and 3, Figure 4 does not provide output for each event. Not only that, but this output contains no information about any events at all. Rather, it looks like nothing more than literal text, generated from a PUT statement in one event. By placing this statement in an early event, this can be generated without a PROC being run.

```
proc template ;
   define tagset helloworld ;
      define event initialize ;
         put "HELLO WORLD" ;
      end ;
   end;
run;
```

## THE FREQ EXAMPLE
We have now added an important tool to our toolbox – the mapping tagsets. This will prove to be valuable in identifying events of interest.

The FREQ procedure for the production of cross tabular output provides some opportunity for output customization. Throughout these examples we will use the following code.

```
proc freq data=sashelp.class ;
   title "Tagset example";
   tables sex*age / missing norow nocol nopercent;
   label sex='Gender' age='Age as of Dec. 31';
run;
```

Some quick observations are noteworthy here. First, note the use of labels for each of the variables being analyzed. Second, the combination of options in the TABLES statement ensures that only the frequencies will appear in the table cells. Our initial output generated from the SAS-supplied PHTML tagset (ODS PHTML file=...) is below.

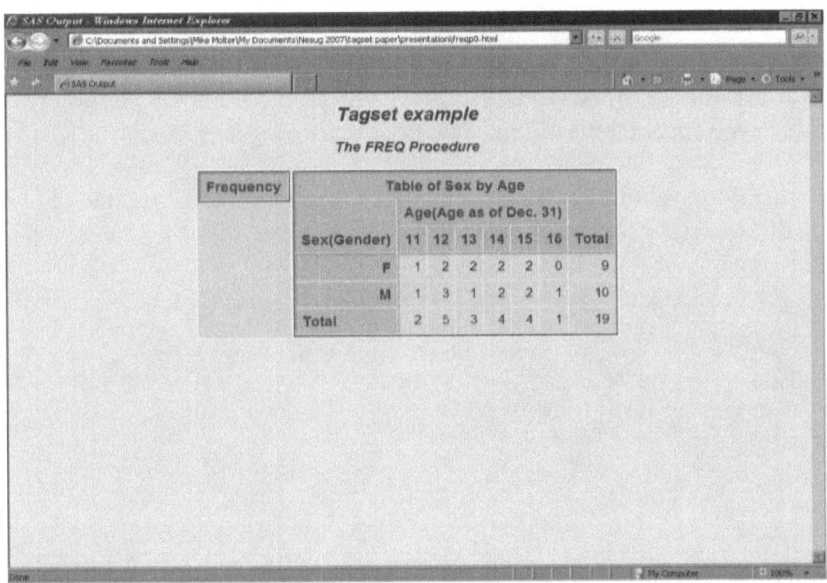

Figure 6

## THE PROC TITLE

Our first task will be to do something with "The FREQ Procedure". We know that "Tagset example" came from a TITLE statement, but this text comes by default with FREQ output. If we are going to do something about it, we need to pinpoint which PHTML event was responsible for generating it. We first look to the event map. This is done by running the above code using the following ODS statement, or any of its equivalents.

```
ods tagsets.event_map file="file name.xml" ;
```

Below is a small piece of the XML output. Below is a small piece of the XML output.

```
- <proc_title_group event_name="proc_title_group"
trigger_name="attr_out" class="Body" colcount="1" index="IDX"
just="c">
<proc_title event_name="proc_title" trigger_name="attr_out"
class="ProcTitle" value="The
```

```
FREQ Procedure" colcount="1" index="IDX" just="c" />
</proc_title_group>

- <proc_branch event_name="proc_branch" trigger_name="attr_out"
class="ContentProcName" value="Freq" colcount="1" name="Freq"
label="The Freq Procedure" index="IDX" just="c"
url="freqem0.xml#IDX" hreftarget="body">
```

In this piece, we see that "The Freq Procedure" is the value of the VALUE variable in the PROC_TITLE event, but also the LABEL variable in the PROC_BRANCH event. At this point, either of the events could have generated the output. We need to investigate further.

Another good resource is the markup itself. By opening the output with a plain text editor such as Notepad, we discover the following contained within the file.

```
<noscript></noscript>
<div class="branch">
<a name="IDX"></a>
<h1 class="c">Tagset example</h1>
<h2 class="c">The FREQ Procedure</h2>
<p>
<div>
<div align="center">
```

From this, we see that the text is contained within the h2 tags. Whichever of the two events were responsible, it probably also generated this tag. We now look at the PHTML tagset code, do a simple search for "<h2", and discover the following:

```
define event proc_title;
    put "<h2";

    trigger align;
    put ">";
    put VALUE;
    put "</h2>" NL;
end;
```

We do not see the "The FREQ Procedure" as literal text in this event, but all the clues point to this text as being the value of the VALUE variable. Assuming this, we can do what we want. We can inherit the tagset and re-define the event as an empty one, as below, thereby suppressing the text.

```
proc template ;
    define tagset freq1 ;
        parent=tagsets.phtml ;
```

```
      define event proc_title;
      end;
   end;
run;
```

We can also substitute another variable for VALUE, substitute literal text such as "The FREAKY Procedure", or we could create a memory variable in the event and replace VALUE with a reference to it, as in the following.

```
proc template ;
   define tagset freq1 ;
      define event proc_title;
         set $myvalue "THE FREAKY PROCEDURE" ;
         put "<h2";

         trigger align;
         put ">";
         put $myvalue ;
         put "</h2>" NL;
      end;
   end;
run;
```

Not all PROCs use the PROC_TITLE event, and for those that do, the ODS PROCTITLE global statement can be turned on and off to control whether this kind of text is displayed or not. In reality, rather than using a tagset to customize this text, one might choose to turn off its generation and substitute it with another title. The value in this example is more in the lessons we have learned than in the usefulness of this feature. We have seen examples of the tagset structure, the event structure, how statements are used, how events call each other, and the syntax. Maybe more importantly, we have gained experience as a detective. We learned about different resources available to pinpoint the responsible event. This was done by a combination of mapping tagsets (either EVENT_MAP, SHORT_MAP, or a homemade tagset), examination of the markup itself, and simple searching through the parent tagset. Finally, we have made more sense of an ODS feature that in the past, was another example of ODS magic. Issue a statement and somehow this text would appear in, or disappear from the markup. We now know that the text "The FREQ Procedure" is just one example of a piece of information internal to this PROC, and passed, through an event variable, to ODS for output delivery when this statement is turned on. By turning the statement off (ODS PROCTITLE=OFF) and running the PROC through the event map, we would see that the PROC_TITLE event is never used. As is the theme with tagsets in general, we have gained a better glimpse into the inner workings of this PROC, and we have gained control over a piece of the markup that was at one time untouchable.

## "SAS OUTPUT"

If you look carefully at the upper left corner of the browser window in Figure 6 above, you will see the text "SAS Output." If you are using Internet Explorer version 7, you will see the same text in the tab (as is the case in the figure above). Let's see if the investigative techniques we used above will help us to get to this text. Unfortunately in this case, we do not find this text in the event map XML file. Maybe this is something specific to HTML. Looking at the markup, we find the following.

```
<title>SAS Output</title>
```

A search for "<title>" in the tagset code turns up three possible events — TOP_TITLE, DOC_TITLE, and CONTENT_TITLE. What's different about this example is that the text we are trying to get to, in each of these possibilities, appears to be written out as literal text. In each case, the text is being generated under the condition that VALUE does not exist. If it does, then its value will be generated. Although it's not definitive evidence, TOP_TITLE can probably be ruled out, because the literal text it is putting out is "SAS Output Frame". It's possible that VALUE=SAS Output, in which case, this event could be responsible, but more likely it is one of the other two, each of which would generate "SAS Output" when VALUE does not exist. We can always return to this other possibility if these two events prove innocent. By returning to the event map output, though the text is never found, when searching for CONTENT_TITLE, we discover that this event was never used, leaving DOC_TITLE as our leading suspect. We test our suspicion by inheriting the PHTML tagset or even the FREQ1 tagset from above, and customizing this event the way we did with the PROC_TITLE event. Sure enough, DOC_TITLE turns out to be the guilty party.

## SUPPRESSING ROW AND COLUMN VARIABLE NAMES

When the row and/or column variables have labels attached to them, PROC FREQ tends to display in the table the name of the variable followed by the label inside parentheses. Let's see if we can get rid of the variable names and parentheses, leaving only the labels. Because this text plays the role of a header, this might be a good place to start looking in the event map. Unfortunately, we would not like what we find. The generation of the row header is much different than that of the column header, forcing us to treat them separately.

We will begin with the row header. An excerpt from the event map that contains it is below. Pay close attention to the values of VALUE.

```
- <header event_name="header" trigger_name="attr_out" out-
put_name="CrossTabFreqs" output_label="Cross-Tabular Freq Table"
section="head" class="Header" value="Sex" rowspan="2" row="2"
data_row="0" colcount="1" col="1" type="string" index="IDX"
just="c" vjust="b">
<put_value event_name="put_value" trigger_name="attr_out"
output_name="CrossTabFreqs"
output_label="Cross-Tabular Freq Table" class="Header" value="("
colcount="1" index="IDX" just="c" vjust="b" />
<put_value event_name="put_value" trigger_name="attr_out"
output_name="CrossTabFreqs"
output_label="Cross-Tabular Freq Table" class="Header"
value="Gender" colcount="1" index="IDX" just="c" vjust="b" />
<put_value event_name="put_value" trigger_name="attr_out"
output_name="CrossTabFreqs"
output_label="Cross-Tabular Freq Table" class="Header" value=")"
colcount="1" index="IDX" just="c" vjust="b" />
```

What is disturbing is that the text "Sex(Gender)" is split across four event uses, with the variable name Sex in the HEADER event, and the rest in separate uses of the PUT_VALUE event. Let's start with the HEADER event. When looking at this event definition in the PHTML tagset definition, you will see that it triggers another event, CELL_VALUE, which is what is responsible for the generation of the output. Here you will find VALUE being generated, under the condition that the event variable URL does not exist. That's only because when that variable does exist, VALUE will be output in another event that includes text to create a hyperlink. Because we do not want to generate the variable name, we have another instance to suppress output generation. Now because HEADER (and in turn, CELL_VALUE) is responsible for several parts of the output, we have to place tight conditions on suppressing this particular variable name. One condition would be to insist that the row number is 2. Row 1 will always contain the label of the table (in this case, "Table of Sex by Age". Of course we do not want to suppress everything in row 2, so we need more conditions. We also know that this label will span two rows, the first of which contains column headers, the second that contains column variable values. We are getting closer, but the Total column also spans two rows. A third condition could be that the column number is 1. This should uniquely identify the text to suppress. The PUT statement in the CELL_VALUE event is now modified to contain extra conditions, as in the following.

```
put value /if ^exists( URL) and ^(cmp("2",row) and cmp('2',rowspan)
and cmp("1",colstart));
```

EXISTS is a function that returns true when all the variables in the list have values. The carrot (^) negates the result of any function, and CMP checks for equality among its two arguments. ROW and COLSTART hold the row and column number of the current cell respectively, and ROWSPAN holds the number of rows spanned by the current cell.

That takes care of the variable name – now it's time for the parentheses. By looking again at the event map, it turns out that this is the only cell that calls on the PUT_VALUE event. By looking at the PHTML tagset definition, we see that all this event does is write out the value of VALUE. We now simply add the condition that this value not be an opening or closing parenthesis.

```
define event put_value;
   put VALUE / if value not in ("(",")");
end;
```

We have now trimmed down "Sex(Gender)" to "Gender". We now want to reduce "Age(Age as of Dec. 31)" to "Age as of Dec. 31". The good news is that this is found all together from one event in the event map.

```
<header          event_name="header"          trigger_name="attr_out"
output_name="CrossTabFreqs" output_label="Cross-Tabular Freq Ta-
ble" section="head" class="Header" value="Age(Age as of Dec. 31)"
colspan="6"    row="2"    data_row="0"    colcount="1"    col="2"
type="string" index="IDX" just="c" vjust="b" />
```

The bad news (ok, it's not that bad) is that it's in the HEADER event. We will again have to impose tight restrictions to make sure this is the only cell we affect. Though many combinations would work, we should be able to count on ROW=2 and ROWSPAN not existing. The question now is what to do under these conditions.

Recall that HEADER leaves it up to CELL_VALUE to generate the text – specifically, VALUE. Under these conditions, we want it to generate just a portion of VALUE. For that reason, we will use DATA step functions in HEADER to parse VALUE, storing the result in a memory variable. In CELL_VALUE, we will output the value of this variable when it exists. When it does not, we will generate what we did before under the conditions that were added above.

It's important to remember here that HEADER is still passing something to CELL_VALUE for generation. That means we do not want to re-move anything from the current definition of HEADER – we still want to generate the tags and trigger the same events. We just want to have our new value ready before CELL_VALUE is triggered.

It's also important to know that when parsing a string, tagsets do not react very well to nested functions, so a few more lines of code may be necessary. We begin by finding the occurrence of the first open parenthesis.

```
do / if cmp("2",row) and ^exist(rowspan);
eval $pos index(value,"(") ;
```

Notice that we have begun a statement block with DO under the conditions stated above. We then used EVAL to create a numeric variable with the familiar INDEX function. Since we want nothing before this open parenthesis, or either of the parentheses, we will use SUBSTR starting one position after the result of our INDEX function.

```
eval $pos $pos+1 ;
set $val substr(value,$pos) ;
```

This is nice, but we still have a closing parenthesis at the end. We can chop that off with some help from the LENGTH function.

```
eval $len length($val) ;
eval $len $len - 1 ;
set $val substr($val,1,$len) ;
unset $len ; unset $pos ;
done ;
```

This statement block has been added to the HEADER definition immediately before the call to the CELL_VALUE event (TRIGGER CELL_VALUE). We now alter CELL_VALUE to generate this when it's available.

```
do / if $val ; put $val ; unset $val ;
else ;
    put value /if ^exists( URL) and ^(cmp(row,"2") and
    cmp('2',rowspan) and cmp("1",colstart));
done;
```

Under the ELSE statement is what we came up with earlier. The condition in the DO statement that appears not to have an operator works like an EXISTS function. Maybe the most important part of this is the UNSET statement. Keep in mind that memory variables hang around forever until you explicitly do something with them. Without UNSET, $VAL will persist and its value generated whenever this event is called.

## SUPPRESSING THE "MINI" TABLE

The cross tabular PROC FREQ generates two tables – of course the main table with all the frequencies in it, and the second is the one-by-one table to the left that tells you what each number in any cell represents. Having suppressed all but the frequencies, let's see if we can suppress the generation of this mini table.

Suppressing an entire table means suppressing a bigger chunk of markup, starting with markup that begins with the text "<table". A little investigation reveals that the TABLE event is responsible for this. The temptation at this point might be to look for something in the event map that distinguishes this table from the main table. Unfortunately, the variables that EVENT_MAP shows us do not show any difference. You could write your own mapping tagset to look for such a variable, but that can take a while, and in the end, probably is not worth the effort. The reason is because the TABLE event has several events nested within. Whatever condition you find will have to be imposed on all those events so that they too do not generate any output. Rather, we will make use of the stream variable. With this approach, we minimize the amount of modification to existing code, and add one new, short event.

Streams can be initialized with the SET statement or the OPEN statement. When we initialize a stream variable with an OPEN statement, output from all PUT statements is redirected to the stream instead of to the file, until the stream is closed. For that reason, with all the PUT statements contained in the TABLE event, we do not have to change anything in the current TABLE event, as long as we make sure that when this is called for the mini table, a stream is open, and when for the main table, no stream is open. What we will do to the current TABLE event is rename it, say, to MYTABLE. We will then redefine TABLE to manage the opening and closing of the stream. TABLE will then trigger MYTABLE. The code is below.

```
define event table ;
   start:
   open dump / if ^exist($is_table) ;
   trigger mytable ;


   finish:
   trigger mytable ;
   close ;
   set $is_table "true" ;
end;
```

The memory variable $IS_TABLE manages the stream. Since the mini table is generated first, we want to open the stream at the first use of the TABLE event. Since $IS_TABLE has yet to be initialized, the condition for opening DUMP is true at this point. Now all the markup generated by MYTABLE (normally TABLE) that creates a table, as well as everything generated by nested events before the FINISH state, is directed to the stream. When we finally reach the FINISH state, we trigger the FINISH state of MYTABLE which generates the closing table tag (</table>), finalizing the creation of a table. We can now close the stream and initialize $IS_TABLE, so that the stream is never open again, and all subsequent PUT statements direct text to the file.

## PHTML VS. HTML – A MATTER OF STYLE

The main difference between these two ODS destinations is in styling. Once again we encounter an aspect of ODS output that once was a mystery, but now becomes clearer with the tagset. We know that we can change the way our output looks by specifying the name of a style definition with the STYLE= option on the ODS statement. Furthermore, we can use style definitions provided by SAS, or we can create our own by setting attributes for each of the different style elements. Some PROCs also allow us to define style attributes "on the fly" as a way to temporarily override the attribute values defined on the style template being used. TITLE and FOOTNOTE statements also allow for this kind of manual override, or what is also referred to as inline styling. Regardless of the method used, the question still remains: how do these specifications get into the markup? We are now in a better position to answer that question.

We saw earlier after turning on the EMBEDDED_STYLESHEETS statement which style events ODS uses. The main event is called STYLE_CLASS. Each time this event is called, another element from the style definition is loaded – the name of the element (defined in the style definition) becomes the value of the variable HTMLCLASS, and all of the attribute values become variable values, all accessible in the tagset (e.g. if BORDERCOLOR is defined for the DATA element as green, then when STYLE_CLASS loads this element, HTMLCLASS=DATA while BORDERCOLOR=GREEN). With these variables populated, simple PUT statements create valid stylesheet syntax, either at the top of the markup file when EMBEDDED_STYLESHEETS is turned on, or in an external file when one is specified on the ODS statement. PHTML, however does not define the STYLE_CLASS event. Rather, PHTML uses a more manual method of creating its stylesheet with the SHORTSTYLES event. Instead of loading each of the style elements in the definition, this event triggers a small number of events, each of which specifies one element to load. As with STYLE_CLASS, variables become populated and, PUT statements create a much smaller stylesheet.

Though the stylesheet PHTML generates is quite a bit shorter than that from the HTML destination, this difference is not always seen by the user. The reason is that the few elements that are loaded are the ones users care about most of the time – BODY, SYSTEMTITLE, PROCTITLE, TABLE, DATA, HEADER. Therefore changes to these elements in the style definition will be realized by the PHTML destination. A much more visible difference between the two destinations is the inability of PHTML to handle inline styling.

Without knowledge of tagsets, no logical explanation can be offered for how we can change the font color of the title by changing the Systemtitle element definition in the style definition, but we cannot change it with the statement.

```
title color=red "Why cannot I change title colors?" ;
```

As mentioned above, Systemtitle is loaded by the PHTML destination. Inline style attributes, however, never become part of an element definition. Their values still populate variables, but they do so during the event being used to generate that part of the output – much later than when STYLE_CLASS and SHORTSTYLES are used. When the above statement is issued with the HTML destination, the value of FOREGROUND is populated when the SYSTEM_TITLE event is used. This ultimately calls the STYLE_INLINE event that generates inline style attributes inside the tag that produces the title. The DATA event does the same thing. Oddly enough, though the STYLE_INLINE event that the HTML destination calls is actually defined in the PHTML tagset (HTML tagset inherits from PHTML), the SYSTEM_TITLE and DATA events defined in PHTML never call STYLE_INLINE.

## THE BY STATEMENT

Another noticeable difference is seen when a BY statement is used with a PROC. When this happens the BYLINE event is used. The PHTML and HTML destinations define this event differently. The following illustrates the differences.

```
PHTML output:
<h1 class="c">Sex=F</h1>

HTML output:
```

```
<div class="c Byline">Sex=F</div>
```

The CLASS= attribute inside an HTML tag tells the browser where to look in the stylesheet to get style instructions. The style sheets in both destinations contain the text .c {text-align: center }; CLASS="c" means look at this part of the stylesheet for instructions. In this case, the instruction is to center align the text. With PHTML, text-alignment values such as these are the only values provided in this attribute. Without any other style instructions, the browser looks to the element in the stylesheet named for the tag itself – h1. As it turns out, PHTML puts all of its titles in h1 tags too. For that reason, By lines in this destination look just like titles.

On the other hand, with the HTML destination, the browser has one more place in the stylesheet to look for instructions – the Byline class. This class defines the same attributes as the h1 class with different values, giving the Byline its own unique look.

```
.Byline
{  font-family: Arial, Helvetica, sans-serif;
   font-size: medium;
   font-weight: bold; font-style: normal; color: #0033AA;
   background-color: #B0B0B0; }
```

The dot in front of the class name means that any element can reference this class inside the tag. The STYLE_CLASS event loads each element defined by the style definition and creates classes such as this one in the stylesheet, named for the element. The SHORTSTYLES event used by PHTML also creates classes named for the few elements it loads, but omits the dot, meaning that references to the class are permitted only inside the tag with the same name. Additionally, each destination adds classes for text alignment. Since Byline is not one of the elements that PHTML loads, it does not get added as a class to its stylesheet, and there is no opportunity to reference it in any of the tags. For that reason, Byline attributes have to be borrowed from one of the few classes it does have. Let's see if we can create a tagset inherited from PHTML that will load the Byline element and add it as a class option to the above output.

The SHORTSTYLES event in PHTML does nothing more than trigger several events, each of which has the same basic structure illustrated below.

```
define event titlestyle;
   put "h1 {" NL;
```

```
    trigger stylesheetclass;
    put "}" NL;
    style = systemtitle;
end;
```

The PUT statement in this example is beginning to generate the class that only h1 tags can use. The STYLESHEETCLASS event will generate a few attributes (e.g. font face, font size, font weight, plus a few others) and their values retrieved from variables. STYLE=SYSTEMTITLE means that these variables are populated with values defined by the SYSTEMTITLE style element.

Following this convention, we inherit the PHTML tagset and add a new event called BYSTYLE.

```
define event bystyle ;
    put ".byline {" NL; trigger stylesheetclass; put "}" NL;
    style = byline;
end;
```

Note that we have added the dot in front of the class name so that we can reference it from anywhere. We are also loading the style element BYLINE, the same one loaded by the HTML destination that gives this part of the output its own unique look. We can now add this event as one to be triggered by the SHORTSTYLES event. All that remains is adding the reference alongside the "c" in the text <h1 class="c">. After generating "<h1", the current PHTML definition triggers the event ALIGN, which generates the CLASS= attribute above, including the closing quotation marks following the c. By changing the event triggered to CLASSALIGN, before the closing quote gets generated, the value of HTMLCLASS (in this case, BYLINE) gets generated. The new event looks like the following.

```
define event byline;
    put "<h1";
    trigger classalign;
    put ">";
    put VALUE;
    put "</h1>" NL;
end;
```

The attribute inside the h1 tag now reads class="c byline", which tells the browser to look to both the "c" class and the "byline" class for styling instructions.

## TAGSET PARAMETERS

Version 9.1.3 introduced the ability to parameterize our tagsets similar to the way we parameterize macros, with two main differences. While macro parameters are declared on the %macro statement, tagset parameters are never declared. The second difference is that while each macro parameter value is stored in its own macro variable, each tagset parameter is stored in the same dictionary variable. A dictionary variable is one of two ways we can create arrays in the tagset. Before moving on, let's look at this capability in a little more detail.

## TAGSET ARRAYS

In addition to the variables we have seen up to this point, the SET statement can also create list and dictionary variables, each of which works like an array. Of the two, the list variable is more like the familiar DATA step array. In addition to the name of the variable, we add a set of square brackets and an optional index, as in the following.

```
set $mylist[1] 'first element' ;
```

The index specifies which particular element in the list will hold this value. Providing two square brackets without an index in between (i.e. set $mylist[] 'last element') adds another element to the end of the list to hold this value. References to the variable are the same as references to a DATA step array element.

```
put 'The 24th element of this list variable is ' $myl-ist[24] ;
```

The only difference that dictionary variables offer is that instead of associating element values with integers, they are associated with other character strings.

```
set $states['Michigan'] 'MI' ;
set $states['North Carolina'] 'NC' ;
```

Note the use of quotation marks surrounding the character index inside the brackets. Referencing is the same as with list variables, but again with quotation marks.

```
put 'The abbreviation for Michigan is ' $states['Michigan'] ;
```

As an alternative to integer and string indices, arrays can also use the name of another variable as an index, as in the following.

```
eval $loop 1 ;
do / while $loop < $mylist ;
   put "The current value of the MYLIST variable is " $myl-ist[$loop] nl ;
```

```
    eval $loop $loop + 1 ;
done ;
```

Other differences from the DATA step array exist too. Note that with both types of tagset arrays, array elements can be added at any time. This differs from the DATA step array where the ARRAY statement serves the purpose of declaring ahead of time exactly how many elements it will hold. Also, the DATA step has the DIM function whose argument is the name of the array, and returns the number of elements in the array. This information is available for list and dictionary variables by referencing the name of the variable without an index or brackets.

```
put  'The  number  of  elements  in  the  variable  $states  is'
     $states ;
```

## THE $OPTIONS DICTIONARY

Each tagset parameter becomes the name of an individual element in a dictionary variable called OPTIONS. Parameter values are provided by the user on the ODS statement that opens the destination in the following manner.

```
ods markup tagset=tagset-name options(
    parameter-name-1 = "parameter-value-1",…
    parameter-name-n = "parameter-value-n") ;
```

We reference these parameter values in the tagset the way we reference any other dictionary elements, except for the following: regardless of how the user refers to the parameter name in the ODS statement, references to the parameter names in the tagset definition must be in all caps.

```
proc template ;
   define tagset caps ;
   define event initialize ;
   putlog "The value of the parameter is" $options["PARM"] ;
   end; end;
run;

ods markup file='test.txt'
tagset=caps options(parm="hello world");
ods markup close;
```

Note the reference to the dictionary element on the PUTLOG statement without ever having defined a variable. The user, rather than the author of the tagset, becomes responsible for defining the $OPTIONS dictionary variable with the OPTIONS option and its attributes.

The Proctitle and SAS Output examples illustrated earlier are begging for

parameterization. In the Proctitle example, multiple options were suggested. The one illustrated had us creating a memory variable with the
PROC_TITLE event, and referencing it in a PUT statement in the same
event. Though this does allow for customizing this part of the output, it's
about as desirable as asking a user to modify macro code. This example
becomes much more user friendly by rewriting the event as below.

```
proc template ;
   define tagset freq1 ;
   define event proc_title;

   /* set $myvalue "THE FREAKY PROCEDURE" ; */
   put "<h2";
   trigger align;
   put ">";
   put $options["PTITLE"] ;
   put "</h2>" NL;

   end; end;
run;
```

The user supplies a parameter value in the following manner.

```
ods markup file='myproctitle.html' tagset=freq1
options (ptitle="THE FREAKY PROCEDURE");
```

We can make a similar change to the DOC_TITLE event so that "SAS
Output" becomes what we want it to be. We change this event…

```
define event doc_title;
   put "<title>";
   put "SAS Output" /if ^exists( VALUE);
   put VALUE;
   put "</title>" NL;
end;
```

To this event

```
define event doc_title;
   put "<title>";
   put ' " ' $options["DOCTITLE"] ' " ';
   put "</title>" NL;
end;
```

where DOCTITLE is the name of the parameter.

Let's go back to the styling of the By line. In this example we created a
tagset that added a class to the stylesheet and added a reference to that
class in the h1 tag. By adding style=byline to the new Bystyle event, we
loaded the Bystyle style element and its unique attributes. Let's now pa-

rameterize that tagset to allow for a user to have control over some of those attributes.

Recall that adding the class reference to the h1 tag was done by modifying the BYLINE event. We can leave that part alone. In order to change attributes, we need to change the class definition itself in the stylesheet. This was controlled by the new BYSTYLE event, and more specifically, the STYLESHEETCLASS event that it triggered. STYLESHEETCLASS is responsible for generating attribute-value output with tagset statement such as the following.

```
put "  font-family: " FONT_FACE;
put ";" NL / if exists( FONT_FACE);
```

The value of FONT_FACE comes from the style element loaded (BYLINE). A simple change to this produces the font face chosen by the user.

```
put "  font-family:  " $options["BYFONT_FACE"] ;
put "  font-family:  " FONT_FACE / if
^exists($options["BYFONT_FACE"]);
put ";" NL / if any($options["BYFONT_FACE"], FONT_FACE);
```

The first statement simply replaces the variable inherited from the loaded style element with the parameter input, where BYFONT_FACE is the name of the parameter. In case this was not specified by the user, we will go back to generating the font face loaded with the style element. The third statement, similar to the second in the original, generates the semicolon if either of the variables has a value. STYLESHEETCLASS is filled with pairs of statements like these, one for each attribute to be generated. It's certainly not much of a stretch to parameterize other attributes in the same way. If you are willing to go a bit further, do the same for other areas of the output, such as the titles, the Proctitle, table headers and even data. Depending on how many areas you do decide to affect, you may choose to make these changes directly to the STYLESHEETCLASS event, or create a separate event to be triggered, or if it's just one area of the output you want to parameterize such as the Byline, replace the trigger STYLESHEETCLASS statement with statements like these.

Of course an alternative way to gain the same functionality would be to change the style template. Templates, though, are in some ways like macros – we like to keep them relatively stable by avoiding making less-than-fundamental changes to them. Parameterization is a concept designed just for these kinds of changes. Inline styling offers the same convenience but we saw earlier how this is not accessible to PHTML (though an alternative to this might be a tagset that makes inline styling accessible). Either way, we avoid the sometimes difficult task of defining style definitions, and the style definitions that we do have each maintain their individual identities that makes each of them unique. All of this is accomplished by directly controlling the markup that ODS is generating.

## THE REPORT EXAMPLE

Our final example re-emphasizes a theme touched on at the end of the last example. Without that tagset, if a user suddenly decides he wants the Byline to have Times New Roman font, he is going to have to do some prep work before running the PROC – namely, creating a new style template that is different from the style template he was going to use in only a trivial way – the font of the By line. By creating a parameterized tagset, this prep work was eliminated, and the price (other than the initial tagset development) was a simple addition of an option (for specifying the parameter value) on the ODS statement.

PROC REPORT is one of the most versatile reporting PROCs we have. It's capable of generating not only a detailed report of your data, but also a summary report with all the basic descriptive statistics SAS has to offer, customized summary lines, and also custom inline styling. For these reasons, it's also one of the most widely used PROCs.

What the PROC is capable of is one thing, what clients want is sometimes another. It's common for clients to request for certain pairs of descriptive statistics to be combined into one column. PROC REPORT is perfectly capable of calculating the mean and standard deviation, but there's no easy way to get them into one column with the standard deviation inside parentheses, or combine the minimum and maximum with a dash in between. For that reason we often find ourselves, as in the last example, preparing the data ahead of time, this time by computing the statistics that PROC REPORT is capable of computing ahead of time (maybe with the MEANS procedure) and then using PROC REPORT for display purposes only. In our final example, we will eliminate that prep work by creating a parameterized tagset that combines two columns according to a pattern.

In this example, we will use the following basic PROC REPORT.

```
proc report nowindows data=sashelp.class split='^' ;
    column sex age=meanage age=stdage ;
    define sex / group 'Gender' ;
    define meanage / mean 'Mean^Age' format=8.1;
```

```
   define stdage / std 'Standard^Deviation' format=8.2;
run;
```

This code creates a three-column report in which the second column represents the mean age for the current value of SEX and the third column represents the standard deviation of the age. The goal of the tagset is to allow the user to ask for the second and third column to be combined into one column (thereby making it a two-column report), with the standard deviation being wrapped in parentheses. The parameter would be specified in the following way.

```
ods markup tagset=squeeze file='squeeze sample.html'
options (pattern="{2} ({3})");
```

The numbers within the braces represent column numbers calculated by PROC REPORT – in other words, as they would be with a "default" display of the report. In this case, we are saying that columns 2 and 3 of the default report (the mean and standard deviation) should be combined into one column by putting a space between them and the value of the third column in parentheses.

Though not always necessary, it's a good idea, when possible, to have in mind how you expect the markup to be changed. By running the above code with the PHTML tagset, the markup contains the following.

```
<colgroup>
<col>
<col>
<col>
</colgroup>
<thead>
<tr>
<th scope="col" class="c">Gender</th>
<th scope="col" class="c">Mean<br>Age</th>
<th scope="col" class="c">Standard<br>Deviation</th>
</tr>
</thead>
<tbody>
<tr>
<td class="l">F</td>
<td class="r">    13.2</td>
<td class="r">    1.39</td>
</tr>
<tr>
<td class="l">M</td>
<td class="r">    13.4</td>
<td class="r">    1.65</td>
</tr>
```

Since we are reducing the table to two columns, we should eliminate one of the <col>s. We will also eliminate the second <th tag and the second <td tag within each <tr> tag, but in each case, we want to hold onto cell text (the value of VALUE, found between the opening and closing tags – e.g. Gender) so we combine it with its counterpart in the third tag. For example, the following will replace the first set of <td tags.

```
<tr>
<td class="l">F</td>
<td class="r">     13.2 (     1.39)</td>
</tr>
```

The following list of tasks describes the general plan of attack when it comes to writing the tagset.

Parse the parameter. The user can specify any characters to separate the values from the two columns (parentheses, dashes, commas, etc.). We will find it handy to have a nice comma delimited list of the columns affected (column numbers still in braces). At the same time, we will also want to know which of the two columns comes before the other. When processing the first of the two columns, we want to do two things – hold onto its value, but also suppress any output generation. We will use a memory variable to accomplish the first, and we will open a stream variable to accomplish the second. When processing the second of the two columns, rather than generating the value of VALUE, we will create a memory variable simply by using the DATA step's TRANWRD function, replacing the number corresponding to the first column in $PATTERN with the value held from when that column was processed, and replacing the number corresponding to the current column with the current value of VALUE.

The first of these tasks can be done any time before the beginning of table creation (e.g. DOC event). A sample of the logic follows.

```
set $numbers com-press($options["PATTERN"],"1234567890{}","k") ;
set $numbers tranwrd($numbers,"}{",",",{") ;
set $temp1 scan($numbers,1,",") ;
set $ctemp1 compress($temp1,"{}") ;
eval $ntemp1 inputn($ctemp1,'12.') ;
```

The first statement begins the creation of a memory variable called $NUMBERS that simply removes from $PATTERN everything but numeric digits and braces. The second statement inserts a comma between each set of braces. This gives us the comma delimited list of affected columns, which makes it easy to use the SCAN function to process each specified column one at a time. After stripping away the braces to create $CTEMP1, the last statement is used to turn the column number into a number. Subsequent statements do the same with the second column, and logic is used to determine which is bigger. Whichever of $TEMP1 and $TEMP2 holds the largest column number gets stored in $CSECOND, and the smaller in $CFIRST. $SECOND and $FIRST hold the numeric counterparts.

Two new events are added. One is called SUPPRESS and is defined as below.

```
define event suppress ;
    start:
    open dump  / if cmp(colstart,$cfirst) ;
    set $col colstart ;
    finish: close ; flush ;
end;
```

As you can see, the start state opens a stream called DUMP when the current column number (COLSTART) is the first column specified in the parameter ($CFIRST) and the finish state closes and flushes it. The current HEADER and DATA events are modified simply by triggering this event at the beginning of the start state and at the end of the finish state. This saves us from having to add conditions to all the PUT statements. Note also that the memory variable $COL is created to hold the value of the column number. The reason for this will become clear soon.

The second new event is called SETVALS, and serves the purpose of creating the necessary memory variables when either of the two columns specified in the parameter are being processed. The event is defined as below.

```
define event setvals ;
    do / if cmp($col,$cfirst) ;
    set $hold value ;
    else / if cmp($col,$csecond) ;
    set $val tranwrd($options["PATTERN"],$first,$hold) ;
    putlog "$VAL:   " $val ;
    set $val tranwrd($val,$second,value);
    putlog "$VAL:   " $val ;
    done;
end;
```

A memory variable called $HOLD is created when the first of the two column is being processed, simply to hold onto that value. When the second column is being processed, $VAL is created – first by substituting the held value of the first column into $PATTERN, and second, by substituting the current value of VALUE in for the second column. The only question that remains is how and when this event is used.

The header of the table is generated in the same way other PROCs generate it. – by calling the HEADER event. In PHTML, this event calls the CELL_VALUE event which contains the PUT statement that generates the output. On the other hand, unlike other PROCs, the DATA event does not generate output. It contains the column number (COLSTART) but does not contain VALUE. Instead, PUT_VALUE, an event that contains nothing but the PUT statement, generates the output (this is the reason we created the memory variable $COL to hold onto the column number). Yes, the DATA event calls CELL_VALUE which has the PUT VALUE statement, but since VALUE is empty, this statement has no effect. Data cells have to wait until PUT_VALUE is called to have output generated.

In our case, whether its header or data output, we do not necessarily want VALUE being output, depending on whether it's a column in the parameter specification or not. So here's what we do. The PUT statement in the current CELL_VALUE event is executed if the variable URL is populated. We replace this conditional PUT statement with a TRIGGER statement, triggering a new and improved PUT_VALUE event that triggers SETVALS, and then generates $VAL if it exists, VALUE if it does not.

```
define event cell_value;
    start:
    trigger preformatted /if asis;
    set $close_hyperlink "true" /if exists( URL);
    trigger hyperlink /if exists( URL);
    trigger put_value /if ^exists( URL) and
    ^cmp("DATA",EVENT_NAME);

    finish:
    trigger hyperlink /if exists( $close_hyperlink);
    unset $close_hyperlink;
    trigger preformatted /if asis;
end;

define event put_value;
    trigger setvals ;
    do / if exists($val);
    put $val ;
    unset $val ;
    else ;
    put value ;
    done ;
end;
```

Keep in mind that the HEADER event contains a populated VALUE. When called, it triggers CELL_VALUE which then triggers PUT_VALUE. After checking with SETVALS to see if the current column is one that was specified with the parameter, it either writes $VAL or VALUE to the file. On the other hand, DATA does not contain a populated VALUE. For that reason, it does no good to call the PUT_VALUE and SETVALS event, which is why the TRIGGER statement in CELL_VALUE has the added condition that the name of the event is not DATA. We do know that, unlike other PROCs, REPORT calls PUT_VALUE on its own so that EVENT_NAME=PUT_VALUE. This is when the statements of PUT_VALUE execute for data cells.

These are the basic elements for the SQUEEZE tagset. It should be noted that what we have described above does not account for spanning headers. This and other things may have to be considered to make it more robust. It is left up to the user to add more functionality such as combining more than two columns, having more than one combination column, or allowing for spanning headers.

## CONCLUSION

We may never fully understand how the magician pulls the proverbial rabbit out of the hat, but in this chapter we have made significant progress. We have gained a more detailed understanding of the relationship between ODS and the PROC. We have seen how the tagset, with a toolbox that contains familiar tools like variables, arrays, conditional and iterative logic, and PUT statements allows us to exploit this relationship in order to directly control the markup without having to manually create the whole file. By choosing examples that focus on customizing output, we have only scratched the surface of what we can do with tagsets. Hopefully it was enough to spark curiosity that leads to further research. With enough practice, users who need their data in a custom XML format may find tagsets the answers to their prayers. Users needing Excel spreadsheets may find the highly parameterized EXCELXP tagset useful. If something is missing from it, add to it. Many users need RTF. Though no usable RTF tagsets exist yet, stay tuned for version 9.2. Want to customize your graphic output? Be sure to research in 9.2 the tagsets that lie underneath the new graphic templates. This chapter used HTML for its examples, which meant close examination of HTML markup, but the lessons learned apply to any formats – get to know the events that ODS and the PROCs use and in what order they use them; play detective and use resources such as examination of the markup, mapping tagsets, and text searches of inherited tagsets in order to identify the source of a given piece of markup; and of course, get to know tagset syntax. A mastery of these skills will allow you to dictate the markup without relying on magic.

## REFERENCES

Gebhart, Eric "ODS Markup, Tagsets, and Styles! Taming ODS Styles and Tagsets." Proceedings of the SAS Global
Forum Users Group International Conference, April 2007.

# twelve

# Using Proc Contents Output to Perform Quality Control Checks on SDTM Datasets

**Jennifer Srivastava**

This chapter focuses on using SAS Proc Contents output as a tool for performing Quality Control (QC) checks on SDTM datasets. Although the code applies to SDTM data, it could easily be used for other applications as well.

The SAS code presented in this chapter will be using the Variable Name (NAME), Variable Number or position within the dataset (VARNUM), and Variable Label (LABEL) fields from the Proc Contents output dataset, along with the Data Step and Proc Compare to perform two different types of QC checks on SDTM datasets.

## INTRODUCTION

Proc Contents is often employed by programmers as a way to learn more about the details and attributes of a SAS dataset. In addition to the primary use of Proc Contents, the SAS programmer can also save the Proc Contents output as a dataset, and use it to perform a variety of Quality Control (QC) checks.

In the pharmaceutical industry, it is becoming increasingly common for submissions to the Food and Drug Administration (FDA) to have data presented in a standard format as defined by the Clinical Data Interchange Standards Consortium (CDISC). The analysis datasets submitted to the Food and Drug Administration (FDA) are typically created or revised to follow the Study Data Tabulation Model (SDTM). For the remainder of the chapter, these analysis datasets will be referred to as

SDTM datasets.

The code presented in this chapter is used to perform QC checks on SDTM datasets. However this code could easily be applied to other types of data as well.

If a programmer uses Proc Contents to create an output dataset, he or she may consider using the NOPRINT option to avoid printing out the contents. The Proc Contents output dataset will contain the 40 variables as listed below. As the reader can see, there is a lot of information available in this dataset. This information is often referred to as metadata or data about data. The SAS code presented in this chapter will be using the Variable Name (NAME), Variable Number or position within the dataset (VARNUM), and Variable Label (LABEL) fields.

Alphabetic List of Variables and Attributes from a Proc Contents Output Dataset

```
Variable Type Len Format Label
CHARSET Char 8 Host Character Set
COLLATE Char 8 Collating Sequence
COMPRESS Char 8 Compression Routine
CRDATE Num 8 DATETIME16. Create Date
DELOBS Num 8 Deleted Observations in Data Set
ENCRYPT Char 8 Encryption Routine
ENGINE Char 8 Engine Name
FLAGS Char 3 Update Flags (Protect Contribute Add)
FORMAT Char 32 Variable Format
FORMATD Num 8 Number of Format Decimals
FORMATL Num 8 Format Length
GENMAX Num 8 Maximum Number of Generations
GENNEXT Num 8 Next Generation Number
GENNUM Num 8 Generation Number
IDXCOUNT Num 8 Number of Indexes for Data Set
IDXUSAGE Char 9 Use of Variable in Indexes
INFORMAT Char 32 Variable Informat
INFORMD Num 8 Number of Informat Decimals
INFORML Num 8 Informat Length
JUST Num 8 Justification
LABEL Char 256 Variable Label
LENGTH Num 8 Variable Length
LIBNAME Char 8 Library Name
MEMLABEL Char 256 Data Set Label
MEMNAME Char 32 Library Member Name
MEMTYPE Char 8 Library Member Type
MODATE Num 8 DATETIME16. Last Modified Date
NAME Char 32 Variable Name
NOBS Num 8 Observations in Data Set
NODUPKEY Char 3 Sort Option: No Duplicate Keys
NODUPREC Char 3 Sort Option: No Duplicate Records
NPOS Num 8 Position in Buffer
POINTOBS Char 3 Point to Observations
```

```
PROTECT Char 3 Password Protection (Read Write Alter)
Variable Type Len Format Label
REUSE Char 3 Reuse Space
SORTED Num 8 Sorted and/or Validated
SORTEDBY Num 8 Position of Variable in Sortedby Clause
TYPE Num 8 Variable Type
TYPEMEM Char 8 Special Data Set Type (From TYPE=)
VARNUM Num 8 Variable Number
```

When creating SDTM datasets there is a requirement to place variables in a specific order as defined by the CDISC Specification Guide. One way to do this is to place a RETAIN statement after the DATA statement in the final data step of the program. Below is an example using an Adverse Event (AE) dataset.

```
DATA AE;
    RETAIN STUDYID USUBJID AESEQ AESTDT AEENDT AESEV AESER AETERM
    PETERM SOCTERM;
    SET AE;
RUN;
```

To verify that the variable order in the dataset matches the variable order in the CDISC Specification Guide, the programmer can refer to the Proc Contents output to see the variable order. Specifically, the programmer would want to look at the NAME and VARNUM variables.

If a dataset is small, it may be a relatively easy task to check the variable order manually. However, if a programmer is dealing with a large dataset containing many variables, or if he/she has to check many smaller datasets, the programmer may consider doing these checks programmatically. The following page displays the CHKORD macro, which contains some code to complete this task. This code assumes that there is a development dataset as well as a QC dataset. The QC programmer can add this code to his/her QC program to compare the variable order between the two datasets and to print out results with mismatches flagged.

```
*********************************************************;
*** Check the Variable Order in a SDTM  Dataset   ***;
*********************************************************;

%macro CHKORD(lbd=,lbq=,ds=);
%* lbd=development libname reference, lbq=qc libname reference,
ds=dataset name ;
%* Contents of the Development Version of the Dataset;

proc contents data=&lbd..&ds out=cont_dev(keep=name varnum re-
name=(varnum=devnum)) noprint;
run;

proc sort data=cont_dev;
```

```
   by name;
run;

%*Contents of the QC Version of the Dataset;
proc contents data=&lbq..qc_&ds out=cont_qc(keep=name varnum re-
name=(varnum=qcnum)) noprint;
run;

proc sort data=cont_qc;
   by name;
run;

%*Compare the Development and QC Versions and Flag any Mismatches;
data comp;
   merge cont_dev cont_qc;
   by name;
   if devnum ne qcnum then mismatch=1;
run;

proc print;
   title "Check Variable Positions for &ds";
   where mismatch=1;
run;

%mend CHKORD;

%CHKORD(lbd=SDTM001,lbq=SDTMQ001,ds=AE);
```

If a programmer has a set of SDTMs that have already been pro-
grammed, passed QC review and passed a senior- level review, he/she
may want to compare the variable names and labels from his/her current
set of SDTMs to those in the final set of SDTMs. This would be another
way to confirm that the variable names and labels conform to what is
listed in the SDTM Specification Guide. The macro CHKPRV contains
code to perform this task.

```
*********************************************************;
* Compare Variable Names and Labels in the Current Protocol's
Dataset to those from the Previous Protocol *;
*********************************************************;

%macro CHKPRV(lbc=,lbp=,ds=);
%* lbc=current development libname reference, lbp=previous
development libname reference, ds=dataset name ;
%*Contents of the Development Dataset from the Current Protocol;
proc contents data=&lbc..&ds out=cont_cur(keep=name la-bel);
run;

proc sort data=cont_cur;
   by name;
run;

%*Contents of the Development Dataset from the Previous Protocol;
proc contents data=&lbp..&ds out=cont_prev(keep=name la-bel);
run;
```

```
proc sort data=cont_prev;
   by name;
run;

%*Compare the Variable Names and Labels from the Previous and
Current Versions of the Development File;
proc compare base=cont_prev compare=cont_cur listall max-print=(15
10000);
   id name;
   var label;

   title1 "&ds: Compare the Variable Names and Labels from Previous
Protocol &lbp to those in Current Protocol &lbc";
   title2 "Base=Protocol &lbp , Compare=Protocol &lbc";
run;

%mend CHKPRV;

%CHKPRV(lbc=SDTM002,lbp=SDTM001,ds=AE);
```

## CONCLUSION

In conclusion, the Proc Contents output dataset can be a useful programming tool for anyone who needs to perform QC checks on SDTM
datasets or other types of data. These techniques can help the user save
time and allow him/her to check their data in a programmatic and systematic way resulting in a higher quality finished product.

# thirteen

# Extending SAS Data Integration Studio with Java: Custom GUIs and SAS Server

### Christopher Treglio

This chapter introduces the concept of extending the functionality of the SAS Data Integration Studio client application through its Java plugin facility. Making use of this facility gives programmers access to significant features built into the SAS Data Integration Studio API, which enable full interaction with the SAS Metadata and Workspace servers. Both metadata objects and SAS data sets can be created, read, deleted, and modified. Data written by the SAS Data Integration Studio application can be read and reported on, and extended metadata can be authored and manipulated.

This chapter will explain the advantages of building a Java client upon SAS Data Integration Studio over building an independent standalone application, and give a tour of the basic API made available to its plugins. Additionally, it will cover topics like creating new objects within the metadata, editing existing SAS metadata, and modifying SAS data sets with either SAS or SQL code.

Finally, the chapter will profile three working applications which have been built and deployed on the SAS Data Integration Studio platform to standardize the generation of CDISC SDTM 3.1 submission data sets. The applications make extensive use of SAS Data Integration Studio GUI classes and backend connection APIs. They include a variety of innovative features, such as our Java/SAS persistence layer built with O/R mapping techniques that saves Java objects in SAS data sets over the workspace server connection.

## CORE FUNCTIONALITY

Developing within the application framework means that certain core client application functions are built for you. Additionally, utilities and APIs are available for some SAS OMA interaction that would be complex to code independently. Among the core application components that SAS Data Integration Studio provides are:

- Logging and Error Display
- Properties
- GUI Base Classes

### LOGGING AND ERROR DISPLAY

By turning on the "debug" log with MdObjectFactory.getInstance().setDebug(true), you can output error messages to the message window in the DI Studio application, with Util.printOutputln("message").

Also, with the MdObjectFactory.getInstance().setLogginEnabled(true), you can output the metadata queries that SAS Data Integration Studio issues to the Metadata Server for debugging.

### PROPERTIES

SAS provides the com.sas.plugins.PluginResourceBundle class for properties and other resources. Simply instantiate the resource bundle with the Class of a class in the package where the "PropertyBundle.properties" file exists, and your String and int properties, as well as images, will be available with simple getter methods. Note that there is a special property – "ImageLocation.notrans" – that holds the base directory for image files gotten this way.

SAS's PluginResourceBundle, like the standard Java one, can be internationalized with the addition of the appropriate country code to the file name, like "PropertyBundle_DE.properties".

The typical way to use this PluginResourceBundle class is to put properties files in the same package as the class that uses them, and distribute them within the .jar file of your plugin. For example:

```
PluginResourceBundle rb = new
PluginResourceBundle(GuiExample.class);
```

In this case, the PropertyBundle.properties file should be deployed within the same package as the GuiExample.class file.

However, sometimes it's convenient to have properties files outside the .jar file, so they can be changed without rebuilding and redeploying your plugin. The PluginResourceBundle class offers an alternative constructor that takes an InputStream. You can construct a simple FileInputStream as follows:

```
FileInputStream externalStream = new
FileInput-Stream("plugins"+System.getProperty("file.separator")+
"exter-nal.properties");

PluginResourceBundle rb = new PluginResourceBun-
dle(externalStream);
```

This resource bundle would load properties from the "external.properties" file, found in the "plugins" directory of your DI Studio installation.

## GUI BASE CLASSES

The SAS Data Integration Studio GUI is built with Java Swing, and all Swing and AWT classes can be used within plugins. To give your plugins the same GUI look-and-feel as the rest of the application environment, you may want to use the base GUI classes SAS provides. Two GUI layouts in particular are easy to build with SAS GUI base classes as listed here:

- Standard Dialogs, with the WAStandardDialog
- Wizards, with the WAWizardDialog and with WAPropertyTab pages

The simpler is the standard dialog. Here's a example WAStandardDialog subclass:

```
public class ExampleDialog extends WAStandardDialog {
    public ExampleDialog(Frame frame, String title) {
        super(frame, title);
        WAPanel mainPanel = new WAPanel();
        JLabel someLabel = new JLabel
            ("Some text          content....");
        mainPanel.add(someLabel);
        // add more components as appropriate here        . . .
        mainPanel.setPreferredSize(new
            Dimension(200, 200));
        setMainPanel(mainPanel);
}
```

This code creates a dialog like this:

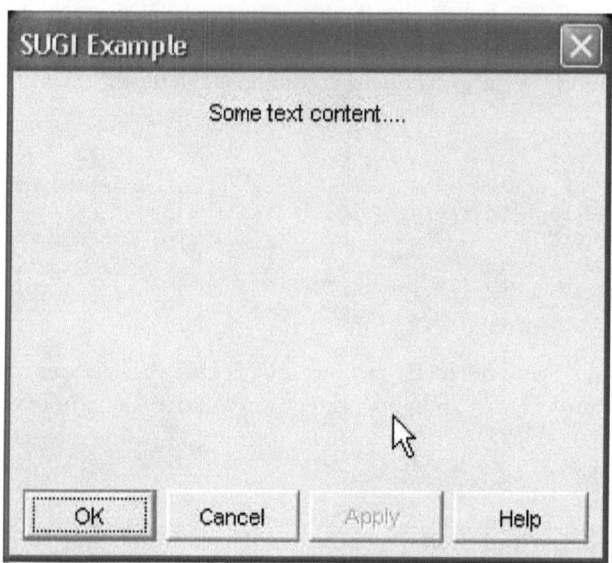

WAStandardDialog offers methods you can override to provide functionality for the four buttons displayed by default. Similarly, the WAWizardDialog can be used as follows:

```
public class ExWizard extends WAWizardDialog {
    public ExWizard(Frame frame) {
        super(frame);
        WAPropertyTab tab1 = new WAPropertyTab();
        tab1.add(new JLabel("Default layout for a tab is "
        + tab1.getLayout().getClass().getName()));
        this.addTab("Page 1 Title" ,"PAGE_ONE",
            tab1, false);
        WAPropertyTab tab2 = new WAPropertyTab();
        tab2.add(new JButton("Some Action"));
        tab2.add(new JTextField(40));
        this.addTab("Page 2 Title" ,"PAGE_TWO",
            tab2, true);
    }
}
```

This results in:

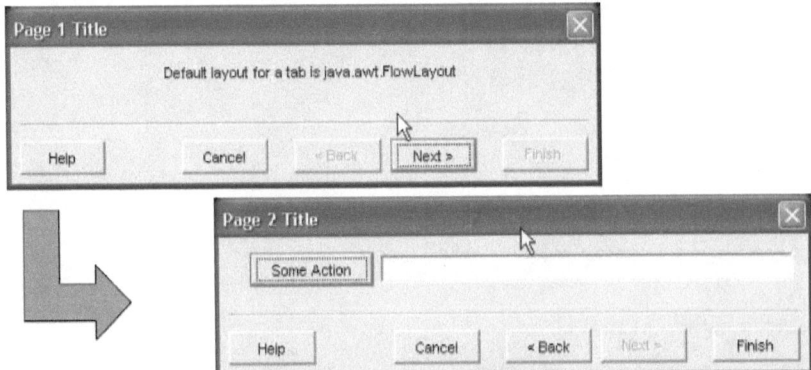

Notice that the "Finish" button is available on the second page – this is controlled by the last Boolean argument of the WAPropertyTab constructor.

In real use, these WAPropertyTab objects would probably be subclassed to perform more substantial work. Also, these WAPropertyTab objects are WAPanels, just like the panel set as the "main panel" in the first example. The WAPanel can be much more sophisticated than either example shown above, providing functionality for validating data and moving data between GUI components and the "model". These functions are documented more fully in SAS's online API docs.

## ASSEMBLING A PLUGIN.JAR FILE

Of course, somehow we have to deploy your code within SAS Data Integration Studio. To accomplish this, you will need to put a .jar file in the "plugins" subdirectory of your installation (which at the time of this writing is still called "ETLStudio"). That .jar file needs to contain a MANIFEST.MF file that has these entries, minimally:

```
Manifest-Version: 1.0
Created-By: 1.4.2_06-b03 (Sun Microsystems Inc.)
Plugin-Init: examplePlugin.ExLauncher.class
Copyright: Copyright (c) 2006 Yourcompany Inc.
```

The highlighted entry above is the important one. The Plugin-Init field must name the class in your plugin that implements the com.sas.wadmin.plugins.ShortcutInterface, which provides the following methods.

```
public void onSelected() {
    //this method is called when the user invokes the plugin
}
public Icon getLargeIcon() {
    // the 32 x 32 icon shown in the "shortcut" bar
}
public JMenuItem getMenuItem() {
    // complex menu items can be constructed, or just new JMenuItem()
}
public int getLocations() {
    // return SHOW_ON_SHORTCUT, SHOW_ON_MENU, or SHOW_ON_ALL
}
public void initPlugin() {
    // initialization method called when the plugin is loaded
}
public void dispose() {
    // use this method to clean up any resources used
}
public String getDescription() {
    // description of the plugin
}
public Icon getIcon() {
    // smaller icon used for the Menu
}
public String getName() {
    // name displayed in the shortcut bar
}
```

Our customary practice is to build a "Launcher" class that implements this ShortcutInterface, which then kicks off our GUI dialog within its onSelected method. This arrangement allows the GUI dialogs (which are typically subclasses of javax.swing.JPanel) to be run independent of the SAS Data Integration Studio environment, for debugging purposes.

## EXAMPLE: THE DI LOGVIEWER

With only the above information, we can already code a useful application. The plugin application demonstrated below is called the "Logviewer." This plugin does three things:

- It turns on metadata conversation log on, with the MdObject-Factory.getInstance().setLoggingEnabled(true), discussed above.
- It filters the logging stream to provide for appropriate formatting for Windows clients.
- It displays a simple GUI window showing the log as it is written.

The Logviewer is comprised of 3 classes

- Viewerlauncher, implementing Shortcutinterface
- LogViewDialog, extending JFrame

- LogFilter, extending FilterOutputStream

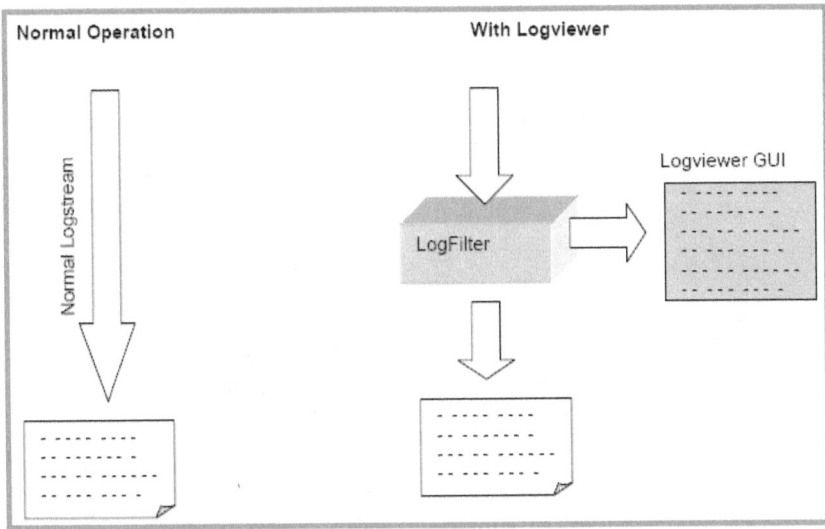

The Logviewer plugin intercepts the standard logging stream, and writes its contents to both the viewer window and to the file for which it was originally destined. (In the process, it corrects a "quirk" in the format of the log stream to ensure that the log contents has OS-appropriate line breaks – the normal log is not legible for Windows clients.)

## THE MANIFEST.MF FILE
The Manifest for the Logviewer jar file is as follows:

```
Manifest-Version: 1.0
Ant-Version: Apache Ant 1.6.5
Created-By: 1.4.2_06-b03 (Sun Microsystems Inc.)
Plugin-Init: diplu-gin.example.logviewer.ViewerLauncher.class
Copyright: Copyright (c) 2006 Bayer HealthCare Pharma-ceuticals
```

This manifest was created with an Ant script as follows:

```
<property name="jar_location" location="."/>
<property name="logviewer_jar" value="logviewerPlugin.jar"/>
<jar destfile="${jar_location}\${logviewer_jar}" base-
dir=".\antTemp">
<manifest>
    <attribute name="Plugin-Init"
value="diplugin.example.logviewer.ViewerLauncher.class"/>
    <attribute name="Copyright" value="Copyright (c) 2007 Bayer
HealthCare
Pharmaceuticals"/>
    <!--
```

```
    the jar manifest spec allows arbitrary name-value pairs to be
    included...
    <attribute name="Name" value="Value"/>
    -->
</manifest>
</jar>
<!--
the jar manifest spec allows arbitrary name-value pairs to be
included...
<attribute name="Name" value="Value"/>
-->
</manifest>
</jar>
```

## THE VIEWERLAUNCHER

The diplugin.example.logviewer.ViewerLauncher.class listed above in the
"Plugin-Init" attribute refers to the class in your plugin that implements
the ShortcutInterface class. Ours looks like this:

```
public class ViewerLauncher implements ShortcutInterface {
    private String pluginTitle;
    protected static PluginResourceBundle rb = new
        PluginResourceBundle(ViewerLauncher.class);
    private LogViewDialog dialog;
    /**
    * Notice that this method is capable of both opening and clos-
    ing the dialog.
    */
    public void onSelected() {
        if (dialog.isVisible())
        {
            // close window
            dialog.setVisible(false);

        } else if (!dialog.isVisible())
        {
            // open window
            dialog.setVisible(true);
        }
    }
    /**
    * This method gets the image named in the log.plugin.icon en-
    try in the property file, and returns it as an Icon.
    *
    */
    public Icon getLargeIcon() {
        ImageIcon i = rb.getImageIcon("log.plugin.icon");
        return i;
    }
    /**
    * This cannot be null if the getLocations indicates that the
    plugin should be shown in the menu.
    */
    public JMenuItem getMenuItem() {
        return null;
    }
```

```
/**
 * We are only showing the plugin on the Shortcut menu sidebar
 */
public int getLocations() {

return SHOW_ON_SHORTCUT;
}
/**
 * This method runs when the plugin class is loaded. Here, it
gets the plugin title from a property file, and
 * instantiates the dialog that will be shown when the plugin
icon is clicked
 */
public void initPlugin() {

    pluginTitle = rb.getString("log.plugin.title");
    dialog = new LogViewDialog(pluginTitle);
}
/**
 * Nothing done here.
 */
public void dispose() { }
/**
 * This description is unused.
 */
public String getDescription() {
    return "DESCRIPTION";
}
/**
 * This method can return null, because we are only showing the
plugin in the shortcut menu. The icon we use is
 * gotten from the {@link #getLargeIcon()} method.
 */
public Icon getIcon() {
    return null;
}
/**
 * This becomes the String shown in the shortcut menu.
 *
 */
public String getName() {
    return "Toggle Log Window On/Off";
}
}
```

Perhaps the most important method above is the onSelected, which determines what happens when the plugin icon is clicked. Also note that uncaught exceptions thrown in the init method will hang SAS Data Integration Studio.

## THE LOGVIEWDIALOG

Above we saw the init method instantiating – and the onSelected method making visible – an object of the LogViewDialog class. This is what that class looks like:

```java
/**
 * When instantiated, this JFrame subclass lays itself out. Note that
 * it is still invisible, until the ViewerLauncher makes the window
 * appear.
 *
 * @param title
 */
public class LogViewDialog extends JFrame {
    OutputStream logToFile;
    JTextArea window;
    LogFilter filter;

    public LogViewDialog(String title) {

        super(title);
        JPanel contentPane = new JPanel(new BorderLayout());
        // if a Log stream already exists, take note of it
        if (Util.getLogStream() != null)
        {
            logToFile = Util.getLogStream();
        }
        // if no log stream exists, use System.out
        else
        {
            logToFile = System.out;
        }
        window = new JTextArea();
        LookAndFeel laf = UIManager.getLookAndFeel();
        window.setBackground(
            laf.getDefaults().getColor("Label.background"));

        JScrollPane scrollingResult = new JScrollPane(window);
        scrollingResult.setPreferredSize(new Dimension(800, 300));
        contentPane.setBorder(BorderFactory.createEmptyBorder(
        12,5,5,5));
        contentPane.add(scrollingResult, BorderLayout.CENTER);
        this.setContentPane(contentPane);
        pack();
    }
    /**
     * This method instantiates the LogFilter, which splices the
     * application's output stream. The content is routed to both the
     * "window" object and to its original output location.
     *
     */
    private void startLogToWindow()
    {
    filter = new LogFilter(logToFile, window);
    Util.setLogStream(filter);
    boolean oldLogState = MdObjectFacto-
    ry.getInstance().getLoggingEnabled();
    MdObjectFactory.getInstance().setLoggingEnabled(true);
    // tag the beginning of the log window with this stamp
    window.append("****************************************\n");
    window.append("LogViewer version 1.0, logging state was " +
    oldLogState);
    window.append("\nstarting log filtering " +
```

```
DateFormat.getDateTimeInstance().format(new Date()) + "\n");
window.append("*****************************************\n");
}
/**
 * This method removes the LogFilter from the OutputStream,
 * reattaching the original log directly to the application's
 * output log.
 *
 * @throws IOException
 */
private void endLogToWindow() throws IOException
{
    // empty whatever might remain.
    filter.flush();
    // reset original output stream
    Util.setLogStream(logToFile);
}
/**
 * This method is called by the onSelected method of our
 * ShortcutInterface.
 */
public void setVisible(boolean open) {

    if (open)
    {
        startLogToWindow();
    }
    else
    {
        try {
            endLogToWindow();
        } catch (IOException e) {
            e.printStackTrace();
        }
    }
    super.setVisible(open);
}
}
```

This log window JFrame displays the content it sees being logged by the application by instantiating a LogFilter filter stream (which is not shown in detail here). This subclass of FilterOutputStream corrects the line breaks for the client OS, prints the content to this dialog's window, and passes it along to the original log stream. The whole application looks like this:

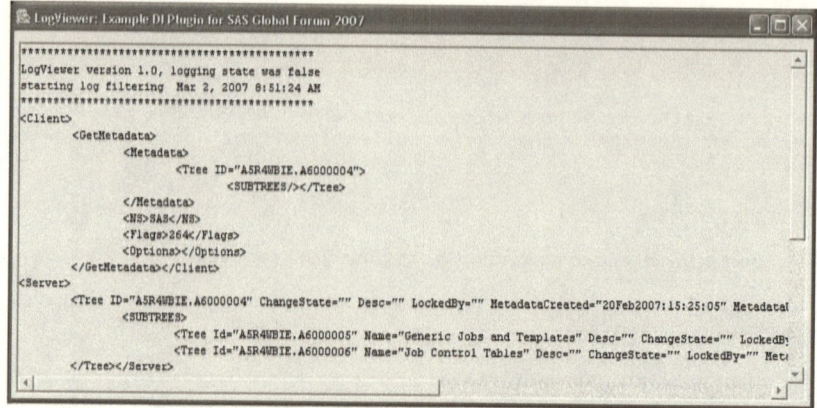

When you interact with SAS Data Integration Studio's interface, the metadata conversation between the client and the server appears in the window. Above, we see the query and response from opening a Tree with the ID "A5R4WBIE.A6000004." The server responds with a list of sub trees, one named "Generic Jobs and one named "Templates" and "Job Control Tables."

Upon close, this dialog disconnects the filter stream and reconnects the original log stream back to the application. Note that only one of these dialogs will be instantiated by the ViewerLauncher class – subsequent clicks to the shortcut icon will simply redisplay the one dialog, so you would not lose previously logged content.

## QUERYING, UPDATING, AND SAVING METADATA OBJECTS

Within the DI Studio architecture, interacting with the Metadata Server (often still called the "OMR" in SAS API documentation) is simple. The following methods – the same methods that are available in typical SAS code – are available from either the MetadataUtil or the MdOMIUtil utility classes:

- AddMetadata
- CheckinMetadata/CheckoutMetadata
- CopyMetadata
- DeleteMetadata
- GetMetadata
- GetMetadataObjects/ GetMetadataObjectsSubset
- GetRepositories

- UpdateMetadata
- Etc.

There are two distinct ways of interacting with the Metadata Server – through the MetadataUtil for single connection applications, and through the MdOMIUtil for mid tier applications. The methods in these classes are almost identical, but through interacting with the MetadatUtil, you will retrieve and operate on objects in the com.sas.metadata package, while the MdOMIUtil will get you objects in com.sas.metadata.remote. For simplicity, this paper will deal with single connection applications working with the MetadataUtil.

Additionally, there's generic method "DoRequest" which can execute any of the above methods, formatted as XML.

## QUERYING OBJECTS

Let's say, for example, that we want to query the Metadata Server about SAS Libraries that have been defined there. Because we are interested in multiple metadata objects, we want to use the GetMetadataObjectsSubset method above. The code looks something like this:

```
String id= Workspace.getWorkspace()
.getDefaultRepository().getFQID();
MdStore mdstore = MdObjectFactory.createObjectStore();

List objects = MetadataUtil.getMetadataObjectsSubset(
    mdstore,
    id,
    MdFactory.SASLIBRARY,
    0, // this would be any of the MetadataUtil.OMI_ ... flags
    "" // options, like an XMLSELECT filter
    );

for (Iterator iter = objects.iterator(); iter.hasNext();) {
    SASLibrary library = (SASLibrary) iter.next();
    // do something with the library
}
```

Note that the GetMetadataObjectsSubset method returns fully-fleshed out metadata objects, while the etMetadataObjects returns only "root" objects, which are less useful (but faster to retrieve).

The query above gets a list of all the SASLibrary objects within the specified repository, but this is rarely the kind of query you will want. More often, you will need to retrieve objects based on some criteria, and those criteria can be based on an object's attributes, or its associations.

- Attributes are simple pieces of data about a metadata object: strings, integers, or dates.
- Associations are connections between metadata objects

Criteria-based queries are built using the XMLSELECT element. For example, instead of getting all the SASLibrary objects in the repository, perhaps we only want to retrieve the one library with the libref of "TEST". The XMLSELECT for that would define a simple attribute-based query, as follows:

```
<XMLSELECT search="@Libref='TEST'"></XMLSELECT>
```

Another identical way of expressing the same query would be:

```
<XMLSELECT search="SASLibrary[@Libref='TEST']"></XMLSELECT>
```

which can be read as "all SASLibrary objects with the Libref attribute of 'TEST'". Either of these XMLSELECT can be used to query the Metadata Server.

Because we are now looking for just one object, you might be inclined to think that we can use the getMetadata method. However, experiment with that method and you will realize that it requires an Object ID, which we do not have (we only have a libref String). Besides, we do not know that we are going to get one object – only the object ID is considered a unique identifier, there may very well be multiple libraries in the Metadata Server with the libref of 'TEST.' As a result, we will need to use the same getMetadataObjectsSubset we used before, and check to make sure that the List returned contains only one object. That code looks like this:

```
MdStore store = MdObjectFactory.createObjectStore();
String select = "<XMLSELECT
search=\"@Libref='TEST'\"></XMLSELECT>";

List objects = MetadataUtil.getMetadataObjectsSubset(store,
    Workspace.getWorkspace().getDefaultRepository().getFQID(),
    MdFactory.SASLIBRARY,
    MetadataUtil.OMI_XMLSELECT, // this flag needs to be set now
    select);
    // check to ensure that 1 and only 1 object was returned.
    if (objects.size() != 1)
    {
```

```
        throw new RuntimeException(objects.size() + " libraries
        with libref " + libref + "returned!");
}
SASLibrary library = (SASLibrary)objects.get(0);
```

Where before we had sent a "0" as a flag to the getMetadataObjectsSubset method, we now need to send the OMI_XMLSELECT flag. (This indicates that an XMLSELECT element is coming – without the OMI_XMLSELECT flag, our search would be ignored!)

These queries are getting more useful, but let's say we wanted to query for the path that the Metadata Server has associated with the libref TEST. To do so, we are going to need to query for more than attributes – now we need to query for associations.

The Metadata Server stores the path associated with a library in a separate object, appropriately called a Directory. The path of a library (the Directory object attached to the SASLibrary object) is connected through the UsedByPackages association. So, to get the actual path string, we are looking for a Directory object, but the only information we have about that Directory object is that it's attached to a SASLibrary with the libref TEST. This is expressed in the XMLSELECT search as follows:

```
<XMLSELECT
search="Directory[UsedByPackages/SASLibrary[@Libref='TEST']]">
</XMLSELECT>
```

Notice that the Directory object is the object named outside the outermost brackets. That means that we are going to get Directory objects back from our query. Put it all together like this:

```
MdStore store = MdObjectFactory.createObjectStore();
String select = <XMLSELECT
    search=\"Directory[UsedByPackages/SASLibrary[@Libref='TEST']]\
    ">
    </XMLSELECT>";
List objects = MetadataUtil.getMetadataObjectsSubset(store,
    Workspace.getWorkspace().getDefaultRepository().getFQID(),
    MdFactory.DIRECTORY, // <- notice this has changed!
    MetadataUtil.OMI_XMLSELECT,
    select);
    // check to ensure that 1 and only 1 object was returned.
if (objects.size() != 1)
{
    throw new RuntimeException(objects.size() + " Directories with
    SASLibrary libref " + libref + " returned!");
}
Directory dir = (Directory)objects.get(0);
String path = dir.getDirectoryName();// <- this is our answer
```

## N.B.

If we wanted to reverse the query – look for SASLibraries that had a known path string – we would have to change the association name. The UsedByPackages association shown above is the name of the association from the Directory to the SASLibrary. The reciprocal association from the SASLibrary to the Directory is called "UsingPackages."

## MODIFYING OBJECTS

Once you have retrieved objects from the Metadata Server, modifying objects is also possible simply by changing the object's attributes and asking the object to "update its metadata".

```
library.setDesc("new description . . .");
library.updateMetadataAll();
```

Creating wholly new objects is also possible. Simply ask the MdObject-Factory for a blank copy of an object, modify it as necessary, and update it as above.

```
SASLibrary newLibrary =(SASLibrary)
    MdObjectFactory.createComplexMetadataObject(
        mdstore,
        null,
        "NewLibName",
        MdObjectFactory.SASLIBRARY,
        reposID);
newLibrary.setDesc("new description . . . ");
newLibrary.updateMetadataAll();
```

# INTERACTING WITH SAS DATASETS

Above we were interacting with the Metadata Server, retrieving and modifying metadata objects. Of course, a time will come when you want to actually work with SAS data as well. This can be done through the Workspace Server.

## CONNECTING TO THE WORKSPACE SERVER

The easiest way to make a connection to the Workspace Server within SAS Data Integration Studio is to let the Workspace (the singleton object that offers access to the SAS Data Integration Studio GUI application running behind your plugin) to "make" you an application server, with the simple code:

```
AppServer appserver= Workspace.getWorkspace().makeAppServer();
```

Because the username and password to access these servers may be different from the username and password used to log in to DI Studio itself, this call will display login windows as follows:

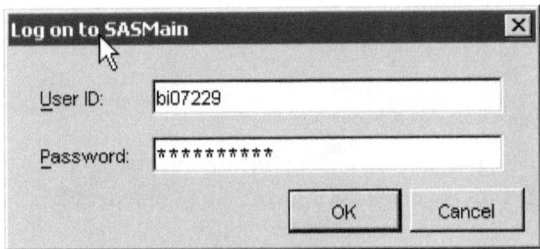

The AppServer object offers two useful functions, allowing access to data sets both via SQL and via standard SAS code.

## QUERYING, UPDATING, AND SAVING DATA WITH SQL SYNTAX

Once an AppServer object is "made" for you by your Workspace object, building JDBC-style interactions with the workspace server is quite easy. First, set the SAS library you would like to interact with the SASLibrary metadata object (remember, we retrieved SASLibrary objects above, while working with the Metadata Server) as follows:

```
appserver.assignLibref(saslibrary);
```

and get a java.sql.Connection object as follows:

```
appserver.makeSQLConnection();
java.sql.Connection conn = appserver.getSQLConnection();
```

Now, use any SAS standard SQL (as you would within a PROC SQL) with typical Java SQL techniques. Building on the previous example, this code snippet returns the names and last modified dates of the tables in our library.

```
appserver.assignLibref(saslibrary);
appserver.makeSQLConnection();
java.sql.Connection conn = appserver.getSQLConnection();
StringBuffer statement = new StringBuffer();
statement.append("Select memname, modate from DICTIONARY.TABLES");
statement.append(" where libname='");
statement.append(saslibrary.getLibref());
statement.append("';");
try {
    Statement sqlstatement = conn.createStatement();
    sqlstatement.execute(statement.toString());
    ResultSet rs = sqlstatement.getResultSet();
    while(rs.next())
```

```
        {
        String tablename = rs.getString(1);
        long moddate = rs.getTimestamp(2).getNanos();
        // etc. . . .
        }
    } catch (SQLException e) {
        System.out.println("Error in query: " + statement.toString());
        e.printStackTrace();
    }
}
```

Why would we want to query the dictionary for information like this, since the members of a SAS Library are available through the Metadata Server? Usually, we would not, but there could be a difference between the data sets in the library directory and those registered in the Metadata Server. Furthermore, data like "last modified data" changes frequently and without the Metadata Server's knowledge, and is not available there.

## QUERYING, UPDATING, AND SAVING DATA WITH SAS SYNTAX

SQL is not the only way to interact with SAS data sets through the App-Server object. Standard SAS code can be submitted to the AppServer with a call like this:

```
int resultCode = appserver.submitSrc("SAS CODE");
```

This method returns a 0 result code for a normal completion, or throws an "AppServerException" if it encounters an error. Log output is available from the "getLog()" method, as follows:

```
String log = appserver.getLog().toString()
```

Output is also available, but it comes back as a String array. You can work with it as like this:

```
String[] out = appserver.getListLinesHolder().value;
StringBuffer outBuffer = new StringBuffer();
for (int i = 0; i < out.length; i++) {
    outBuffer.append(out[i] + "\n");
}
```

At this point you are logged on to the "appserver" object as the user who supplied their login information in the dialog box shows above, not the user who logged in to DI Studio. Permissions to libraries, etc. are determined based on this login.

## APPLICATION EXAMPLES

The techniques described above have been used in production applications for approximately a year now at Bayer. Three DI Studio plugins are now deployed.

### DEFINE XML PLUGIN

One of the standard documents required by the CDISC (Clinical Data Interchange Standards Consortium) for clinical submissions is the "define.xml". The define.xml is a table-of-contents style document detailing each data set (and its variables) included in a submission to the FDA. Since we have used SAS Data Integration Studio to create our submission data sets, all the tables and variables in our submission are registered in our SAS Metadata Repository, and generating the define.xml is simply a matter of systematically querying the repository, and writing the XML file to the local disk.

Since some of the fields required for the define.xml file are beyond the typical metadata registered in the repository, this application makes heavy use of "ExtendedAttribute" objects. ExtendedAttribute objects can be added to any metadata object stored by SAS, and provide a simple and powerful way to add custom name-value annotations to your repository. ExtendedAttributes are shown through the "Extended Attributes" tab in the properties window, for all metadata objects.

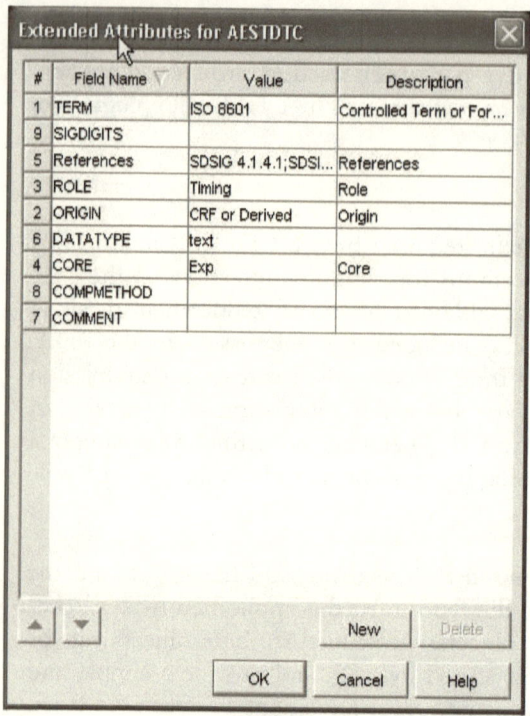

Since entering our sometimes-complex annotations in these windows would be inconvenient for our users, we have deployed a plugin which offers a more user-friendly way of editing them.

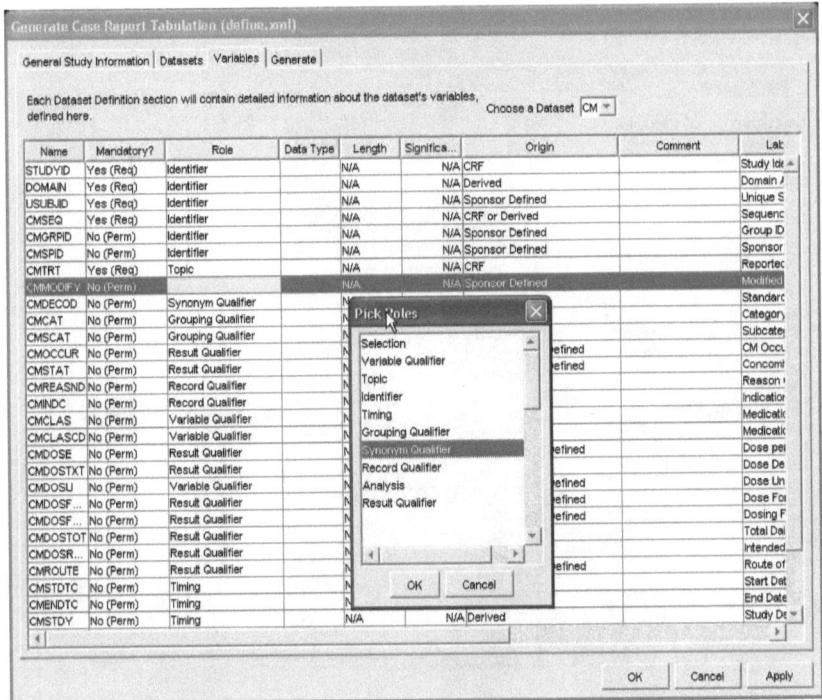

In the above screen capture, we see the Define.xml GUI modifying the extended attributes of a SAS variable (represented in the Metadata Server by a Column object). The GUI is built with a com.sas.workspace.WATabbedPanel object, with each tab an instance of com.sas.workspace.WAPropertyTab. The table and all the editing features are standard javax.swing classes.

## SDTM MAPPING PLUGIN

To generate our submission data sets, we use a custom "mapping" technique whose logic is held in a series of SAS data sets we call "Control Tables." These control tables are read by our SAS Data Integration Studio jobs, which have been enhanced with SAS Macros capable of translating their contents into programmatic logic. The SDTM Mapping plugin is responsible for giving our users a friendly GUI to write this logic into our control tables. Unlike the Define XML plugin above, the SDTM Mapping plugin primarily interacts with raw SAS data sets over the Workspace Server, rather than SAS metadata objects through the Metadata Server.

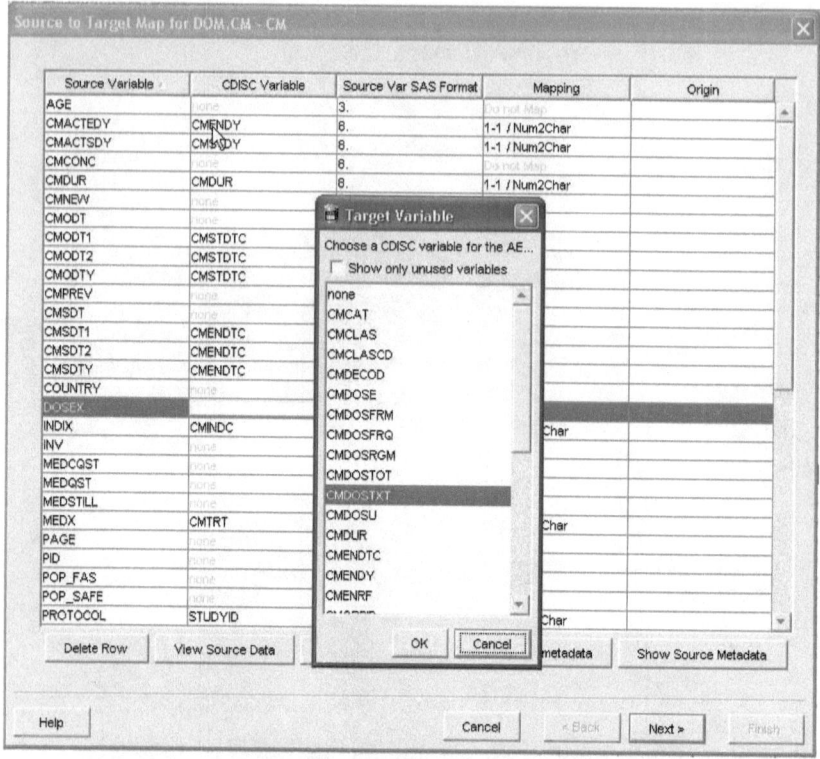

To read and write the Control Table data sets, we could have used simple SAS or SQL as described above. But to simplify our interaction, and to avoid repetitive SQL, our SDTM Mapping Plugin instead uses a "persistence layer" capable of automatically building SQL to read, write, and delete data within these data sets. Like an Object/Relational mapping framework (like the popular Hibernate), it links fields in our Java objects with variables in our data sets. Because this "Object/SAS" persistence layer can automatically load and unload data to and from memory, it frees us from manually coding SQL.

## ADMINISTRATION PLUGIN

Our third application is call the Administration Plugin. Certain administrative tasks, like initializing our Metadata Repositories for use with our other plugins, would be tedious and error-prone without some kind of automation. Certain users, identified as "administrators" by our business, have access to our Administration plugin, which handles tasks like initializing our repositories, locking our repositories when an FDA submission is complete, and copying metadata from one repository to another for reuse in later projects.

Use of our Administration plugin takes some of the burden off our administrative support group, and ensures that administrative tasks are performed by appropriate staff, in a controlled way.

## CONCLUSION

Data Integration Studio offers a good foundation for developing custom functionality for the SAS environment. As the Metadata Server becomes the core part of many SAS architectures, being able to interact programmatically with it becomes an invaluable skill, both for administration and for custom extensions to our business users' applications.

## REFERENCES

The API for all the SAS based GUI classes mentioned above can be found here:
http://support.sas.com/rnd/gendoc/bi/api/workspace/index.html

The API for Metadata Server interaction can be found here:
http://support.sas.com/rnd/gendoc/bi/api/metadata/index.html

More general information about metadata structure can be found in SAS Help, under the heading "SAS Open Metadata Architecture."

www.ingramcontent.com/pod-product-compliance
Lightning Source LLC
Chambersburg PA
CBHW020734180526
45163CB00001B/231